The Great Tamasha

The Great Tamasha

Cricket, Corruption, and the Spectacular Rise of Modern India

James Astill

BLOOMSBURY

NEW YORK · LONDON · NEW DELHI · SYDNEY

Published by Bloomsbury USA, New York

All papers used by Bloomsbury USA are natural, recyclable products made from wood grown in well-managed forests. The manufacturing processes conform to the environmental regulations of the country of origin.

LIBRARY OF CONGRESS CATALOGING-IN-PUBLICATION DATA
Astill, James.
The great tamasha : cricket, corruption and the turbulent rise of modern India / James Astill.
pages cm
Includes bibliographical references and index.
ISBN: 978-1-60819-917-4 (alk. paper)
1. Cricket—India—History. I. Title.
GV928.I4A77 2013
796.3580954—dc23
2013011749

First U.S. Edition 2013

1 3 5 7 9 10 8 6 4 2

Typeset by Saxon Graphics Ltd, Derby
Printed and bound in the U.S.A. by Thomson-Shore Inc., Dexter, Michigan

For my parents

Contents

Introduction

Outside the New Delhi bureau of *The Economist*, where I lived and worked for four years, was a small public garden in which a privileged section of north-Indian society was often on display. A narrow brick pathway tracked the perimeter, around which the local householders paraded in slow circuits early in the morning, before the sun boiled up the sky, or in the lesser heat of dusk.

The women wore loose Punjabi pyjamas or bright, unflattering tracksuits. Their husbands, wealthy businessmen and senior civil servants, took their turns in small groups and sleeveless shirts and slacks. Almost all wore gleaming white trainers and many brandished swagger sticks, brigadier-style, to ward away the colony dogs. Sometimes they were serenaded by a screeching of peacocks from the neighbouring zoo. Every hour or so, a tiger wretchedly groaned.

The garden enclosed by the walkway was used by the servants of these wealthy Delhi wallahs. Drivers, guards, housemaids and handymen – launderers of tracksuits, scrubbers of trainers – they loitered off the path in dowdier clothes, smoking, teasing the dogs, snoozing beneath dusty trees or tending the vegetable plots that some had dug slyly beside them. And on a bumpy patch of lawn, especially from October to April when the temperature in Delhi mercifully drops, their children gathered to play cricket.

Though poor, they were lovingly turned out, often brushed and combed for the school day. Yet they were recognisably of north-Indian servant stock. Skinny boys with the delicate, milk-chocolate features of north-eastern Assam, Darjeeling and Manipur charged in to bowl at dark-skinned Biharis and Bengalis. A pair of skilful Muslim boys, wearing lacy white skull-caps, smashed a worn-out tennis ball to the garden's furthest corner, where a tiny Christian girl, with plastic rosary beads joggling around her neck, might be sent to retrieve it.

Snatches of Tamil (or so I was told) marked out the children of the local cooks – Tamil food, low-fat and vegetarian, having become prized in high-cholesterol north India. But mostly the children spoke Hindi, interspersed with the shouted words of English – 'Bowl it!' 'Sixer!' 'Catch it!' 'Out!' – that form the lexicon of India's favourite game.

This was a scene that, during those four years, I grew attached to. I am a 'cricket tragic', in the smug but acute self-description of John Howard, Australia's former prime minister, and can enjoy watching almost any exhibition of the game. And the more I watched these games, as I paced the pathway, clearing my head of whatever politics or business I was reporting on at the time, the more I enjoyed them.

I started to recognise and look out for the best batsmen and bowlers, and, over the years, I saw them grow taller and improve. The distance one teenager, with the Asiatic features of the north-east, hit the ball was amazing. And his skills seemed all the more impressive after I, just once, asked to have a go myself and found the splice of the bat he was using was broken almost in two. Swinging that bat without it coming apart in mid-stroke required a difficult grip that my school cricket coach had not taught. I could hardly hit the ball. How the children rifled it high over the trees, endangering passing cars and sometimes their parents' slowly turning employers, I couldn't imagine.

There is scarcely a more poignant image of India than this: of poor children gathering in a crowded Asian city to play cricket. It is suggestive, first of all, of cricket's spectacular success in India. From northern Kashmir to Kolkata in the east and down to the Tamil south, come monsoon or dry, every day millions of Indians watch and play cricket. When India's national side plays a big game, perhaps 400 million people gather around television sets, to shout, pray and groan; India's biggest cities appear to empty – the government, at great cost to the economy, sometimes calls a national holiday.

India has made an English summer game its own, and in the process changed it. Indian cricket is more popular, more manically followed and, at its infrequent best, more delicately skilful than the game played by any non-Asian country. No English cricket crowd is like the churning, hallooing throngs that fill Indian stadiums. Cricket is India's national theatre – its great *tamasha*, a Hindi word for 'entertainment', which Indians use promiscuously, in half a dozen languages, to mean a show, a performance or a scene.

No other British legacy in India, save perhaps the English language, has proved more popular or enduring than cricket. Nothing unites Indians, in all their legions and diversity, more than their love for it. No other form of entertainment – not even Bollywood or politics – is so ubiquitous in India's media, and no Indian celebrity more revered than India's best cricketers. 'God has a new House' – that is how the *Times of India* recently splashed on the news that Sachin Tendulkar, the most adored Indian player, had been gifted a seat in parliament.

And this cricket hysteria – as distinct from the simple game of bat and ball – is itself popular. Indians, segregated by class and divided by Hindu caste and religion, find in all-in-this-together cricket love a reassuring idea of national unity. A clue to this is the stories they love to tell of the real die-hard cricket crazies, half-demented by devotion to the game. Sudhir Gautum is India's best-known cricketing mendicant. A poor Bihari, he travels the length of the subcontinent to see India play, with his body painted in the colours of the Indian flag and 'Tendulkar' written in white paint across his famished belly. In the world of sport, perhaps only Brazilian football plays such an exalted role in national life as cricket does in India.

Yet the story of Indian cricket is not only about cohesion and success. It is also deeply pathetic. The poor children who play cricket on India's streets and parks have almost no chance of emulating their heroes and playing for India. They are unlikely even to play an organised game of cricket, with a good bat and leather ball. That is because real cricket, as opposed to street games, is dominated by members of a small and privileged middle-class, albeit to a rapidly diminishing degree. In part, that reflects Indian cricket's 19th-century origins. It was, from the start, an elite game, picked up by those ambitious to emulate or impress their British masters. Yet India's failure – over the ensuing 150 years – to spread more cricketing opportunity to its cricket-hungry people is nonetheless lamentable. It is the main reason why India is much less good at cricket than it should be – only fairly recently has India, despite its enormous cricket obsession, become consistently competitive with the teams of much smaller cricketing populations. In a country with a poor record of harnessing the talents of its vast population, this is a significant failure.

Elite and popular, unifying and exclusionary, polite and uproarious, Indian cricket is as contradictory in nature as India itself. For a cricket-loving foreign correspondent, this offers rich pickings. Watching, playing and, more often these days, talking about cricket are among my greatest pleasures, and India has provided unrivalled opportunity to indulge them. There must be Indian politicians, businessmen and taxi-drivers who do not like to discuss Tendulkar's batting or India's prospects against the Australians, but I have rarely met them. Cricket, the shared inheritance of the British Commonwealth, is how I have got closest to India.

It has also given me a more than useful vantage on to it because, in cricket, a lot of India is revealed. It is not always pretty. Indian cricket is perhaps, on balance, a force for unity. Yet caste, religious and regional differences have been played out on many Indian cricket fields; with plenty of ugly nationalism evident in the stands. These are the big conflicts of modern India, great wrestlings over community and identity, and throughout its history Indian cricket has reflected, and sometimes been shaped by, them.

That is the rough end of Indian cricket politics; the everyday version, the game's administration, is also pretty unforgiving. Controlling cricket has always been a big prize in India, vied for between princes, businessmen and politicians. But in the past decade or so, that contest, waged in boardrooms and even the Indian parliament, has become a lot more vicious. This reflects the enormous wealth that has flooded into the game – due to the wildfire spread of Indian television and the accelerating economic growth underlying it. When Tendulkar began his long international career in 1989, India had roughly 30 million television households. By the 2011 World Cup, in which Tendulkar played, it had 160 million. This media revolution is transforming India on a scale that is still hard to comprehend, spreading popular culture and a trickle of prosperity to the furthest parts of the country. And cricket, as the most valuable, popular and ubiquitous product in Indian media, is at the heart of this. In a time of great change, Indian cricket is the zeitgeist.

The Great Tamasha is the story of this phenomenon, the conquest of India by cricket. The first three chapters are broadly historical. They trace the history of the Indian game, from its genesis on the maidans of Victorian Bombay to the recent explosive growth in the TV-cricket economy. Here we will meet some of the great figures of Indian history – including graceful Ranjitsinhji, who won a kingdom with his bat, the one-eyed Nawab of Pataudi, India's greatest captain, and the leonine Kapil Dev, a genuine Indian world-beater, inspiration to small-town Indians and, incidentally, regular perambulator around the garden outside my office. The three chapters that follow are more explicitly concerned with politics. The first examines Indian cricket administration – which I take to be a rather discouraging case study in how power operates in India. The two that follow explain, first, the vexed role of Muslims and Pakistan in Indian cricket; and, second, that of Hindu caste. These are the dominant themes; the subjects are Indians themselves, politicians, entrepreneurs, cricketers well known and unknown, and many ordinary fans. They are the protagonists in India's great sports-cultural drama, and their stories, inspiring or pitiful, are also part of it.

The last three chapters are, directly and otherwise, about the great cricketing event of my time in Delhi – the launch of the Indian Premier League. A domestic Indian competition, founded in 2008 and contested by privately owned, city-based teams, the IPL is the biggest trauma to strike cricket in decades. It uses a new fast-paced, short form of cricket, Twenty20, employs the world's best players on wages previously unimagined in cricket, plus a lot of shouted American-style razzmatazz. Amazingly, at the time it was introduced, many questioned whether India's millions of cricket-hungry fans would go for this confection. They have gorged on it. After three six-week seasons, the IPL was estimated to be worth over $4 billion in annual revenues. Even by India's recent standards, this was eye-watering growth.

In a venal age, the tournament's financial success was also part of its appeal. Middle-class Indians, the main beneficiaries of India's growth spurt, were intoxicated by it. Inevitably the tournament also drew in a powerful horde of investors and chancers – film stars, politicians and billionaire tycoons. The IPL was for many an image of the new India. It was rich, fast and powerful. And it had Western cheerleaders too – white girls in hot pants, dancing with pompoms.

But then the IPL imploded amid allegations of grand political interference and corruption. It really was, it turned out, an image of the new India – just not as its cheerleaders had sold it. *The Great Tamasha* describes these events, including through the eyes of the IPL's divisive Svengali, Lalit Modi. It also examines the league's recovery and return to soaring growth – calamitous as this may prove for cricket as we know it. The IPL is in a sense the book's leitmotif. It is the apogee of India's cricket mania – emblematic of a giant nation's thrilling, yet fatefully turbulent, rise.

A Note on Names and Numbers

Over the past two decades or so, many of India's biggest cities have been renamed, typically to restore an original place name at the expense of a British colonial garbling of it. Thus, Bombay became (or, some would say, reverted to being) Mumbai, Madras became Chennai, and Calcutta became Kolkata. Poona was rewritten as 'Pune' a little earlier, in 1976. Like most Indians, I take a flexible approach to this political name game. When referring to events in these cities in the distant or colonial past, I use their former British-given names; otherwise I use the modern replacement. But I have kept faith with 'Bangalore' – its intended successor, 'Bengaluru', or 'the city of cooked beans', having so far failed to catch on.

With the essential exception of the word *tamasha*, I have tried to avoid using Indian words and terminology that are incomprehensible to anyone unused to Indian English. However, it has been impossible to avoid two elements of Indian numbering: a *lakh* means '100,000' and a *crore* 'ten million'.

CHAPTER ONE

Mastering the Game

The first of December 1926 was a normal, workaday Wednesday in Bombay, the busiest city in India. But thousands of men and boys awoke that morning with no plans to work.

By 9am, as the pale morning sun was gathering heat, burning off the night-time haze that hangs over Bombay's western seaboard, they could be seen streaming towards a grassy park near the island city's southernmost tip. Known as the Maidan, it was the location of the Bombay Gymkhana, a whites-only sports club with the best pitch in the capital city of Indian cricket.

A two-day game was in progress between the Marylebone Cricket Club, a proxy for England's national side, and the Hindus of India. It was one of the biggest social and sporting events in the city for years. The MCC was playing its first game in Bombay on its first ever tour of India. It was also the first major tour of India by foreign cricketers for over two decades, a lag that reflected the intervening war years, but also the low esteem in which Indian cricket was held.

According to that morning's *Times of India*, on sale in Bombay's streets as the men and boys streamed by, the first day's play had been watched by 'vast crowds which thronged the stands, tents, and every possible vantage point, both inside and outside the ground'. Over 20,000 people were said to have attended, including the cream of Bombay's British society, filling the Gymkhana's splendid neo-gothic pavilion and lining the seats in front of it. Everyone else was packed into temporary stands built around the boundary's edge, covered by billowing Mughal-style awnings called shamianas.

It was a well-informed crowd. The stands either side of the pavilion were reserved for the members of Bombay's other main sports clubs, the

PJ Hindu Gymkhana, under whose aegis the Hindus side was raised, the Parsi Gymkhana, the Islam Gymkhana, the Catholic Gymkhana and so on. The general public was restricted to some seats at the far end of the ground, backing on to the rest of the Maidan. The cheapest were available for one rupee – almost a mill-worker's daily wage in Bombay at the time.

It was, in short, a crowd befitting India's most cosmopolitan, prosperous and cricket-loving city; and, on that first day of the game, it had had a treat. After winning the toss, the MCC had scored 363, including a roistering innings of 130 by the Somerset amateur Guy Earle, with eight sixes, one of which had smashed a window in the pavilion. The Englishmen were all out shortly before the close of play; and the Hindus ended the day uncomfortably on 16 for one.

This was the sort of dominance the tourists had come to expect in India. They were not the best cricketers England could put out, the England captain A.W. Carr and stars such as Walter Hammond and Herbert Sutcliffe having declined to tour. But it was a strong party, led by a former England captain, A.E.R. Gilligan. It included another six current and future Test players, among them the fast-medium bowler Maurice Tate and an ancestor of mine, Ewart Astill, a flaxen-haired Leicestershire professional who bowled off-spin and medium-pace cutters. On a six-week sweep of Sind, Punjab and Rajputana – the first leg of a grinding run of 34 matches in four and a half months – the Englishmen were unbeaten. They had won only three of their 12 games; but, had more of the contests been played over three days, instead of two, they would have won many more. No Indian batsman had scored a century against them.

Even so, Bombay's cricket fans had been counting on the Hindus to put up a stiffer fight. They were also a strong side, picked from across India to compete in Bombay's annual cricket tournament, the Quadrangular. A two-week autumn festival held at the Gymkhana Ground, the Quadrangular pitted the Hindus against three other teams defined by race or religion: the Europeans, the Muslims and the Parsis.

It was India's toughest cricket contest – also by far the most popular – and the Hindus had won it in three of the previous four years. They could therefore claim to represent not only their co-religionists, but all India. 'India expects Bombay to do its duty – to check the victorious passage of the visitors,' sounded the *Indian National Herald*, a nationalist rag, in the run-up to the MCC game. 'We depend upon the Hindus to resist the invaders.'

At 10.30 on a bright sunny morning, the Hindu batsmen walked out to begin the second day's play. They started well. But then two more wickets fell, putting the Indians in a sticky position at 84 for three. The English bowlers sniffed blood. Yet warm applause for the next Hindu batsman, a tall and lean 31-year-old, walking briskly towards the wicket, signalled that the crowd still had hope. This batsman's name was C.K. Nayudu.

'CK', as he was known, was the best and most popular cricketer in India. An officer in the army of Holkar, a small princely state of central India, he was lithe and fit, a superb fielder and handy medium-pace bowler. But he was mainly a hard-hitting batsman, who had been the Quadrangular's leading run-scorer almost every year for the past decade. He was a wonderful striker of a cricket ball, famous across India for the massiveness of his hits. And having watched Earle's pyrotechnics the day before, Nayudu arrived at the Gymkhana wicket with a point to prove.

He treated his first two balls with respect. He smashed the third straight back over the bowler on to the roof of the pavilion. As it clunked down the tiles, the crowd gave a rousing cheer. This was more like it. The English bowler, a Hampshire spinner called Stuart Boyes, wheeled in again. And Nayudu lofted him for another six, then another, as the crowd went wild, clapping, cheering and yelling his name.

Nayudu reached 33 in no time, then Astill came on at the Maidan end. He was short and no big spinner of the ball, but a clever and accurate bowler, who had already taken a lot of wickets on the tour. And sure enough, he almost did for Nayudu, who leapt out to a full-pitched ball and mishit it high into the air, presenting the bowler with an easy catch. Astill steadied himself under it but, with the sun in his eyes, poor fellow, he fluffed the chance. So Nayudu hit him for a celebratory six and reached his fifty.

There was no radio in India at this time. Yet word of Nayudu's exploits somehow got about Bombay, and during the lunch interval thousands left their places of work and study and came flooding on to the Maidan. The crowd swelled to 25,000; thousands more loitered outside the shamianas, hoping for a peek of the action, or merely to hear the yelling of those within.

After lunch, Nayudu resumed the assault, hitting three more sixes off Astill. One of his hits – outdoing Earle's best effort – sailed clean over the pavilion and into the tennis courts beyond. 'The crowd was roaring like anything,' recalled one who was there that day, Vasant Raiji. 'There was a tremendous atmosphere, people were clapping and cheering and stamping with their feet on the wooden stands.'

Raiji, who would go on to play first-class cricket for Bombay and Baroda, was only six at the time. This was the first game of cricket he had ever seen. When I called on him at the flat he shared with his wife in Malabar Hill, a lovely coastal part of south Mumbai, as Bombay is called today, he was almost certainly the last surviving witness to Nayudu's heroics. He was now 92, slightly deaf, and anxiously confessed to having no very good memory of the game. He had been more preoccupied at the time, he said, with his father's promise of an ice cream and a bottle of Duke's raspberry pop. But Raiji could still remember the excitement that Nayudu's hitting had inspired. 'It was wonderful entertainment,' he said, 'not a picnic but something like that, a great outing for everyone,' he said. 'People had come to enjoy themselves.'

It was a great tamasha. But it had to end. Nayudu was caught on the boundary off the bowling of Astill's Leicestershire team-mate, George Geary. He had by then hit 153, including 11 sixes, more than anyone had previously hit in a first-class innings. As Nayudu marched back to the Gymkhana pavilion, ramrod straight, the thousands of spectators, British and Indian, stood to applaud and cheer. It was said the noise could be heard halfway across the city.

The Hindus were all out for 356 (with Astill, for consolation, taking five wickets) and the match was inevitably drawn. Yet something historic had happened. Nayudu had taken a top-class English bowling attack apart – in Bombay, the home of Indian cricket. The Englishmen must have been amazed: Indian cricketers were not generally thought capable of such feats. Under a banner headline 'Naidu's brilliant century against the MCC,' the next day's *Times of India* made the point as delicately as it could. 'There can be no doubt', it remarked, 'that the MCC side is more than surprised by the high standard of play revealed by their first opponents in Bombay.'

In fact, the Englishmen's view of Indian cricket was badly out-of-date. The last time Indian cricketers had faced top English opposition was 15 years before, when an All-India side had toured England, captained by the cricket-loving Maharaja of Patiala. They won only two of the 14 first-class games, thus confirming the English cricket establishment's low opinion of the Indian game. 'Notwithstanding their multitudes,' opined the MCC's president Lord Harris, 'I doubt if they are going to turn out a team of all India as good as the best of our county clubs.'

Harris was held to be an authority on the matter. A former captain of Kent and England, he had also served a five-year stint as governor of Bombay in the 1890s. Indian cricket, he believed, would be held back by its poverty, for this would prevent regular tours to expose Indian players to English first-class standards. But Harris had also detected certain preternatural inferiorities in the 'excitable Asiatic' cricketer. 'It is in the matter of patience,' he wrote, that 'the Indian will never be the equal of the Englishman.'

He was a man of his time. Yet Bombay and its cricket had come a long way in the three decades since Harris had presided over them. The 1890s were tough years for Bombay, marred by bouts of Hindu–Muslim rioting inside the city and hunger in the surrounding villages. In 1896 a famine swept central India in which a million people starved. Thousands of famished fugitives were driven to Bombay, where an outbreak of bubonic plague ensued, claiming 20,000 lives, and driving many back to the countryside. In 1899 there was another famine there.

Yet better times followed. The plague spurred a major overhaul of Bombay, including heavy investment in sanitation and transport. This enabled the city to absorb a lot more people. Between 1900 and 1905 more than half a million migrants flooded in, which in turn provided labour for Bombay's cotton-mills and textiles factories just as they were beginning a sustained boom. In 1914 the city received over 87 per cent of India's capital investment. With the outbreak of war in Europe, demand for its cloth and thread soared. Over the course of two decades Bombay was transformed 'from a cluster of distinct localities into an industrial megapolis'.

By the early 1920s this growth had spawned a sizeable middle class whose members enjoyed weekends off and a modicum of discretionary income. These are the basic ingredients of organised leisure: it was no coincidence that this was the decade in which the Hindi film industry became established in the city. By 1923 Bombay's cinemas were taking so much money at the box-office the state government started taxing them. This was also when Bombay's other great amusement, the Quadrangular (or Pentangular as it would become known in 1937, following the addition of a team of Buddhists, Jews and Indian Christians known as 'the Rest'), began to flourish. It was 'the climax of the cricket (and social) season,' as the *Bombay Chronicle* put it.

Fuelled by a growing rivalry between India's most populous communities, Hindus and Muslims, the tournament was hugely popular. 'When the Pentangular was on the whole of Bombay talked about nothing else,' the tournament's last surviving player, Madhav Mantri, recalled. A wicketkeeper for the Hindus during the 1940s, Mantri was now aged 90. When I called on his small flat in an appropriately named Mumbai district, the Hindu Colony, he was comfortably arranged in his pyjamas, watching cricket on television. 'People would reserve their leave for those weeks,' he said, recalling the annual tamasha. 'It was something people looked forward to and it made them happy. The Pentangular was a great occasion and when the Hindus played the Muslims ... phew, big crowds.'

Noisy too. Indian cricket crowds were rarely hushed like English ones. The people who gathered on the Gymkhana Ground, where Quadrangular games were played, beat drums, sang songs and flew kites in the stands. When their heroes hit a century, they rushed on to the pitch to place garlands of flowers around their necks; when they got out cheaply, the spectators booed as if they were pantomime villains. Right from the start an Indian cricket ground was as much a popular theatre as a sporting venue, with the crowd playing a part in the drama. One or two spectators became stars in their own right. For example, Charlie, a short, fat Parsi clown, whose trademark piercing whistle could be heard all around the ground, and who once scurried between the legs of the enormous Maharaja of Patiala while he was preoccupied watching the play. Happily, the cricket-loving Maharaja saw the funny side, and rewarded Charlie with a gold chain.

This was the sophisticated city and cricket culture to which the MCC cricketers had unwittingly pitched up. Bombay was taking its place as a great global commercial capital, swelling in confidence. And the Englishmen would also play a part in this transformation. Astill would enjoy a fine, long career; he won nine Tests for England and was the first working-class professional captain of Leicestershire. Yet it is hard to think he played a more important game of cricket than on the Maidan against the Hindus. For most historians of Indian cricket, Nayudu's onslaught was its moment of arrival.

The post-match celebrations were tremendous. The Hindu cricketers were honoured with a felicitation ceremony at the Bombay Theatre, followed by a performance from Hirabai Barodekar, a 'world-renowned popular young songstress of gramophone name'. Another congratulatory gathering was held at the Damodar Thackersey Moolji Hall, in the suburb of Parel, at which the cricketers were entertained with a performance of *The Taming of the Shrew* in Marathi, and presented with medals by a local jeweller. Nayudu's medal was made of gold.

Gilligan was also impressed. Before leaving the city, the MCC's captain gave a speech in praise of Nayudu's 'polished batting' and the general quality of cricket his team had encountered in Bombay. Later in the tour he also gave the Maharaja of Patiala some historic advice. Over drinks at the shady Roshanara cricket ground in Delhi, he urged him and a group of local businessmen to form a governing body for the Indian game. This would be the first step towards India getting membership of the Imperial Cricket Conference, and thereby Test-playing status. The Board of Control for Cricket in India was duly formed in 1928 and plans were drawn up for another MCC tour of India, in 1930–31. This, it was expected, would include an inaugural India–England Test match in Bombay.

The tour had to be cancelled, however, because of another milestone in India's progress. In March 1930 Mohandas Gandhi emerged from his ashram in Ahmedabad with 78 apostles and began trekking 241 miles to the Arabian Sea to make salt. In defiance of the British salt laws, which gave India's rulers a monopoly on its production, this act of civil disobedience and the Raj's iron-fisted response to it triggered protests across India's main cities. By the end of the year 80,000 protesters had been jailed and there was no question of Test cricket being played in Bombay.

But India's cricketing baptism was not long postponed. The following year an Indian party toured England and, in June 1932, played a Test match at Lord's. Nayudu was India's captain for the match, as he should have been for the tour. That honour went to a prince, Natwarsinhji Bhavsinhji, maharaja of the tiny western state of Porbandar. He was a 'keen cricketer', in the words of one of his biographers, though 'handicapped by being almost useless'. Porbandar, a specialist batsman, scored 42 runs in his entire first-class career, and only two on the 1932 tour. His biggest contribution to Indian cricket was having the decency not to pick himself for India's first Test match.

Yet the tour was a triumph. England won the Test with ease, despite some fine fast bowling from the Indian opening pair, Mohammad Nissar and Amar Singh. Yet nothing, not undeserving princes or even defeat, could dim the glory of the occasion. India, while still a colony, had joined England, Australia, New Zealand and the West Indies as the fifth fully fledged international cricket team. In cricket, if not yet politics, India was its own dominion.

There was no guiding hand behind India's adoption of cricket. It was not part of a grand colonial design. Though many British administrators, schoolmasters and missionaries worked hard to spread cricket in India, their efforts were ad hoc and only really significant from the late-19th century, by which time many Indians had already embraced the game on their own initiative. The lead was taken by members of the Indian elite, in business and politics, who were impressed by the lofty prestige that the British reserved for cricket. In time, Indians found other reasons to play, watch and support the game, which had nothing to do with the British. Yet the original Indian regard for British values and favour was the main reason for cricket's early growth in India. Without this, the game would not have spread as it did.

Cricket was brought to India by British soldiers and sailors: there is a record of British Jack Tars playing the game in Gujarat in 1721. But it was not organised on the subcontinent until the late-18th century when the Calcutta Cricket Club was formed by officers of the East India Company. This was the first cricket club established outside Britain. It played on a grassy plain outside the walls of Fort William, Calcutta's great stone citadel, which had been kept free of native dwellings to ensure a clear line of fire for its cannon. The oldest surviving Indian scorecard records a 'Grand Match of Cricket' played on this ground between Old Etonians and the Rest of Calcutta. This was also the occasion of the first recorded century on Indian soil – by one Robert Vansittart, an OE and son of a former governor of Bengal.

This was the prototype for the games of colonial cricket that were increasingly played across India during the 19th century, as the British extended their grip. 'Wherever they may be, north, south, east or west, sooner or later, provided a sufficient number are gathered together, there is certain to be a cricket match,' wrote a 19th-century British traveller through India, A.G. Bagot. 'And climate has little or no effect on their ardour, for you will find them playing on the burning sand of the desert with as much zest as if it was the best possible pitch in the Old Country.'

More often, the British played in the pleasant sports clubs they founded in every Indian city, garrison town or railway junction where more than a handful of white sahibs were posted. Havens from heat, dust and bothersome natives, these establishments were sacred terrain for the British in India. Here, within the privacy of a smartly-painted picket fence, they acted out a caricature of British upper-class life, modelled on the English public schools that most had attended. Club-life included such indelible idioms of Britishness as sticky puddings, *The Times* (two months old and respectfully ironed), in-house slang and an unforgiving club committee to enforce idiosyncratic house rules and, despite much heavy drinking, a certain decorum.

Ostensibly, the clubs were dedicated to playing sport, to which, like most public-schooled Victorians, the 19th-century British in India were addicted. The gymkhanas – a word derived from the Urdu *gend-khana*, meaning ball-house – often had superb facilities for golf, tennis, football, rugby, hockey and badminton, all British inventions, which their members played avidly. Yet no game was half so dear to them as cricket, for it was a caricature of Englishness even before it left England.

Cricket had emerged, in something like its present form, in the 16th century, among the peasants of south-west England. Its popularity grew rapidly in the 17th century, after it was taken up by the British aristocracy. Upper-class bucks loved to bet on the game. They also patronised talented players, artisans and peasants, to play for the teams that many raised. In cricket, almost uniquely, commoners and gentry mingled, if not as equals then as team-mates.

Another strain of aristocratic cricket was more exclusive. Games of country house cricket, played by gentlemen wearing parti-coloured blazers and caps, were designed to suggest aristocratic virtues, such as duelling, decorum and languor. Cricket's varied rhythms were naturally suited to this interpretation. With its moments of intense jousting between bat and ball, followed by a pause for the ball to be returned by the fielders, cricket can be staged as a chivalric game. This was the character of the colonial cricket played in India.

Such class-based oddities gave English cricket a somewhat paradoxical reputation. It was at once popular and elite. It was exclusive yet, as a rare forum for gentry and commoners to interact, a source of social cohesion. Hence the historian G.M. Trevelyan's famous claim that the French aristocrats would have spared themselves the guillotine if they had only played cricket with their serfs. But it was not the case that in cricket class distinctions were forgotten. Rather cricket, having its own hierarchy – of batsman, bowler and fielder, of captains and team-players – accommodated them. Where the upper and lower orders met to play cricket, gentlemen batted and working men bowled.

As cricket's popularity increased, it became fashionable to see the game as uniquely representative of English society. By the early years of Victoria's reign, this once playful notion had become a cardinal English belief. Cricket was not merely held to reflect the tastes of English society. It was considered to contain within its form certain intrinsic qualities of Englishness. 'The game of cricket, philosophically considered, is a standing panegyric on the English character,' wrote James Pycroft, an Anglican parson and early cricket theorist, in 1851. 'None but an orderly and sensible race of people would so amuse themselves ... cricket is essentially Anglo-Saxon.' Almost a century later, Lord Harris would find nothing to disagree with in that. Cricket, he wrote, was 'English you know, quite English.' This made it both great and, because patriotism, sport and moral standing were intertwined for the Victorians, also good. Cricket, wrote Harris, was 'more free from anything sordid, anything dishonourable, than any game in the world. To play it keenly, honourably, generously, self-sacrificingly is a moral lesson in itself, and the class-room is God's air and sunshine.'

It was no wonder the British did not, by and large, set out to proselytise cricket in India. It was, alone among all their games, a treasured badge of national identity. For the self-aggrandising Britisher in India, playing cricket was what separated him from the natives outside the club gates. Only the English played cricket; Indians could hardly be expected to master the game if they tried. And that is precisely why they did try.

***

The first Indian cricketers were Parsi Zoroastrians, members of a fire-worshipping community whose ancestors had fled the onrush of Islam into Persia in medieval times. They landed in Gujarat where, their legend has it, they were given refuge by a local raja on an understanding that they must not attempt to spread their faith. The Parsis kept that promise, assimilating some aspects of Gujarati culture, including its language and cuisine, but maintaining a proud and exclusive identity. In the way of nomadic minorities, this helped them thrive in business. And when Bombay emerged under the East India Company as an important trading port, many Parsis migrated to the city, seeking the security and opportunities provided by British rule.

India's white rajas were quick to recognise the Parsis as potential allies. The British admired their commercial flair and fairer-than-average complexions. By the late-18th century Parsi merchants were among the most prominent investors in Bombay's shipping industry, and in its spice, cotton and opium trade. As they prospered, many adopted European education, dress and manners. They were soon considered by other Indians, often resentfully, to 'represent themselves as being like the British'. It was only a matter of time before they started laying bat on ball.

That happened, according to Parsi chronicles, in the 1820s or 30s, on the same Bombay park where, a hundred years later, Nayudu would put the MCC bowlers to the sword. It was bigger then, and lay to the west of another British citadel, Fort George. Bombay's European residents called it the Esplanade and rode their horses or promenaded across it, enjoying a ripple of sea breeze. Indians called it the Maidan, an Urdu word, from the Persian for 'town square'.

It is easy to imagine the Maidan back then, looking much the same as many Indian parks today. There would have been a few supple geriatrics performing yoga contortions; the odd courting couple, seeking a furtive escape from parental eyes; and gaggles of sexually under-exercised youths blocking the pathways, greedy for a view of an uncovered female face. But, unlike today, there would have been no Indians playing cricket. Instead, they would have played traditional Indian games, like kabbadi, a cross between military training and game of tag, or gilli-danda, which involves flicking a small stick into the air and whacking it with a bigger one. But then the Parsis crossed over.

Shapoorjee Sorabjee, one of four Parsi cricket chroniclers writing at the end of the 19th century, has provided a fanciful description of the event. He imagined that: 'Parsee boys began with a mock and farcical imitation of European soldiers and officers playing at Fort George, Bombay, their chimney-pot hats serving as wickets, and their umbrellas as bats in hitting elliptical balls stuffed with old rags and sewn by veritably unskilful cobblers. Some enthusiastic boys at first only gleefully watched from a distance the game played at Fort George, and then hunted and returned the balls from the field to the players. For such gratis services rendered heartily and joyfully the officers sometimes called them to handle the bat, which was done with extreme pleasure and delight. Thus were learnt the initiatory practical lessons in cricket by the Parsees ... the more they watched the game the intenser grew their desire to play it.'

Maybe. Another report suggests a British schoolmaster in Bombay, by the name of Boswell, started teaching the game to his Parsi pupils in the late 1830s. At any rate, there is little doubt that soon after Parsi youths started playing cricket the elders of their community were encouraging them to practise it. The first Parsi club, the Oriental Cricket Club, was launched in Bombay in 1848. Two years later it was superseded by the Young Zoroastrian Club, founded with financial support from two wealthy Parsi families, the Tatas and Wadias. All three are still thriving. The club still plays cricket on the Maidan. The Tatas still patronise venerable British institutions: in recent years the family business, the Tata Group, has bought the remnants of British Steel and Jaguar Land Rover. It also still supports Indian cricket – as do the Wadias, who in 2008 added a stake in the Kings XI Punjab IPL side to their property, textiles and airline empire.

Thus provided for, Parsi cricket flourished. At least 30 Parsi cricket clubs were formed in the 1850s and 60s, mainly in Bombay. The British played little or no part in this development. According to Sorabjee – an early Indian cricket nationalist – they were often disdainful of Parsi cricket. He describes an occasion in 1868 when Parsi boys were banned from playing cricket on the Maidan after a 'random ball struck, not in the least injuriously, the wife of a European police constable whilst enjoying a stroll around the cricket field'. But the Parsis were not without British champions. The main source for Sorabjee's account of this incident was a letter that ran in the establishment *Bombay Gazette*, protesting against the ban. It was written by a British judge, Sir Joseph Arnould, who wrote: 'Tastes differ, but for my part it does my heart good to see and hear these vigorous lads so earnest about their manly game.'

The Parsis must have been glad of his support. A successful minority, they were needful of their rulers' goodwill. But they were no one's lackeys. The leading Parsi families were among the richest and most sophisticated in the British Empire. They dominated Bombay's municipal politics, founded several newspapers and were prominent in the city's flourishing theatrical and literary circles. If, as some have claimed, the Parsis adopted British culture as a means to ingratiate themselves with India's rulers, their use of it expressed their own genius.

In 1886 a team of Parsi cricketers went on the first self-funded tour of England by non-Europeans (a team of poor Australian Aborigines had toured in 1868). To improve their chances of success, the community had shipped over to India a Surrey professional, Robert Henderson, to help them prepare for the tour. It was nonetheless a sporting disappointment. The Parsi cricketers won only one of their 28 games, and lost 19. 'In arranging the fixtures, the powers of the players have been much over-rated,' said *Wisden*. Yet their reception in England was gratifying. The Parsis were honoured with a game at Lord's against the MCC, including the great W.G. Grace, but were bowled out for 23 and 66, mainly by W.G. Their final game was at Cumberland Lodge in Windsor Great Park and attended by members of the royal family.

Two years later, in 1888, the Parsi cricketers returned to England and this time performed better. They won eight of their 31 games, and had frequently the best bowler on either side in Dr M.E. Pavri. A fast, round-arm bowler, inevitably known as the 'W.G. Grace of the Parsis', Pavri took 170 wickets on tour at an average of 11.66. After bowling one of his victims at Eastbourne, one of the dislodged bails was said to have flown nearly 50 yards.

In England the Parsis were treated almost as equals. But back in Bombay, playing cricket was not quite the same passport to white society. Having largely ignored the Parsi cricketers, Bombay's British rulers proceeded to incense them, in 1877, by enclosing a quarter of the Maidan for the sole use of the newly formed Bombay Gymkhana.

Making matters worse, the Gymkhana's polo players raced their ponies on the rest of the Maidan, which cut up the Parsi cricket pitches horribly. Enraged by the injustice of this, Sorabjee launched a campaign to have the European polo players evicted from the Maidan, or else for an alternative area to be made available for Parsi cricket.

In a series of elegantly worded petitions, he berated Bombay's rulers for their inconsideration and double standards. The effect was like being gently massaged with acid. On 27 October 1881, for example, Sorabjee sent the following missive to Bombay's then governor, Sir James Ferguson, on behalf of 460 Parsi cricketers. It expressed their view that it was:

> ... a little unfair that the comforts and conveniences of the half-a-dozen gentlemen, who generally play polo, should be preferred to the necessary healthful recreation of over five hundred native youths ... Your petitioners need scarcely remind your Excellency in Council how much good cricket depends upon the state of the turf, and if any proof of the fact were wanted it would be furnished by the circumstance that the Gymkhana carefully preserves its own cricket field from being trampled on by the ponies and even by passers-by.

The Parsi struggle for a more level playing field, meticulously recorded by the historian Ramachandra Guha, can be viewed in a broader context. It coincided, in 1885, with the formation in London of the All-India Congress party by some Hindu, Parsi and British members of the occultist Theosophical Society. Their purpose was no more inflammatory than was that of Sorabji and his fellow petitioners. Imbued with British education, manners and prejudices, they were intent on winning more freedom for Indians within the parameters of British rule. In politics as in cricket, India's increasingly forthright elite were demanding not revolution, but merely fair play.

The Parsi cricketers succeeded first. In 1887 the Parsis were granted a parcel of land for a gymkhana of their own, on newly reclaimed land a mile or so west of the Maidan. This triumph was swiftly followed by the first victories by Indian cricketers over white opposition in India. In 1889 the Parsis beat the Gymkhana's cricket team. Then, in 1889, they claimed a bigger scalp, an English touring side led by the Middlesex amateur G.F. Vernon. Records of this two-day game show how popular

Parsi cricket had become by this time. According to the Parsi captain, J.M. Framji Patel, it drew a crowd of over 12,000 to the Gymkhana Ground, and 'the dark-eyed daughters of the land for the first time mustered strongly'.

After the first day's play, the honours were even. The English side were bowled out for 97. In their reply, the Parsis scored 80 for nine then declared. In the second innings, the English were skittled for 61, with Pavri, the Parsi slinger, taking seven for 34. The Parsis proceeded to win by four wickets, whereupon the crowd went wild, celebrating their heroes. According to Framji: 'The imaginative and emotional Parsi youth felt for a day or two that he was the victor of the victors of Waterloo.'

One or two of those vanquished victors, the British in other words, did not like it one bit. 'The crowd that "demonstrated" at the close of that game was more attractive to the artist than to the administrator,' wrote one horrified British witness to the Parsi triumph, Captain Philip Trevor. 'Few of us who saw it will forget that surging, lowing, multicoloured throng. Its reproduction defied the pen and the brush. But the faces of those who composed it wore an ugly expression. Of that vast multitude not a thousand knew the name of the thing at which they were looking, not a hundred had even an elementary knowledge of the game of cricket. But they were dimly conscious that in some particular or another the black man had triumphed over the white man, and they ran hither and thither, gibbering and chattering and muttering vague words of evil omen.'

There were many British who felt uneasy about risking the myth of European inconquerability on the playing field. Set against that, however, was a counterview that the Parsis' enthusiasm for cricket affirmed the superiority of British culture – from which Indians would surely benefit. Hence, from this time on, the increasing British support for the Indian game. Yet, though Indian cricketers would long remain keenly motivated to beat white opponents, the cricket culture that was emerging in Bombay owed less and less to the British example. As more Indians took to cricket, their fiercest rivalries were increasingly between themselves.

The first Hindu cricket clubs were formed in Bombay the 1870s. Many were backed by the Parsis' main rivals on the Bombay stock exchange, the Gujarati merchant communities that had founded it. Bombay's first Muslim cricket clubs were founded in the 1880s. Both communities soon demanded land for a gymkhana of their own. Two matching parcels of land were duly allotted to them, on the same strip of reclaimed land as the Parsi Gymkhana occupied, by Lord Harris in 1892. All three sports clubs – the Parsi, PJ Hindu and Islam Gymkhanas – are there to this day, facing what is now one of Mumbai's most fashionable boulevards, Marine Drive. But Harris refused to make any more such handouts – thereby disappointing the Bombay Jewish Cricket Club and Mangalorian Catholic Cricket Club, which were also formed around this time.

Cricket was by now spreading to other Indian cities too. High-caste Hindus in Madras (later Chennai) picked up the game from the local British in the late 1880s. This would spawn an annual grudge-game, known as the Presidency Match, between teams of Indian and European cricketers. Cricket in Karachi, a few days west of Bombay by dhow, was at first dominated by Parsis and high-caste Hindus, the latter forming the Young Hindu Cricket Club in 1899. In these and India's other great cities, cricket's growth was unplanned, organic and almost exclusively on sectarian lines.

What explains this chauvinism? Some Indian authorities consider it the result of British divide-and-rule tactics at their worst. Thus, the Parsis learned their cricketing apartheid from the British, the Hindus copied the Parsis, the Muslims followed suit; and the British then institutionalised the arrangement by providing all three communities with land. That is incontestable. Yet the communal organisation of Indian cricket also reflected how most Indians lived. Even in cosmopolitan Bombay, people mostly socialised and almost always married within their religious or caste-based communities. It was only natural that cricket should be similarly arranged, with Hindu cricket additionally subdivided on the basis of caste – thus the formation of the Kshatriya Cricket Club and Gowd Saraswat Cricket Club, two Bombay clubs named after the high Hindu caste of their members.

That cosmopolitan Bombay was no less sectarian than anywhere else in India was also unsurprising. It was India's commercial capital, and Indian business networks were invariably founded upon sect or caste. It was indeed no coincidence that the first Indian cricket clubs were started by members of two of India's most successful business communities, the Parsis and their Gujarati rivals. Playing cricket within these communities, much like marrying within them, became a means of reinforcing a valuable network. Seen in this light, Bombay's Parsi and Hindu cricket clubs operated less like atavistic dens than golf clubs the world over.

These days the communal Gymkhanas are no longer exclusive, following a decision of the Islam Gymkhana to offer membership to non-Muslims in 1949. But many lesser Indian cricket clubs still operate in the traditional way. On a visit to what remains of the Maidan, to pay homage at the Gymkhana Ground, I got chatting to a group of cricketers waiting their turn to bat on one of the public pitches adjoining it. Seated under a dirty canvas awning, they were of different ages, skinny teenagers and paunchy middle-aged men. But all were of the same Gujarati Brahmin stock. Indeed they were mostly related to each other. Their team was named after the ancestral village, near the Gujarati city of Ahmedabad, from which their grandfathers and great-grandfathers had migrated almost a century before.

Out on the worn and tussocky pitch, their opponents – also of Gujarati Brahmin extraction – were playing for the honour of a neighbouring village, whence their own forefathers had come. The game was part of a tournament contested by eight teams, each representing its members' ancestral village. It was an astonishing show of fidelity to tradition. Yet the cricketers also showed how India is changing. Their migrant forebears had all been bookkeepers – a traditional Brahmin occupation – but the cricketers were all businessmen. 'Some in textiles, some in packaging, all very well settled,' one of them, Mukesh Pandya, told me, as he sat padded up and fiddling nervously with his bat handle. Busy with their work, they struggled to keep up with each other these days. Their annual cricket tournament was therefore an increasingly important way to keep their community intact.

I strolled on to the next pitch, set in front of a shabby tin-roofed hut that bore the legend 'The S.F. Sassanian Cricket Club ESTD: 1873'. It was on this rutted ground, in 1988, that a 14-year-old schoolboy called Sachin Tendulkar and his friend Vinod Kambli, aged 16, broke a world record. Playing for their school side, Shardashram Vidyamandir, they put together an unbroken stand of 664. Today the pitch was hosting some less distinguished cricket. The batting side, sprawled along the boundary in the morning sunshine, was younger and more boisterous than the Brahmins. I asked their scorer, a young man with a muddy tattoo on his writing arm, who they were.

'We are the Marwari cricketers,' he said, giving the name of one of India's most prosperous Hindu business castes.

'And who are you playing against?'

He looked up in surprise: 'They're Marwaris too.'

The habits of centuries die hard. As this might suggest, the communal organisation of early Indian cricket reflected how Indian society was arranged. This made it displeasing to a small, but increasingly vocal, group of Bombay liberals, who viewed sectarianism as an obstacle to India's development. Yet it was also the main reason why the Bombay Pentangular was so successful.

The tournament originated in 1892, in an annual fixture between the Parsis and Europeans of Bombay. In 1907 the Hindu Gymkhana was admitted, to make a Triangular contest, and the Hindu–Parsi games soon became especially popular. The Parsi crowd, which prided itself on its knowledge of cricket and the prowess of its players, barracked the Hindus mercilessly, calling them '*Tatyas*', or 'bumpkins'. The Hindu spectators responded by calling the Parsis '*Kakdas*', a nickname derived from the Hindi word for 'crow', which referred to the Parsis' custom of leaving their dead to be picked to pieces as carrion.

The Muslims were accepted into the tournament in 1912; and pretty soon the Hindus against the Muslims became its most fiercely contested and popular game. By the time Gilligan's men came to Bombay, in 1926, the Parsis, whose tiny community represented less than 1 per cent of India's population, were slipping behind. They had won the Quadrangular in six of its 14 years and would win it once more, in 1928. But afterwards the Hindus or Muslims won every year and the Parsis began to fade from Indian cricket. The contribution of these remarkable people had been enormous. They had injected the game into the bloodstream of Bombay's middle-class society, where it would thrive.

Yet they and the Pentangular were not the only reasons for Indian cricket's rapid spread in the early 20th century. Outside the cities, a major new source of cricket patronage was emerging.

***

It was the first day of half-term and the car park outside the Rajkumar College in Rajkot, Gujarat, was in chaos. Children and luggage were being packed into family cars for the holidays. Boyish goodbyes were being shouted from open windows as the cars pulled away … then stopped, so a door could be opened and a seat belt retrieved. It was a familiar sort of chaos. The only difference from the British school scenes of my youth was the presence of servants, who were everywhere, loading the luggage and driving the cars, creating some of the confusion and most of the order.

I walked through the school gates into a handsome stone quadrangle, where more servants were clearing away folding chairs that had been set out for a concert the night before. I asked one of them for the headmaster and was directed to the cricket pitch. I would have been surprised had he been anywhere else.

The Rajkumar is one of four public schools known as the Chiefs' Colleges, which were founded in north India in the late-19th century; the others are in Indore, Ajmer and Lahore. Their founding mission, in the words of Lord Curzon, was 'to fit the young Chiefs and Nobles of India, physically, morally and intellectually, for the responsibility that lay before them'. This was a British objective of the utmost importance.

With never more than 900 British colonial officers in India – ministering to a population of 450 million at its height – the Raj functioned through dependable local allies, of whom the Parsis were a minor example and princely rulers by far the most important. They controlled 565 states, to varying degrees independent from the British, which accounted for a third of the subcontinent's area and two-thirds of its population. The Chiefs' Colleges were founded to turn their princeling sons into loyal British proxies. They were modelled on British public schools, with a strong emphasis on character-building and team sports. Cricket was very much on the curriculum.

At the Rajkumar's cricket pitch, which is one of only a handful of turf wickets in arid southern Gujarat, a broad-shouldered fast bowler was running in, kicking up puffs of dust with every step. The game was the first of an intra-school tournament, and pitted the school's secretaries against the servants. The bowler, it turned out, was one of the Rajkumar's gardeners; he bowled pretty fast and straight.

As I stood watching, the headmaster, Vinodkumar Thakkar, approached carrying my business card in an outstretched hand. He was short, bald and extremely courteous, despite my having called at a busy time and unannounced. 'Welcome to the Rajkumar College,' he said as we shook hands and I told him why I had come. But, of course, he knew already.

The Rajkumar is the alma mater of the first great Indian cricketer, Kumar Shri (His Royal Highness) Ranjitsinhji – though Ranji, as he was called, played for England. After leaving the Rajkumar at the age of 16, he proceeded to Cambridge, in 1890, where he won his blue, then went on to play for Sussex and England. He played 15 Tests between 1896 and 1902, a time of great cricketing fervour in England, later romanticised as the 'Golden Age of English cricket'. And nothing was so romantic as Ranji. His feats of run-scoring are dazzling to this day. He was the first man to score a Test century before lunch, the first to score centuries on his home and overseas Test debuts, the first to score 3,000 runs in an English season. He remains the only man to have hit two centuries, in separate innings, on the same day.

Mr Thakkar invited me on a tour he must have given many times. It started at the school's Victorian cricket pavilion, and as we walked towards it the headmaster explained the principles on which the Rajkumar was run. 'Our philosophy is education through cricket and that means real cricket. It means the right sort of cricket, it means ...' he said, pausing as we stepped into the gloom, '... the cricket played by these fellows.'

Inside the pavilion was a shrine to the school's cricketing old boys. The far wall was hung with honours boards, listing the names of the 42 Rajkumars who had played first-class cricket, mostly for the local first-class side, Saurashtra, and of the six Rajkumars who had played international cricket, for England, India and Kenya. Another wall was dedicated to Ranji. It was hung with a board showing his vital statistics: his Test batting average of 44.95, his highest Test score of 175, and so on. It also displayed half a dozen sepia photographs of Ranji in rigid batting poses, frozen for the Victorian camera's slow exposure.

On the opposite wall was a similar shrine to Ranji's brilliant nephew, Duleepsinhji, also of Sussex and England. Duleep's record was if anything better than his uncle's: a batting average of 58.52 from 12 Tests, with a top score of 173. Yet Ranji is better remembered, because of his novelty and the time in which he played. 'For us …' said Thakkar, pausing dramatically, 'Ranjitsinhji was the greatest player the Rajkumar College has ever produced.'

One might go further. He was for a time the world's best batsman, one of the most famous Asians of the Western world. In late-Victorian England Ranji was a sensation. And it was not only his prodigious run-scoring that won him this reputation, but also the style of it. Slender, light-footed, with sharp eyes and supple wrists, Ranji batted with a balletic, back-footed grace never seen before in England. He didn't step forward and thwack the ball, as Nayudu would; he stood back and dabbed and guided it, with cuts and glances just sufficient to accelerate its passage to the boundary. He is credited – also uniquely – with inventing two cricket strokes, the leg-glance and the late-cut. 'For the first time,' as another Indian princely cricketer once said in homage to Ranji, 'a game of forearm became a game of wrist.'

That this genius was an Indian, and a prince to boot, made him all the more irresistible. 'In the 1890s the game was absolutely English; it was even Victorian,' wrote Neville Cardus, that florid cricket writer who, as a boy, had watched Ranji batting at Old Trafford. 'It was the age of simple first principles, of the stout respectability of straight bat and good-length balls; the flavours everywhere were John Bull's. And then suddenly this visitation of dusky, supple legerdemain happened; a man was seen playing cricket as nobody in England could possibly have played it. The honest length ball was not met by the honest straight bat, but there was a flick of the wrist, and lo! The straight ball was charmed away to the leg boundary. And nobody quite saw or understood how it all happened.'

There were whispers that Ranji had magical powers. He encouraged the rumours. He claimed to have begun playing cricket in earnest only at Cambridge, a couple of years before he walked out to bat for England. He hinted that his Indian eyes were different from English ones – they were quicker, keener. He never played down reports of his fabulous wealth. He got credit on the strength of them. But this was more legerdemain, because the only thing about Ranji that the English had really understood was the genius of his batting.

From the pavilion Thakkar led me on a stroll through the college grounds. He pointed out the stone bathhouse that Ranji had dedicated to his old school; the war memorial listing the old Rajkumaris who had died fighting in two world wars; the library, with its voluminous college history, life's labour of a whiskery British schoolmaster; and the school hall – where I had a shock.

It was a fine room, like an Oxbridge dining hall, with panelled walls and a high vaulted ceiling. Close to the entrance, two small portraits of Rajkot's most famous sons were hanging. There was Ranji, in a batting pose, and next to him another who had lived in the town as a boy, Gandhi. They made an interesting pair: one great Indian wearing white flannels, the other naked except for his dhoti.

Yet it was the far wall that had startled me. It was hung with a collection of massive oil paintings, darkened by dust and age, of the Victorian royal family. At the centre was the queen-empress herself, festooned in black silk. Hanging about her, inside ornate gilded frames, were portraits of her royal children and cousins, as chinless as the Rajput princes whose portraits lined the other walls. I had never before in India seen such a display of unabashed Anglophilia.

As we turned to leave the hall, Thakkar was telling me how difficult life was getting for the Rajkumar. Boarding schools were becoming unfashionable in India, and male teachers hard to recruit. 'For now the College is managing, but I worry a great deal about the future,' he said gravely. 'I need men to keep these hundreds of youths in line but, since all these computer companies and outsourcing businesses started, all the English-speaking people can earn huge salaries there and rise very fast. They don't want to be teachers,' He paused, then said, 'In India, you know there's not that great a respect for teachers. For a man to say he's a teacher, well, he feels rather shy.'

'But we are trying our best,' he said. 'At least we are trying to preserve that great cricket of the past. I mean real cricket, played with decorum, with good manners, the right sort of cricket.'

Ranji was not really a prince at all, in fact. His family were poor relations of the rulers, or Jam Sahibs, of the small princely state of Nawanagar, located on what is now Gujarat's southern coastline. Yet when Ranji was aged six, one of these despots, a Jam Sahib called Vibhaji, in need of an heir, his own son having attempted to poison him. He was persuaded to adopt little Ranji. And the boy was duly sent to Rajkumar College to begin his training. This was well known to Ranji's adoring English public; yet Ranji, at the height of his fame in England, omitted to mention that, while still at the school, he had been rudely cut off by his adoptive father. A Muslim consort of Vibhaji's had given him a son, so Ranji was longer required. He was able to complete his schooling and proceed to Cambridge only because he had become a favourite of Chester McNaghten, the Rajkumar's cricket-loving headmaster. McNaghten extracted a small compensatory allowance for Ranji from the Jam Sahib and accompanied his favourite pupil to England.

Ranji was already by then a promising cricketer. Yet at Cambridge he set himself to becoming a great one. He practised almost every day to a state of near-exhaustion. Though his batting was beautiful, Ranji's success was not magical or casual, but the result of hard work and steely focus. Having been robbed, as he believed, of his kingdom, he had identified in cricket an alternative route to riches.

Runs for Cambridge and more for Sussex led to Ranji's Test debut, against Australia at Old Trafford. This was despite opposition to his selection from Lord Harris. True to form, his lordship argued that only an Englishman should play for England. Yet the Test side was at that time picked by the bosses of whichever cricket ground was hosting the game – and those in Manchester, defying Lord Harris, picked Ranji. His century on debut confirmed him as a great celebrity. But he was meanwhile, unbeknown to his adoring public, mired in debt, pursued by aggressive creditors and on the brink of serious embarrassment. He therefore returned to India in 1898, while on his way home from touring Australia, to try to cash in on his new fame.

Vibhaji had recently died and Ranji claimed to be the rightful heir to the throne of Nawanagar. There was no legal basis for this claim and the British official adjudicating the matter rejected it in favour of the old Jam Sahib's natural son and anointed heir, Jaswantsinhji. Nonetheless, Ranji received the respectful hearing that was due to a great England cricketer. His claim was subsequently reviewed by the viceroy and debated in the House of Commons. In the process, it became credible.

Ranji returned to England the following year. He then enjoyed four years of tremendous cricketing success while suffering, despite patronage from a couple of sympathetic Indian princes, serious money troubles. Again, this forced him to return to India to press his case for a kingdom – and, while there, Ranji had some remarkably good luck. His rival Jaswantsinhji took ill and died. His doctor claimed the cause was typhoid; it is also rumoured that Ranji had had him poisoned.

He certainly had motive. Jaswantsinhji's death left three claimants to the Nawanagar throne; but only one was a hero of the British Empire. Ranji's claim, though very weak, was accordingly recognised by the British and he acceded to the throne of Nawanagar in 1907. This, his biographer Simon Wilde has calculated, gave him a kingdom of 3,800 square miles, 340,000 vassal subjects, a private army of 2,700, and he had cricket to thank for it. Had he not won such fame in the game, it is inconceivable that Ranji's claim would have been recognised.

In a coronation speech that was not written for his ragged subjects, he seemed almost to acknowledge this. He vowed to 'endeavour to play the game so as not to lose whatever credit I have gained in another field'. He also swore 'to abide loyally by the traditions of this state, in its deep unswerving loyalty to the British throne'.

Ranji consequently devoted more effort to building opulent palaces in Jamnagar, his royal capital, than to cricket. He formed a Nawanagar cricket team, which under his successor was briefly the best in India. But he played little part in developing the Indian game outside his state. He refused to captain the All-India team that toured England in 1911 or contribute to its expenses. He also forbade his nephew Duleep from going on the 1932 Test tour. 'Duleep and I are English cricketers,' he was reported to have said.

This attitude has offended some Indian historians. Ramachandra Guha takes Ranji at his word and does not consider him an Indian cricketer. But this seems wrong. Ranji was born and raised in India, learned cricket in India and his achievements were all the more remarkable because he was an Indian. He also played like an Indian, defining a style of wristy stroke-play that is now one of India's richest cricketing traditions. Yet perhaps above all Ranji demands inclusion in India's cricketing pantheon because of the power he gained through cricket. Many early Indian cricketers sought political advantage by mastering the revered national game of their rulers. But Ranji's success in this regard was unrivalled. It also proved inspirational.

**

Around the turn of the century, several Indian princes became interested in cricket. One of the first was an early patron of Ranji's, Rajendra Singh, the Maharaja of Patiala. Briefly bored with pig-sticking, at which he was superb, the Maharaja formed a cricket team in the 1890s and, like the Parsis, paid for a string of English professionals to come out to coach it. Over the next two decades, following his lead and Ranji's, the princely rulers of Bhopal, Baroda, Holkar, Kashmir, Udaipur, Jodhpur, Dungarpur, Cooch Behar, Rajputana, Nawanagar, Natore and many other states all piled into cricket.

They had various motivations. Patiala, his son and successor Bhupinder Singh, and his son and successor Yadavindra Singh, were talented sportsmen, who also patronised hockey, wrestling, football and other games. Bhupinder and Yadavindra were good enough batsmen to play for India, as they did, on merit. Other princely cricketers, such as Porbandar, were woeful. Of a hapless cricketing maharaja of Kashmir, a British observer left this account: 'He was padded by two attendants and gloved by two more, somebody carried his bat and he walked to the wicket looking very dignified, very small and with an enormous turban on his head. In one of the matches I happened to be bowling and my first ball hit his stumps, but the wicketkeeper, quick as lightning, shouted "No Ball" and the match went on. The only way the Maharaja could be given out was lbw. And after fifteen or twenty minutes batting he said he felt tired and he was duly given out lbw. What the scorers did about his innings, which was never less than half a century, goodness only knows.'

Such vanity was easily mocked. Yet the princes, albeit extravagantly, were only following the British example. A system of upper-class privilege remained embedded in the English game until long after India won independence and princely power was no more. It was built on the distinction between 'gentlemen' amateurs and mostly working-class 'players' that endured until 1962: most English grounds had separate dressing-rooms, dining-rooms and entrances for these two classes of cricketer until then. Lord Harris was a beneficiary of this system. Though a decent batsman, certainly better than Porbandar, he would not have played for England on merit.

This was further proof of the high status the British reserved for cricket. So was the prominence of upper-class cricketers in the high echelons of the Raj. A close contemporary of Harris's, F.S. Jackson, was a former England captain and governor of Bengal. Lord Willingdon, Viceroy of India at the time of Gandhi's salt march, was, like Harris, president of the MCC. By the early 20th century, these cricket-loving sahibs were heartily encouraging the Indian game, attending matches and presenting prizes. Investing in cricket was therefore a good way for the princes to get their attention. 'Cricket was one of the languages of the Raj,' writes the Australian historian Richard Cashman, 'and those who could master its subtle inflection and rhythms could expect to exert a greater influence over colonial policy-makers.'

Whatever their motivations, the princely cricketers provided a big boost to Indian cricket. They imported some of the finest cricketing stars of the era, including Jack Hobbs, Herbert Sutcliffe, Clarrie Grimmett and Learie Constantine, to play for their sides. They also provided jobs in their armies and household staffs for many Indian cricketers. And this largesse, unlike the communal cricket played in the cities, came with little or no regard to a player's caste or creed. In 1898 Patiala's side included four Englishmen (though one was perhaps an Anglo-Indian, a member of a Eurasian community begotten during the freewheeling early decades of the British in India), three Parsis, two Hindus, including Ranji, a Muslim and, in the capacious form of the Maharaja himself, a Sikh.

Poor cricketers were among the beneficiaries of princely patronage. They included four brothers, the Palwankars, who were born into a Hindu caste reviled as 'untouchable' by higher-born Hindus. The eldest and best Palwankar, Baloo, was a star of the 1911 All-India tour to England; his brother, Vithal, was Nayudu's captain on that momentous day in 1926, when CK battered the MCC. During the first three decades of the 20th century, the Hindus team generally had one or another of the untouchable brothers in its line-up. Notwithstanding the genius of Ranji and Duleep, they have a claim to be considered among the first families of Indian sport.

The princes also wrote cheques for India's fledgling national cricket set-up: much of the cost of the 1911 tour was borne by Patiala. He was also partly responsible for launching India's first inter-regional tournament, the Ranji Trophy, in 1934. The contest was of course named after the first cricketing prince, who had declared his innings the previous year. Patiala donated a fine gold cup to be awarded to its winner.

There were also downsides to princely patronage. The princes injected their own medieval brand of politics into the administration of the Indian game – and their feuds could be vicious. One of the most serious, which endured throughout the 1930s, was between Patiala and an eccentric Indian princeling, the Maharajkumar of Vizianagram.

Vizzy, as he was called, ruled a microstate in the holy north Indian city of Varanasi, on a bank of the Ganges. He was short, fat, myopic and cricket-mad. He was a better batsman than Porbandar, but not by much. To improve his chance of runs, Vizzy allegedly had a habit of bribing the opposition bowlers with gold watches to persuade them to bowl gently to him. Even then he rarely scored fifty. Yet Vizzy's lack of talent in no way tempered his burning ambition, which was to captain India.

He realised his ambition on India's second Test tour of England, in 1936. It had been expected that the side would be captained by another Indian prince who had played for England, the Nawab of Pataudi, or else by Nayudu or by Patiala's hard-hitting son, Yadavindra, who was captain of the Hindus at the time. But Vizzy outwitted these rivals through a campaign of brilliant toadying and manipulation. He at first claimed to be unavailable for the tour. Meanwhile, he campaigned among India's recently formed state cricket associations, promising to select their players for India in return for their support. He was also in good odour with the British: having named both a stand at the new Feroz Shah Kotla stadium in Delhi and a splendid silver trophy after the viceroy, Lord Willingdon. One by one, Vizzy's rivals dropped out of the running. Nayudu, a prickly character, lacked high-level support. Yadavindra was unpopular with the Bombay public, and Patiala's standing with the British had dived, partly due to Willingdon's disapproval of his lascivious sex life – the Maharaja had at least ten wives and 80 children. Pataudi, seeing the intrigue and factionalism in Indian cricket, didn't really fancy the job. Whereupon it turned out that Vizzy was available to tour after all.

He arrived in England with 36 pieces of luggage, two personal servants, and a team that already despised him. He did not win its confidence. Unlike Porbandar, Vizzy picked himself for every important game, including the three Tests. He was, besides being a poor batsman, a clueless captain. An official post-tour inquiry led by the chief justice of Bombay, Sir John Beaumont, concluded that Vizzy, 'did not understand the placing of the field or the changing of the bowling and never maintained any regular order in the batting.' Yet the enquiry was occasioned by a bigger problem, a civil war that erupted in the tour-party between Vizzy and Nayudu, which led to disgraceful rows. The most heinous saw Vizzy and his loyal tour manager, Major R. Britton Jones, conspiring to send one of India's best players, Lala Amarnath, home for insubordination.

A rambunctious Punjabi and free-spirited cricketer, Amarnath was a fine and popular all-rounder. On his Test debut, against England in Bombay in 1933, he had scored the first Test century by an Indian. Yet to Vizzy this made him a threat, as also did his friendship with Nayudu. After Amarnath dared to challenge one or two of the prince's idiotic field placings, Vizzy therefore turned against him. He juggled him in the batting order, showed no consideration for his injuries and, when Amarnath complained, Vizzy ignored him. Amarnath did not respond well to this treatment. After telling his team-mates what he thought of it, Britton Jones ordered him back to India.

This incident, which was exhaustively reported in the British press, was a great embarrassment to India, but somehow it did not ruin Vizzy's reputation. After India won independence in 1947 he reinvented himself as an Indian patriot – forswearing the knighthood bestowed on him in England during the 1936 tour. As a cricket administrator in Uttar Pradesh, he also sought to heal the divisions of the past: he invited Nayudu, at the age of 61, to captain the state. Vizzy, at last, became popular in a way – as a famously uninspired cricket commentator on All-India Radio. The joke was that Vizzy hunted tigers – of which he claimed to have bagged over 300 – by placing a transistor radio in the jungle and boring them to death with his commentary.

But at least Vizzy was consistent in his support for cricket: he clearly loved the game. Another drawback of princely patronage was that it was liable to dry up suddenly, when a prince died or found a new toy. The death in 1911 of Sir Nripendra Narayan, the cricket-loving Maharaja of Cooch Behar, thus sparked a dramatic demise in Bengali cricket. And this phenomenon was evident on an India-wide scale after 1947. In the space of just two years, 1947 to 1949, India's new Congress government entreated or bullied more than 500 princely rulers to sign away their states to the newly formed republic in exchange for a generous stipend, known as the Privy Purse. Many left cricket thereafter.

The killer blow to princely cricket came in 1971, when the Privy Purse was stopped. No longer able to afford their cricket teams, most of the remaining cricketing princes withdrew from the game. Some turned their palaces into luxury hotels and lived quietly off the proceeds. Most simply hunkered down, to meditate on their past glories and present fears of falling masonry.

'What a treat for you!' the Jam Sahib exclaimed. 'What a lovely creature!' Through the windscreen, we watched in silence as a tiny fawn took its first trembling steps. Behind it, through a tangle of thorny acacias, I could make out a section of sweeping palace roof. 'What a treat!' sighed the king, a broad-shouldered septuagenarian called Shatrusalyasinhji. 'I must tell you that the spotted deer is in my opinion the prettiest deer in the world.'

He had also been a cricketer, though a much lesser one than his uncle Duleep and great-uncle Ranji. Sat, as he was known to his friends, was also a different character. He was dressed all in white, as a mark of his devotion to the god Shiva, and had a snowy, waist-length beard. He looked a bit like Gandalf.

I had come to Jamnagar, where he lived alone in a small bungalow, to discuss cricket with him. But Sat was more interested in natural history. The moment we had met, he had urged me to join him on a safari to 'a small nature reserve of mine'. This turned out to be a 45-acre walled enclosure, in the middle of Jamnagar, just across the road from the small bungalow where he lived alone. It was one of his palace gardens. The Jam Sahib, as Sat was still respectfully known in Jamnagar, had let it grow wild and stocked it with deer and antelopes that had been brought to him, 'half torn up by jackals', by the villagers of his former ancestral estates.

This was the least of his passion for nature. At one time, Sat said as we drove through the thorn scrub, he had kept 8,000 pets in his palaces. 'There were, you know, a lot of birds and reptiles and things in the bedrooms,' he explained. 'I think you could say it got a bit out of hand.' The main problem was apparently the constant grieving. 'When you keep an animal you get very close to it and when it dies it is, you know, extremely painful. So I said to myself, "Now come on, you've got to harden your heart," and I think that's helped me to deal with everything else, too.'

We trolled on through the undergrowth, braking for a couple of peacocks, and occasionally stopping to view a spotted deer or small herd of nilgai, a muscular Asian antelope. 'We had 135 gardeners working here when I was a boy ...' the Jam Sahib said. And suddenly I gasped in wonder, as the palace came into view. It was vast and ornate, decorated with fairytale turrets, domes and battlements. 'Ah,' he said, observing my surprise. 'It is quite handsome. But completely unaffordable these days, I'm afraid. It's crumbling to pieces. All my palaces are. It's the typhoons mainly that are the nuisance.'

I asked the Jam Sahib how many palaces he had these days. 'Just three at the moment,' he said distractedly, and then sighted a rare albino spotted deer: 'Now look at that chap! There's a story to him, I can tell you!'

We left the nature reserve and proceeded to what Sat described as his Guest Palace. He said he had high hopes we might find, 'fingers crossed, a cup of tea and perhaps even a cheese sandwich' waiting for us there. I had envisaged this building as a sort of coach-house. But it turned out to be even more massive than the first. It was the size of an English stately home and topped with a lofty watchtower and more domes and turrets. Both palaces had been built by Ranji. This one was formerly occupied by Sat's sister. 'But, of course, I had to move her out after the earthquake ...' he said sorrowfully, as we walked up to its massive double doors.

They opened ahead of us, and as we entered the palace I glimpsed an attractive middle-aged woman, wearing a green and red sari, who was standing behind one of the doors with her head bowed. The Jam Sahib swept past without acknowledging her. Then, without a backward glance, he whipped off his white knitted cap and flung it over his shoulder. His cousin caught it cleanly, and closed the doors.

Sat led me down a long corridor filled with large stuffed animals. 'That chap ate 107 people before he was shot,' he said cheerily, pointing to a glass case holding a snarling tiger. 'Ah, here we are!'

We entered a dining room, where a beautiful rosewood table had been laid for two. 'You must sit here I think,' he said. 'And will you not try one of those? If I'm not mistaken, the triangular ones are chicken and these others are made with peanut butter – all the way from America!'

As a boy, Sat had been a fair batsman. After attending public school in England, he had therefore spent three months playing for the Sussex second team, accompanied by his father, Ranji's nephew Digvijaysinhji, who was both Jam Sahib and president of the BCCI. 'It was one of our happiest times,' Sat recalled fondly. 'We attended the matches together. We even carried our own sandwiches!'

I asked the Jam Sahib why he thought cricket had proved irresistible to Indian royalty? 'Well, of course, that is obvious,' he said briskly. 'The rulers wanted to get into the good books of the British by showing what like-minded people they were. It was simply to impress the British.'

Throughout the 1960s Sat played for Saurashtra, a state formed by amalgamating Nawanagar and other princely states. He also dreamt of becoming the first Jam Sahib to play for India. But the days of princely privilege were waning, and he was not good enough to win selection on merit. The highlight of his career was a painstaking 164 for Saurashtra in Pune. It was Sat's first first-class century and on the train back to Jamnagar he wondered if it might qualify him for his other great ambition – which was to wear the cricket blazer of the defunct Nawanagar team.

'But when I came home father said absolutely nothing to me about my innings all day,' he said, with his air of practised sadness.

'A week went by and still he said nothing about it. After a while, I could bear it no longer. So I said to him, "Father, you may have read in the newspaper that I scored a century in Pune. May I now wear the famous Nawanagar blazer?" And father replied: "For scoring 164 in seven and a half hours? Certainly not!" So I never did get to wear the Nawanagar blazer. Father had said nothing doing and, you know, you can't very well award it to yourself.'

CHAPTER TWO

In the Land of the Blind

The nawab surveyed me with his good eye. I had asked him a question but he, seated in an ornate silver chair, had ignored it. 'What I meant to say,' I tried again, 'is that I'd really like to know who's telling the truth …'

I thought this was what he had been expecting, an informal and off-the-record chat about the enormous corruption scandal in which he, Mansoor Ali Khan, the ninth Nawab of Pataudi, had become unwittingly embroiled. This was what we had arranged, here in this very room of his Delhi townhouse, only the previous day. But if Pataudi remembered that, he gave no hint of it. He looked distinctly unimpressed.

'Have you played?' he replied in his rich bass voice. 'Have you played cricket?'

I nodded.

'Where? What cricket have you played?'

'Well, you know, at school and university …' I said, feeling surprised and rather uncomfortably pleased. 'At Oxford, but I didn't get a blue …'

'Oxford. No blue,' said Pataudi, cogitating. 'Fair enough. I imagine you were a bowler?'

I nodded again, wondering whether I should provide details. I would have been glad to, but it might have sounded strange.

'Fair enough. How can I help?'

Pataudi was the fifth and last prince to captain India, and by far the most important. He led India in 40 Tests between 1961 and 1975, more than twice as many as anyone previously had. He was probably India's greatest cricket captain. Pataudi, or Tiger as he had been called since childhood, is remembered as the man who made India win.

Great things had been expected of him from a young age. Tiger's father was the last nawab ruler of Pataudi, a fly-speck state 60 kilometres from Delhi. He was also the only man to play cricket for both England and India – having missed out to Vizzy's machinations in 1936, he led India on a tour to England in 1946, as English cricket roused itself from its enforced wartime slumber. Already in poor health, the nawab died six years later, while playing polo on Tiger's 11th birthday. Tiger then inherited his father's title, though not his ancestral state, which had by then been signed away to India. He had also inherited his father's talent. A born batsman, Tiger was a natural timer of the ball. Untrue to the princely stereotype, he was also a lightning fielder at cover or, before the disaster that would blight his career, short-leg.

At Winchester, Tiger broke the batting record set by his father's old England captain, Douglas Jardine. He made his debut for Sussex – Ranji's and Duleep's old county – as a 16-year-old schoolboy. He then went up to Oxford in 1960 and hit a century in the Varsity match as a freshman, as his father had done before him. He was made captain of Oxford the following year, in which he scored heavily against the best county bowling. With three games left to play, he was top of the English batting averages and within 92 runs of his father's record for the most runs scored in an Oxford season.

But then Pataudi suffered a cruel blow. In July 1961, he was half-blinded in a car crash: a splinter of glass had pierced his right eye, rendering it almost useless. Many assumed his cricket career was over.

'How much could you actually see?' I asked him, after we had been chatting for some time.

Pataudi's face clouded over, and he covered his glassy right eye with one hand. Then he pointed at me with the other and said: 'I can see there's someone standing there. But I can't make out it's you. It's almost useless. Not that people ever believed that, you know. When I got out for a duck, they said I was no good because I'd only got one eye. And when I got a hundred, they said there must be nothing wrong with my eyesight after all. I'm afraid Indians are a very cynical people.'

With one good eye and the peak of his cricket cap pulled low over the broken one, Tiger resumed playing within a few weeks of his accident. At first he struggled: 'I could pick up the line of the ball but I was very troubled by straight bowling. I couldn't really pick the length of the ball. You need two good eyes for that.'

Yet Pataudi made adjustments for his disability. 'If the ball was straight, I tried to be cautious,' he said. 'But anything wide I hit hard, because I knew that a fast straight ball would always get me out in the end.'

Amazingly, the runs began to flow again. He scored a pair of fifties for Delhi, against Indian Railways, and was picked to play for India, against England, only a few months after his accident. In his third Test, in Madras, he destroyed the English bowling in an innings of 103 that included 16 fours and two sixes. This was Nayudu-esque hitting, which had hardly been seen in India since CK's time, most Indian batsmen having put aside their early habit of lofting the ball. But Tiger had no such inhibition. He was maimed yet all the more swashbuckling for it.

He was picked, as vice-captain, to tour the West Indies later that year; whereupon Indian cricket suffered another painful setback. Nari Contractor, India's captain and one of the last top-class Parsi cricketers, was brained by a bouncer from the Barbadian Charlie Griffiths. It took emergency surgery and a blood transfusion from his West Indian counterpart, Frank Worrell, to save his life: his Test career was over. So Tiger, at the age of 21, became India's captain – and the youngest ever in Test cricket.

Plagued by capricious selection and feuding, India had hardly ever had a settled captain before this. Against West Indies in 1958–59 they were led by four different men in five games. No wonder the team was rarely united. But Pataudi changed that. 'Before Tiger, the Indian team was quite parochial,' one of his former charges, the left-arm spinner Bishan Singh Bedi, told me. 'He was the first Indian captain who told us, "OK, you're not playing for Delhi or Madras, Calcutta, Bombay, Mysore, no, you're playing for India. So think India." Tiger was by far the best captain I played under.'

It helped, perhaps, that Tiger's own regional loyalties were distant. It was said he once chastised one of his batsmen, Chandu Borde, for wearing a Maharashtra state cricket cap on India duty; at which Borde pointed out that Pataudi himself often wore his Sussex cap. 'Ah, Chandu,' Tiger replied, 'but Maharashtra is not Sussex.'

Pataudi captained as aggressively as he batted. His predecessors were often timid, happy simply to avoid defeat. But Tiger played to win. He was a gambler, after the fashion of sporting gentlemen, and though his aggressive declarations and eccentric bowling changes sometimes backfired, this was part of the excitement. India's weakness, his leadership suggested, was no excuse not to play with spirit. That was also the message of his monocular batting. 'I was lucky,' he told me. 'There were no very fast bowlers around when I was playing.' But this was too modest. For most of his career – which included six Test centuries – Tiger was India's best batsman.

It was heroic stuff. But the fact that a one-eyed batsman was the best in India also suggested how modest its standard of cricket remained. The improvement in results that Tiger oversaw was, in fact, rather small. When he became captain in 1962, India had been playing Test cricket for three decades and won only five games out of 78. It had taken two decades to record India's first victory. Under Tiger, India won eight victories over a decade, including their first overseas, in a series victory against New Zealand in 1967.

Yet Pataudi's appeal to Indian cricket fans was about more than results. He was a handsome prince, married to a film star, the Bengali beauty Sharmila Tagore. Tiger exuded brio and dash – even if, judged by today's megaphone standards, Indian cricket was a low-key affair in the 1960s. 'There was no television in my day and the reach of cricket was not great,' he said. 'When we were playing in Bombay, it was a big event. Bollywood had to sit down for a week. But at other times, no one made a fuss.'

'Even when we won the first series overseas, in New Zealand, it was not such a big thing,' Tiger continued. 'It was so far away. I don't think most people even knew about it.' On the journey back to India, he recalled, the team plane stopped to refuel in Singapore and the players were invited to step out to be felicitated by some local Indian diplomats. Pataudi, in a state of nervous exhaustion owing to his fear of flying, declined to leave the plane; whereupon an Indian diplomat stepped aboard to berate him. 'He said it was disgraceful of me,' Tiger recalled wryly. 'He said, "just you wait until I tell your mother!"'

That would not happen today, when India's cricket captains are god-like celebrities, richer than film stars, courted by politicians. But Pataudi did not envy them. He was largely unimpressed by India's modern cricket mania. 'There's a great passion for cricket in this country, but little knowledge,' he said matter-of-factly. 'Everyone loves cricket, but very few people have played the game properly. The facilities are too poor. If you're watching a match in England, most of the people around you will have played some sort of cricket. Here there's plenty of enthusiasm, but most people haven't got a clue.'

Hence the success of the IPL, he suggested. Pataudi had until recently sat on the league's governing council – an undemanding role, for which he had been paid $200,000 a year. He had supposed this was some sort of a payback, Tiger's father having captained the father-in-law of the BCCI's then chief, Sharad Pawar, on the 1946 tour to England. Yet Tiger's proximity to the IPL, such as it was, had not improved his view of the tournament. He had only been to see one IPL match, in Delhi, and he had left after a few overs.

'Too noisy,' he said. 'You can't see anything and you can't even hear yourself think. And you know the really sad thing about the IPL? It isn't even very good. I don't think it is ever going to produce great cricket. It's what we call a tamasha, you know, music, lights, fireworks, ladies dancing and all that other rubbish.' Pataudi shrugged. 'Each to his own, but it's not for me. I like watching cricket in a proper environment. You know, hushed crowd, occasional glass of beer, preferably from a deckchair in the village near Horsham where I lived for half my life.'

Tiger had been dropped from his comfortable role in the IPL a few months previously, in a sudden reorganisation of the league. This had been occasioned by a gross corruption scandal, which was then gripping India, and it was to discuss the details of this affair that I had come to see Pataudi. He was happy to tell me whatever he knew of it. But he was not, for all that, terribly interested in the scandal. He found it depressing. 'Nothing seems to raise eyebrows in this country anymore. It seems you can get away with almost anything. Ah well. I'm afraid I went to the wrong school,' he said drolly, shaking his head. 'They didn't teach us to make money at Winchester.'

We had been talking for over two hours and I sensed Pataudi had had enough. So I ventured one last question. 'And what if your accident hadn't happened? How good might you have been?'

Pataudi replied without a pause. 'Well, I suppose twice as good,' he said. 'I should have scored a lot more than I did.'

***

Shortly after midnight on 15 August 1947, the union flag was run down the flagstaff of Red Fort in Delhi and the Indian saffron, white and green tricolour run up. India was now a free country. And in due course many other colonial emblems were erased. British statues were taken down from their plinths in New Delhi and dumped in an Ozymandian park outside the capital. The Imperial Civil Service became the Indian Civil Service. The Bombay Presidency was divided into the states of Maharashtra and Gujarat. Yet India retained much more of the Raj than it threw out.

The civil service, as well as the legal and education systems, was largely unreformed. English remained the language of most government business.

Meanwhile, educated Indians lost none of the regard for British culture that had been imbued in them over the course of two centuries of British rule. When I asked Madhav Mantri, India's oldest living Test cricketer, what the highlight of his career had been, I assumed it would involve playing for India. But Mantri said it was without doubt being introduced to the young Queen Elizabeth at Lord's in 1952. I wondered what Mantri's nephew Sunil Gavaskar, a deeply nationalist (and much greater) Indian cricketer, would have made of that.

This Anglocentric view was strongly represented by Jawaharlal Nehru, India's first prime minister, who ruled until his death in 1964. Educated at Harrow and Cambridge, Nehru jokingly called himself the 'last Englishman to rule India'. To pass the time in prison, where he was often locked up during the freedom struggle, he used to write out lists of great Old Harrovians. He was the sort of accomplished, anglicised Indian the British had sought, as a matter of policy, to create. He was, as Lord Macaulay would have noted approvingly, 'brown in colour, but English in tastes, in opinions, in morals and in intellect.'

For Nehru and other Congress leaders, India's inheritance of British culture and colonial institutions was not a cancer to be cut out. Rather, it formed a part of India's national history and endowment. Naturally, Nehru was also fond of cricket. He enjoyed watching the game and turned out faithfully to play it – enthusiastically but not well – in the annual match between the upper and lower houses of the Indian parliament.

There was a less conciliatory strain in Indian nationalism. Some nationalists understood *swadeshi*, or self-sufficiency – one of the great rallying cries of the freedom movement – to have a cultural as well as an economic dimension. During an outbreak of anti-British protest in Bengal in 1905, such nationalists threw cricket bats on to their bonfires of Lancashire cotton. This recalled a contemporaneous attack on Irish cricket, once one of Ireland's most popular games, by Celtic revivalists. But while Ireland revived hurling and Gaelic football and largely abandoned cricket, in India these protests soon fizzled. Few Indians, it transpired, wanted to go back to gilli-danda.

By the time the British left India, there was little doubt that Indian cricket would continue to thrive. As an elite game, it retained a certain British quality – including a sense, beloved by the well-to-do Indians who mostly played it, that cricket was a morally superior game.

Yet Indian cricket was now a century old and had its own character and traditions. It was also immensely popular. Cricket was written about in newspapers, played in the street and gossiped about at home and around chai stalls across the subcontinent. And cricket's roots were deepest in India's most populous and fastest-growing cities including Bombay and Madras. During the Pentangular, crowds of 40,000 flocked to Bombay's handsome new Brabourne Stadium, which hosted the tournament from 1937.

In Bombay and other big cities, cricket was one of India's most popular entertainments, ranked alongside Hindi films, religious festivals and political rallies. And Indian fans enjoyed cricket and all these diversions in much the same emotional way. A big cricket match was a dramatic event, in which the crowd participated exuberantly. This was not something learned from the British. The theatricality of Indian cricket crowds expressed a striking feature of Indian society – Indians' love of a show. 'We're all drama queens,' the Bollywood actor Aamir Khan once told me. 'Compared to British or Americans, people in India expected their theatre to be that much more. The emotional key here is different.'

Cricket's complicated form was amenable to this Indian sentiment. It provided many, broadly predictable, changes in the pace and rhythm of the game, which the Indian crowds hammed up in delight. As the bowler began his run-up, they would begin to murmur and then, as he accelerated towards the stumps, a rising clamour would build around the ground, until the glorious climax of the delivery. 'Booooowled!' the crowd shouted, as the bowler released the ball from his hand; and if the batsman then hit a boundary or the bowler took his wicket, it would explode into shouting and applause. Then the spectators would settle, murmuring, and the whole process begin again, ball by ball, over after over.

This episodic quality makes cricket, as C.L.R. James has written, an unusually theatrical sport. So do the many micro-dramas it contains within the wider drama of an innings, a game or a series. Thus the duel between a clever spinner and a big-hitting batsman; or a fast bowler and a tailender; or the eternal tension that exists between individual achievement and victory for the team. James compared cricket to Greek tragedy. Yet the game's multitudinous subplots more obviously recall India's epic, the *Mahabaharat*.

Indian cricket had also, by the time the British left India, a fairly well-developed institutional structure. There was the BCCI, its constituent state cricket associations and hundreds of gymkhana, school and company cricket teams. Most had never had much to do with the British, so it made little difference to them that the British were gone. Yet Indian cricket also faced certain difficulties.

One was the demise of its most popular tournament, the Pentangular, which had fallen victim to political events. The tournament was first cancelled in 1930, owing to the protests sparked by Gandhi's salt march. After it resumed four years later, it was increasingly targeted by liberal protesters who considered the tournament, perhaps rightly, an incitement to sectarianism. Asked for his view of the Pentangular, in 1940, Gandhi agreed with these critics. The Mahatma was almost entirely uninterested in cricket. Yet he considered it unseemly that the tamasha should be held while in Europe the 'flower of manhood was being done to death'. Moreover, he added, 'I would like the public of Bombay to revise their sporting code and erase from it communal matches. I can understand matches between colleges and institutions, but I have never understood the reason for having Hindu, Parsi, Muslim and other Communal Elevens. I should have thought such unsportsmanlike divisions would be considered taboo in sporting language and sporting manners.'

This was a painful criticism. Earlier that year India's freedom movement had fractured fatally on sectarian lines – Muhammad Ali Jinnah's Muslim League having issued its demand for a Muslim homeland. In this febrile time, Hindu–Muslim cricket contests were anathema to many in Congress. Yet, contrary to a popular belief, Gandhi's criticisms were not sufficient to end the Pentangular. They persuaded the Hindu Gymkhana to withdraw its team from the tournament that year. But it went ahead without them, and the following year the Hindus, unable to resist a windfall of gate receipts, returned to it. There would be four more Pentangulars, all immensely popular. The Hindus won in 1941 and 1943, the Muslims won a nail-biting final against the Hindus in 1944, and the Hindus won again in 1945–46. But there it had to end. In August 1946, a few weeks before the next Pentangular would have been held, 10,000 people died in the so-called Great Calcutta Killings, the first wave of the Hindu–Muslim massacres that would attend India's calamitous partition. The tournament was cancelled and never revived.

Partition was itself a setback to Indian cricket. It entailed the loss of some of India's richest cricketing terrain, especially Karachi and Lahore, to Pakistan. Some of India's best players, including the fast bowler Mohammad Nissar, were also lost to the new state. As early as 1952 this led India's great batsman Vijay Merchant to predict that India's fast-bowling stocks would suffer as a result. 'Above all, the partition has deprived India of future fast bowlers,' he wrote. 'In the past, India often relied for fast bowling on the North Indian people, who because of their height and sturdy physique, are better equipped for this kind of bowling than the cricketers of Central India or the South.' So it has proved. India's first fast bowlers, Nissar and Amar Singh, were quite possibly the best opening pair India has ever had. While Pakistan has gone on to produce a stream of brilliant pace bowlers, India has hardly produced even one out-and-out quick.

The reduction in princely patronage, between 1947–49, was another blow to the Indian game. But this was offset by growing support from Indian companies, especially in Bombay. The city's prestigious company tournament, the *Times of India* Challenge Shield, to some extent replaced the Pentangular. A big Shield game between such cricketing titans as the Tata Group and Associated Cement Companies, could draw a crowd of 10,000 to the Maidan. This was valuable advertising, which led them and other companies to hire India's best cricketers. During the 1960s Tata's side included five Test cricketers.

Many Indian cricketers, though officially amateurs, could not have played without corporate patronage. Even during Pentangular times, Mantri recalled, the most important fixture for many Hindu players, including himself, was not against their arch-rivals the Muslims, but against the Europeans. This was because it delivered a potentially lucrative opportunity to impress a British boss. 'The Europeans were the top bosses back then, and naturally you wanted to come into contact with them,' Mantri said. He ended up working for Associated Cement, which won the Shield five times between 1952 and 1961.

The rise of corporate patronage reasserted Bombay's primacy in cricket. Because the city was home to India's biggest companies, its players had the best chance of a decent job, ensuring that talented cricketers moved to Bombay in search of one. For a staggering 15 years, between 1958 and 1973, the Bombay side did not lose a single Ranji Trophy game. Until 1990, a third of India's Test players came from Maharashtra, the state of Bombay. Yet at the same time, in a counter-wave, cricket was spreading across India.

Radio played a big part in this. Live Test match commentary was introduced in 1952, and commentary soon became available in Hindi, Marathi, Tamil and Bengali, as well as English. A big increase in international cricket fixtures also raised the game's profile. Between 1932 and 1947 India played seven Tests. Between 1947 and 1957 it played 42. This in turn helped boost the Ranji Trophy, which by the 1960s had become extremely popular. The biggest grudge games, as between Tamil Nadu and Karnataka, or between Delhi and the armed forces could draw a crowd of 30,000.

While cricket spread to the regions, they were seeing serious unrest. During the 1950s, India saw waves of strikes and protests calling for a redrawing of its state boundarires on the basis of language. Sometimes they turned violent – as when, in January 1956, 106 people were killed in Bombay during riots sparked by Marathi-speaking protesters. This led to a major redrawing of India's state boundaries on linguistic lines later that year, spawning Andhra Pradesh, Kerala, Madhya Pradesh and other new states. The rise of regional political movements was another boost for the Ranji Trophy, which became an important means of asserting regional pride. And, because it is always easier to make new constituencies in democratic India than kill off old ones, the tournament also became a unique record of India's changing political map. Thus, many of the states scrapped in the shake-up continued to exist in cricket. Saurashtra, a short-lived conglomeration of former princely states, continues to this day to field a team in the Ranji Trophy, as does its erstwhile neighbour, the now-defunct princely state of Baroda. English cricket, it is interesting to note, has a similarly nostalgic tendency – long non-existent Middlesex is still included in the County Championship.

The relentless rise of Indian cricket is reflected in the much slower growth of India's other main popular sports, football and hockey. Football had delivered one of Indian sport's great patriotic successes: when a team of barefoot Bengalis, Mohun Bagan, defeated the footballers of the East Yorkshire Regiment 2-1 in 1911. The game's simplicity and cheapness, which has enabled it to sweep the world, also made it seem appropriate to India. Yet enthusiasm for football hardly spread beyond a handful of states, including West Bengal, Kerala, Goa and the far north-eastern state of Manipur. The mixed fortunes of Indian hockey are even more striking – because it is a game in which India was not merely somewhat competitive, as it was in cricket, but the world's best.

Between 1928 and 1956 India's hockey players won six successive Olympic gold medals, the third coming at Hitler's 1936 Games in Berlin where they beat Germany 8-1 in the final. Hockey accounts for eight of India's nine Olympic golds, the other being in shooting. Indian cricket has never enjoyed anything like this success. Yet Indian hockey never assumed anything like cricket's importance among India's metropolitan elite. Consequently it never enjoyed anything like the same level of support: the maharajas of Patiala were rare examples of princely hockey patrons. Nor did hockey take off in any big city, with the partial exception of Delhi. At the height of Indian hockey's success, it was played mainly in the small towns and villages of north India. A single Punjabi village, Sansarpur, has produced 14 Olympians at hockey, which says a lot for Sansarpuris but less for the game's national reach.

But why, given how rapidly cricket was spreading, was India's playing record so slow to improve? Indian cricket fans always had fine individual performances to celebrate. Vijay Hazare scored a century in each innings in Adelaide in 1947. Vinoo Mankad scored a total of 256 runs and took five wickets during a Test match at Lord's in 1952. Yet while Indian hockey players swept the world, India's cricketers struggled to win a game. Indeed it took them two decades to win their first Test, at the 25th attempt, against a second-string England side in Madras in 1952.

There were a few reasons for this poor performance. Indian pitches were slower and easier to bat on than foreign ones, which made Indian batsmen ill-prepared for the green seamers they often encountered abroad. India's paucity of fast bowling made this adjustment even harder. It left Indian players woefully unprepared for the barrage of English, Australian and West Indian fast bowling they invariably faced. The result could be humiliating. In a series against England in 1952, Polly Umrigar, a beefy Parsi who was one of India's best players of the 1950s, was visibly terrified by fiery Fred Trueman. Weak leadership and capricious selection also helped sap the Indian players' confidence. Yet the main reason for the national team's underwhelming results was simply that it did not represent the nation.

Though cricket's fan-base was spreading rapidly, the India side's talent pool was stagnant, or even shrinking.

This was another effect of corporate patronage. Where India's princely patrons hadn't cared a hoot who they hired so long as they could score runs and took wickets, Indian companies wanted college graduates. Thus Bishan Bedi, whose father was a small-time businessman in Amritsar, recalled being hired by the State Bank of India in 1968. 'They needed an India player who was a graduate, which I was. So I got a job. If I'd had to pass a test, I would not have made it. I was very lucky. Had I not played the game I'd have been a big zero at home in Amritsar, with nothing to do. But because of my involvement with the game I had a good public sector job.'

According to an analysis by Richard Cashman, of the 143 Indians who played Test cricket up to 1979, half had a college degree, compared to 1 or 2 per cent of Indians as a whole. There were always colourful exceptions to this elite bias; poor men who rose to play for India. Yet they had often received exceptional help. One was Chandu Borde, the Maharashtrian all-rounder chastised over his choice of headgear by Tiger Pataudi. He was one of ten children born to a poor couple in Poona and Tiger's jibe was at least the second time he had been patronised by a prince – at 13 Borde had received a cricket scholarship from the Maharaja of Baroda.

For the vast majority of young Indians, cricket was simply not a viable career option. Niranjan Shah, the longstanding boss of Saurashtra's cricket association, told me that in the 1970s and 80s he had found it hard to persuade the local fathers even to let their sons play. 'It was not like now,' he recalled. 'There was not much incentive for a poor man to play cricket.' To some extent, this shortage of opportunity reflected what was happening in India's economy. Nehru aimed to industrialise India very rapidly, chiefly through massive state-led investment in factories and dams. To provide the engineers and managers required to operate these 'temples of concrete', as Nehru called them, the government invested heavily in India's small, Anglophone middle class. Amazingly, in a country where 82 per cent of people were illiterate, it spent as much on a handful of universities as on primary education. Such policies helped perpetuate the advantages of the metropolitan elite but left hundreds of millions trapped in poverty. India was a democracy in which power and wealth was controlled by a tiny elite. Similarly, Indian cricket, though immensely popular, was an elite game.

It was therefore appropriate that the saviour of Indian cricket was a prince. Tiger Pataudi's greatest contribution to Indian cricket, however, was a down-to-earth observation: that India should stop worrying about what it could not do and play to its strengths. Above all, this meant dispensing with a fiction that it had world-class fast bowlers, cricket's main attacking weapon. Under Pataudi, India started picking three specialist spin bowlers, no matter where they were playing or on what sort of pitch. This was a bold, or eccentric, innovation. It also ensured that, with rarely more than one specialist seamer in the side, India's fast bowling was even quirkier. India's new-ball attack became little more than an exercise in getting the ball roughed up sufficiently for the spinners to grip. This was a service often provided by the batsmen, on occasion by Tiger's own monocular medium-pace. One commentator referred to the tactic as India's 'non-violent bowling policy'. Like the Mahatma, Tiger had turned a traditional form of defence to attack.

It sometimes worked, because India's spinners were at this time superb. Between June 1959 and January 1968 India lost 17 consecutive overseas Test matches, the most wretched away sequence in cricket history. Yet having arrested that run in Australia, they proceeded to New Zealand where, the next month, on a dry pitch in Dunedin, they won their first overseas victory. Led by Erapalli Prasanna, a cerebral Bangalorean off-spinner, the Indian spinners took every New Zealand wicket in the second innings except for two run-outs. India also won the last two Tests, to take the series 3-1. Their spinners, including Bedi, an ungainly Sikh with a bowling action that flowed like running water, took 54 of the 74 New Zealand wickets that fell in the series. New Zealand's own spinners took only 17.

Throughout the next decade India's spinners were among the world's most recognised cricketers. They were dominated by a foursome, immortalised as 'the Quartet', of Prasanna, Bedi and two south Indians, Srinivas Venkataraghavan and B.S. Chandrasekhar, a leg-break and googly bowler. Operating as a trio – and on one occasion all together – they brought a style to Indian cricket which aficionados of the game relished. From 1967 to 1978 India played 68 Tests, including 55 with at least three spinners. They won 14, lost 25 and drew 16. If that was, again, a fairly modest improvement on the previous decade – in which India had won seven and lost 19 out of 56 – the Quartet made Indian cricket gloriously distinctive.

They were different characters: Bedi ebullient, Prasanna gracious, Venkat brooding, Chandra modest and shy. Yet they were a team within a team, discussing the theory and practice of spin between themselves. 'We were very proud of each other. All four of us,' Bedi said. 'If somebody got seven wickets, say Chandra got seven wickets, no one was unhappy for him, we were all thrilled.'

Chandra was the most attacking of the four. He was also another emblem of Indian pluck in adversity – his bowling arm having been cruelly withered by a childhood attack of polio. Yet this disability, unlike Pataudi's, appeared not to hinder his genius. Some said it accentuated it – that his skinny bowling arm cut through the air like a raw-hide whip. There was certainly something uncanny about the steepling bounce Chandra could extract. He himself could never say what the secret was. 'I wasn't good at cricket,' he once admitted, 'but one year it clicked.' On his day, Chandra was unplayable.

Pataudi had made the Indian side more confident and competitive. But he would miss out on the full glory of India's spin-bowling revolution. In poor form, he was replaced as captain for a 1970–71 tour of the West Indies by Ajit Wadekar, a fine Bombay batsman. Tiger then went off to fight a different contest. With a general election looming, Indira Gandhi, Nehru's daughter and successor, had announced a plan to abolish the former princes' state stipend, the Privy Purse, even though it had been promised in perpetuity. Incensed, Tiger announced that he would quit cricket and seek election as an independent, representing his ancestral seat of Pataudi and its environs. His film-star wife, Sharmila Tagore, joined him on the campaign trail.

Yet Congress was at the height of its power and Pataudi's stand won little sympathy. Tiger won less than 5 per cent of the vote. And Mrs Gandhi, promising to abolish poverty, swept the poll. Meanwhile, Wadekar was leading India on a great run of victories.

It began with a 1-0 series win in the West Indies, chiefly due to the batting of two other Bombay batsmen, Dilip Sardesai and the pint-sized debutant Sunil Gavaskar, who scored seven centuries between them. Unlike so many of their predecessors, neither appeared remotely scared by fast-bowling. India had found some steel.

Shortly after, India travelled to England, where in the summer of 1971 they won their greatest victory yet. On the fourth day of a Test match at the Oval, Chandra ripped through England's batting, taking six for 38 to leave India needing 173 for victory. The next day was a propitious one, Ganesh Chaturthi, the birthday of Hinduism's elephant-headed god of fortune. To celebrate, some local Indians hired an elephant from a visiting Russian circus and paraded it around the ground before the start of play. India proceeded to win their first Test victory in England and, due to some rotten weather that had washed out two previous Tests, a 1-0 series victory.

Only four years before, Pataudi's inaugural overseas win in New Zealand had been celebrated fairly nonchalantly in India. Wadekar's victory in the West Indies had also caused little stir. But this win against the old colonial power was a different matter. The team was due to fly back to Bombay, but at the last minute the plane was diverted to Delhi so that Mrs Gandhi could personally congratulate India's heroes. They proceeded to Bombay, and a scene of mass jubilation. More than

100,000 people were estimated to have turned out to cheer the players and shower rose petals on their motorcade as it crawled 35 kilometres from the airport to the Brabourne Stadium. There, in front of a full house, they were welcomed by Dev Anand, the biggest Bollywood star of the time.

The biggest cheers were inevitably for Wadekar, Bombay's victorious captain. 'They could have been heard across the Arabian Sea,' he recalled. Wadekar had no doubt of the significance of his success: 'The victories in 1971 marked the start of a new era. They enabled us to shed the inferiority complex for good. We started believing that we could beat anybody anywhere. I will always remain grateful to my colleagues and, more so, the giants of yesteryear, who sowed the seeds and provided the platform. My generation reaped the harvest.'

India was still no world-beating cricket power. Wadekar's triumph amounted to only two Test wins, in Trinidad and at the Oval. Yet Indian cricket had clearly improved. In 1972–73 England came to India looking for revenge; this time the Indians won 2-1. Their spinners took 71 of the 77 English wickets to fall. Again Indian cricket fans celebrated wildly. Yet when the Indian side returned to England in 1974, it was whitewashed 3-0. In the last game, at Edgbaston, England won by an innings and 78 runs, losing only two wickets in the match. In the circumstances, *Wisden*'s verdict was kind: 'India relied mainly on three spinners, Bedi, Prasanna and Venkataraghavan and with no genuine fast bowler available the attack once more proved docile.' This was the flip side of the all-spin policy – when it went wrong, it could be humiliating.

In India meanwhile, the flip side of India's raised expectations was horribly apparent. Wadekar's house was bombarded with shoes by an irate mob. In Indore a triumphal concrete bat, raised to commemorate the historic victory at the Oval, was smeared with mud and tar. This was enough for Wadekar. As his team fell to feuding, he announced his retirement, which allowed Pataudi to return for a brief swansong.

Later that year, Tiger led India in a home series against the West Indies, which the Indians lost 2-1. That was respectable in the circumstances. India's opponents were taking off on a rather longer winning run than they had managed. For the next two decades, West Indian pace would dominate cricket, not Indian spin. Yet India's brief burst of success was an important marker, nonetheless. In the Quartet, India had a bowling attack admired around the world, and in Gavaskar one of the world's best batsman. And Indian cricket's popularity had soared on the back of their successes. In 1977, 80,000 spectators would turn up to the last day of a Test match against England at Eden Gardens in the sure knowledge that India would lose. In the event, they were beaten after little more than an hour's play.

At least the spectators had known what to expect – because Indian crowds were becoming a lot rowdier. Between 1967 and 1975 Indian stadiums saw four serious riots during Test matches, two each in Calcutta and Bombay. They were attributed mainly to overcrowding. Yet the violence was also a sign of the nationalist sentiments that India's winning streak had encouraged. Cricket, as the opportunistic Mrs Gandhi had appreciated, was now firmly associated with Indian national pride. And many Indians, especially those newly attracted to the game, were no longer prepared to settle for individual heroics and an occasional victory. They had started expecting India to win all the time, and when they lost, as Wadekar found out, their anger was terrible.

The populist strain in India's cricket culture was becoming more prominent. Hence, too, cricket's increasing association with Bollywood-style celebrity. It was not only Pataudi, a debonair man with a beautiful wife, that Indian cricket fans considered glamorous. They thought all cricketers were, especially foreign ones. English and Australian players, even those little known in their own countries, were routinely mobbed in India. 'The Indian public treat a visiting cricket team as English youngsters would treat pop stars – with unquestioning idolisation,' wrote an appreciative England captain, Tony Greig, in 1975. Even a team from the British daily newspaper the *Guardian*, a light-hearted bunch of weekend players, found themselves playing on Test grounds and being presented to the vice-president when they had toured the previous year.

The foundations of India's shrill modern cricket culture were in place. But India was still modest and understated in the 1970s. The failure of the Congress governments' leftist economic policies had left it mired in poverty. Mrs Gandhi's solution, tragically, was to lurch even further to the left. In 1969 she nationalised 14 banks, and state takeovers of coal mines, oil and insurance firms followed. The economic cost was appalling. India's economy grew during the 1970s at 3 per cent a year, a pace since disparaged as the 'Hindu rate of growth'. Poor Indians, denied the opportunities that come with growth, were the main victims of this failure. But middle-class Indians were also, in global terms, hard up. The meagre earnings of Indian cricketers were an indication of this.

In 1971 they received 750 rupees – or around $100 – per Test match. That represented a three-fold increase over the previous decade. But, given that India only played two Tests in 1972, it was hardly a decent wage. India's best cricketers remained dependent on their day jobs, which in turn made them unavailable to play in the great training-ground of West Indian and Pakistani cricketers, English county cricket. This was another reason why their results were slow to improve.

Bedi was one of the few Indians who did make it to county cricket. Having received a special dispensation from his employer, the State Bank of India, he spent six seasons with Northamptonshire, from 1972 to 1977. He was one of the best bowlers in the world at the time. Yet even in England he made little money from playing cricket. 'I'm not at all ashamed to say the first refrigerator I saw in our house was after I became a Test cricketer,' Bedi said. 'I became a Test cricketer on a bicycle. I didn't have any transport, any scooter, any car, nothing. The first car I ever bought was in 1972 after my first season with Northants. It was a VW Beetle. I still have it.'

But a fridge, to be sure, was a considerable status symbol in India at this time. Tiger Pataudi was rumoured to have wooed his film star wife with a gift of one.

The successes of the early 1970s left its mark on Indian cricket, including in the literature it inspired. By the standards of English or Australian cricket writing, the Indian cricket library offers slim pickings. It has no Neville Cardus or Jack Fingleton; nor has the Indian readership much appetite for one. India's leading sports bookshop, Marine Sports, is housed in a cubbyhole – about the size of an American walk-in closet – in a bustling district of central Mumbai. Its Goan owner, Theo Braganza, reckons to sell 100 books in a good week. But his inventory, including dusty piles of obscure tomes, entitled *Vijay Merchant: In Memoriam*, *An Umpire Remembers* or *My Innings in Mumbai* suggests even this modest target may be ambitious.

In the work of Mihir Bose, Ramachandra Guha, Boria Majumdar, Rahul Bhattacharya and others, however, Indian cricket writing has seen a modest flowering in recent years. And in much of their writing is a sense of Indian cricket coming of age in the era of Tiger and the Quartet. This is also implicit in an unusually recondite Indian cricket book, *The Tao of Cricket*, by the respected Bengali sociologist Ashis Nandy.

It opens magnificently: 'Cricket is an Indian game accidentally discovered by the English.' Nandy then argues that cricket's success on the subcontinent was testament to the game's intrinsic compatibility with ancient Hindu culture. With reference to the Hindu epic, the *Mahabharata*, he argues that Indians prefer slow-burning dramas and endless digression, that they have an equivocal view of destiny, in which victory and defeat are always partial. These qualities, Nandy argues, are provided by cricket. Thus, Indians did not merely acquire the game of their colonial occupier – in some deep cultural sense, they owned it all along. On a chilly Christmas Eve in Delhi, I arranged to meet Professor Nandy to hear more of his theories.

We met on a veranda of the India International Centre in central Delhi, a redoubt of whisky-sipping retired bureaucrats and academics, of Gandhians, Fabians and unreformed Marxists. 'Please understand,' said the bearded professor, drawing a soft brown shawl around his shoulders, 'that there's a rhythm, if not an algorithm, to cricket that many South Asians identify with. No one's fully defeated; no one's fully victorious. Just when you think you're fully defeated, someone scores a double-century.'

'But professor ...'

'In cricket,' he continued, 'the opposite is the total opposite. Your heart may bleed, but you have to clap your opponent's century. This is, of course, why Imran Khan is so popular in India. He's a demon, but an attractive one, who plays the game well, even better then the gods ...'

'Yes, but ...'

The professor was uninterruptable. 'Management of ambiguity, chaos and ambivalence, this is the definition of all South Asian society. Please imagine, we have 330 million gods and not one priest. This means that anyone may declare himself a god and you have to gulp it down, you have to digest it! It makes life unpredictable. Cricket is also unpredictable, in cricket you are playing against your own destiny ...'

'But, please, professor. What of this remains in Indian cricket today?'

He paused. Then Nandy shook his head. 'I don't see much of cricket in this IPL business. It is simply a degraded form of the game. What is the point of it? Is it an effort to catch up with other sports? Why? So many sports are so similar. Why can they not allow us to have one game to be different?' He paused, and gazed into space. He looked bereft.

The Tao of Cricket was published in 1989. By then the most popular form of Indian cricket was already unrecognisable from the slow-moving and protracted game on which Nandy's theory was based. This was one-day cricket, less an equivocal contest than a zero-sum run-chase, usually played over games of 50 overs per side. It was the original brattish challenger to Test cricket, a shorter, faster game, more demanding of explosive hitting. Though, like cricket itself, it was developed in England, during the 1960s, one-day cricket seemed like the sort of tamasha cricket that Indian fans had been waiting for all along.

Amazingly, in light of what was to come, India's cricket bosses were slow to embrace the new format. Still obsessed with the prestige of cricket, they considered it rather déclassé and hardly bothered with it. In the first two one-day World Cups, in 1975 and 1979, both of which were held in England, India had won a single match, against the no-hopers of East Africa. Shortly before the third, which would also be held in England, in 1983, India's chairman of selectors, Raj Singh Dungarpur, dismissed the format as 'irrelevant' to India. They entered the 1983 tournament as 66-1 outsiders.

The odds grew longer when, in an early round, the infant cricketing nation of Zimbabwe reduced India to 17 for five and the brink of elimination. However, India's captain, the bustling all-rounder Kapil Dev, played an astonishing innings – 175 not out – and turned the game round. Unexpected victories against Australia and England followed, and India were suddenly in the final against West Indies at Lord's. But still hardly anyone gave 'Kapil's Devils' a prayer of actually winning the tournament. West Indies had won both previous World Cups and were considered more or less invincible at the format. Even the Devils themselves held out little hope.

When I asked one of them, Kirti Azad, whether, on the morning of the final, he had considered victory a possibility, he responded with a noisy guffaw. 'We never, ever thought we could win. We never dreamt it.

We were at Lord's, the Mecca of cricket, playing the West Indies, a team in which everyone was a match-winner. Haynes, Greenidge, Richards, Marshall, Garner, Roberts, Holding – what a team! And we only had two world-class players, Kapil Dev and Sunil Gavaskar, who was the world's best Test batsman, but not a one-day batsman. We thought we had no chance.'

India batted first and scored 183, a modest total. In their reply the West Indies were coasting at 57 for one. But then their best batsman, Viv Richards, got out to a brilliant running catch by Kapil, and the remaining West Indian batsmen collapsed. They were all out for 140, and India, to the amazement of everyone watching, had won the World Cup. As the last West Indian wicket fell, an ecstatic crowd of British Indians surged across the boundary rope, and the players fled for the sanctuary of the pavilion. Azad, a tall north Indian off-spinning all-rounder, got caught and stripped for souvenirs by the mob. 'They even took my trousers,' he chuckled.

Back in India millions, listening live to radio commentary of the game, celebrated in delirium and disbelief. *India Today* marked the victory with a cover story entitled 'Miracle at Lord's'. Mrs Gandhi, recently returned to power after a spell in opposition, again grasped the opportunity for some free publicity – indeed even more hungrily than she had after the victory at the Oval in 1971. She sent a telegram to the players that read 'My slogan is "India can do it". Thank you for living up to it.' These words were emblazoned on state-owned petrol stations across India.

India's World Cup triumph changed Indian cricket dramatically. It turned out that most Indian cricket fans did not want the drawn-out subtleties of Test cricket at all. They wanted a seven-hour hitting contest, an extended climax of action and screaming, with an unequivocal result at the end. And they wanted this all the more because, extending the miracle, Kapil's Devils kept winning. Within two years of their World Cup triumph, they had bagged three more one-day trophies. These victories made the association between cricket and national pride even more explicit. A little over a decade before, Indian cricket fans had supported their team with little expectation of victory. These days millions tuned in to cricket expecting India to win.

Only 18 months after India's World Cup win, a home Test series against England showed the effects of these changes. It was a dramatic series, played against the background of Indira Gandhi's assassination, in October 1984, at the hands of a Sikh bodyguard. Yet the crowds were small by Indian standards: not every ticket for the Tests was sold. The series also suggested how one-day cricket had changed the way India's cricketers were approaching the game. After India won the first Test, most observers expected them to close the series down, by playing for dull draws. But, now addicted to dashing stroke-play, they instead threw away the next two matches and lost the series 2-1.

India's cricket cognoscenti bewailed these developments. Writing in 1988, their doyen, Sujit Mukherjee, warned that, 'It is possible that a new kind of cricket crowd which watches only limited-overs cricket is rapidly growing in India. A large majority of our spectators watch cricket without understanding details of the game ... and their sole interest is being present at an Indian victory.' Nightmarishly, he speculated that India's Test match crowds might one day switch allegiance to the new format. 'There is no denying that this can happen,' he wrote. But the evidence was in fact already coming in. A country once famous for its patience and sloth had lost its heart to the newfangled tamasha cricket.

The Indian cricket board was now happy to provide it. Up to 1983, India had played 48 one-day internationals in nine years. In the decade that followed, they played 134. This was in line with a global increase, yet the cultural shift in Indian cricket was especially pronounced. Almost every one-day game was a sell-out; support for Test cricket was meanwhile drying up like monsoon rains on a Delhi pavement. The Ranji Trophy was even harder hit. As lately as 1977 a Ranji game in Baroda had raised a serious riot. By the late 1980s not even a big regional grudge-match could raise a decent crowd. Many state associations stopped bothering even to charge for Ranji tickets.

But cricket's overall popularity was soaring, bringing new money into the game. This was apparent at every level. In 1982 a small north Indian manufacturer of cricket bats and gloves, Sanspareils Greenlands, launched its own kit brand, SG. Its timing was propitious. India's World Cup victory unleashed huge demand for the company's hand-stitched pads and Kashmiri willow bats. 'Our sales went berserk. That victory had a massive impact,' the company's boss, Triloknath Anand, would recall. 'Sports shop owners, cricketers were coming to our factory and saying *"Jitna maal hai bhej doh"'* (send us everything you have). SG is now the world's biggest manufacturer of cricket kit.

The BCCI's fortunes also improved. On the night of India's World Cup victory, the board was too broke to afford India's heroes a decent dinner. The team celebrated in a burger bar in Piccadilly. Unimpressed, they demanded a fat win bonus, which the board was also unable to stump up. 'We said, "Come on, yeah, we won the World Cup! We don't want tips!"' recalled Azad. To raise money for a bonus of 100,000 rupees (then about £6,400) per player, the cricket board persuaded Lata Mangeshkar, a great Bollywood singer, to perform a benefit concert in Delhi. But its days of penury were numbered.

With demand for one-day cricket soaring, India's cricket bosses found they could make as much from ticket sales for a one-day international as for a five-day Test. Games held in Sharjah, at a stadium built by a Pakistani-educated and cricket-devoted Arab tycoon, Abdulrahman Bukhatir, were especially profitable. They were played before festive crowds of Indian, Pakistani and Sri Lankan expatriate workers and, in a foretaste of the IPL, attended by the Indo-Pakistani glitterati, including politicians, Bollywood stars and fugitive Bombay gangsters.

India's success also made the Indian board more ambitious. Under the direction of a Congress politician, N.K.P. Salve, the BCCI launched a successful bid to host the 1987 World Cup jointly with Pakistan and Sri Lanka. The bid was bankrolled by another great son of Saurashtra, Dhirubhai Ambani, a self-made textiles billionaire. Yet its mastermind was the board's newly appointed treasurer, a Bengali cricket administrator and Marwari businessman called Jagmohan Dalmiya. Suspicious, Machiavellian and committed to monetising Indian cricket's growing popularity, Dalmiya would rule over the Indian game for most of the next two decades.

India failed to retain the Cup in 1987. Yet its staging of the tournament was a triumph. In *Wisden*'s view, 'the fourth World Cup was more widely watched, more closely fought and more colourful than any of its predecessors held in England.' Through cricket Indians were expressing a more hopeful national mood. Mrs Gandhi had been succeeded by her 40-year-old son, Rajiv. Youthful and forward-looking where his mother had grown paranoid and imperious, Rajiv talked of

India's youth and bright future. Reforms were introduced to encourage investments in information technology, laying the way for India's computer services industry. There was talk of staunching India's brain-drain – the thousands of doctors, engineers and researchers who left for richer pastures each year.

Under Rajiv India also began snipping away the scar tissue bequeathed by four decades of Nehruvian socialist rule, a thicket of enterprise-throttling laws and regulations that was known as the 'licence-permit raj'. The extent of these strictures was astonishing. Indian companies could not increase, diversify or reduce production without obtaining the government's express say-so. And obtaining that permission was hard, and sometimes impossible. It involved a process riven with mind-numbing bureaucracy and, inevitably, corruption. Partly as a result of Rajiv's reforms, India's prospects began to improve. The economy grew at an annual average rate of 5.7 per cent during the 1980s. India, at last, seemed to be moving forwards and its success in one-day cricket, a fast and glamorous new cricket format, seemed indicative of that.

The decade also witnessed the beginnings of another great change, of enormous significance to India and its favourite game. This was the rise of television. Introduced to India in 1959, when the state broadcaster Doordarshan ('distant show' in Hindi) was founded, television had been slow to take off. In 1982, when colour television arrived, India had only two million sets. Yet by 1992 it had 34 million. This represented a huge increase in the audience for televised cricket.

Henceforth, India's top cricketers would not be able to walk unmolested through any Indian city. Television made them much more visible – none more so, at this time, than India's Cup-winning captain, Kapil Dev.

If any man represented the 1980s, as Nayudu had the 1920s and Pataudi the 1960s, it was Kapil. He was India's most brilliant one-day cricketer, their match-winner, their most exciting player. It was often said, mostly by Indians, that they had taken so enthusiastically to cricket because they are a sedentary people and it is an unathletic game – not the way Kapil played it. He bounded in to bowl – fast, as no Indian had for decades – flinging himself elastically into his delivery stride. He hit sixes like Nayudu. He was easily India's best fielder. In an era of great all-rounders, of Imran Khan, Ian Botham and Richard Hadlee, Kapil was world-class and led India by aggressive example. Whatever timidity remained in Indian cricket, Kapil abolished it.

He also signalled another sort of change. Kapil's family were by no means poor, as the Palwankars were. Yet by the exclusive standards of Indian cricket, they were parochial and unpolished. India's captain hailed not from Bombay or Delhi but from Chandigarh, capital of Punjab and Haryana. He spoke English clumsily. In this way Kapil augured another watershed in Indian cricket, an end to its dominance by the metropolitan elite. A new breed of hungry, lower middle-class cricketer, introduced to the game by television, would soon begin emerging from India's smaller cities and furthest corners. Kapil was their patron saint.

He was my neighbour in Delhi and I knew him slightly. With another World Cup approaching – to be held in India in 2011 – we arranged to meet one day, over lunch in a plush Delhi hotel, to chat about the past.

Almost three decades after his Cup-winning heroics, Kapil remained an impressive specimen. His hair was greying and his face a little jowlier, yet he was still lean and muscular. It was still possible to imagine him running in to bowl. As he ushered me to a table, in a Chinese restaurant with views overlooking Delhi, he radiated the same nervous energy that he had on the pitch. It made him slightly unrelaxing to talk to – especially, I soon found, on the subject of his modest origins.

'Kapil, you were a different sort of Indian captain ...' I began awkwardly, as he toyed with his mobile phone.

He frowned back. 'How do you mean, "different"?'

'Well, you came from Chandigarh, not Bombay or Delhi,' I said. 'Wasn't that quite unusual?'

But Kapil was still frowning. He looked insulted, which was the last thing I had intended. 'What I mean to say is,' I added cravenly, 'you must have been a particular inspiration to people living in small towns.'

Kapil relaxed slightly. 'Yes, the media are always saying this,' he said guardedly. 'I don't know why they're so interested, but it's true I came from a small town and no one else did. Cricket was all Bombay. For 20, 30 years, people said only big-town boys can play. But that wasn't true. I showed a lot of people I had talent and with the grace of God I showed that boys from the small towns were good too. And now that's where the talent is and the support. In small-town India people are really crazy about cricket. But you can't compare now and then. In our time, not even 15 per cent of people had a television to see our faces, but now 90 per cent have televisions. Cricket has become so much more popular since our day.'

I had seen an illustration of this shortly before, in the hotel's ballroom, where Kapil had joined a clutch of other former World Cup captains – Sir Vivian Richards, Imran Khan and Arjuna Ranatunga – to launch the forthcoming World Cup. They were filmed by a huge battery of television cameras, before several hundred Indian journalists. The tournament, though still more than two months away, was already causing huge excitement in India. Indians expected their team to win the cup for the first time since 1983. And that was, for perhaps the first time, a realistic expectation.

'But still everyone knows us and everyone loves us,' Kapil added, and then fell silent. He didn't look especially happy to be adored. In the pause, I overheard Imran and Richards, who were sitting at the table with us, deep in conversation.

Or rather, I heard Imran, who was now a Pakistani politician and strong critic of American foreign policy. 'You know, if they killed his wife and children, it is not hard to imagine why a man would become a suicide bomber,' he told Richards, who was listening in inscrutable silence. 'Or he would fight them and raise his children against them! If the people in the UK and US knew what was really going on they would rise up and protest. The Americans are destroying us. People are desperate. They say all our leaders are corrupt, only Imran Khan can save us!'

'Is it hard for you to move around in public?' I asked Kapil. He shook his head. 'Very hard. People make it very difficult, even here in Delhi people always want to see me. But the Bengalis are extreme. In Kolkata so many people crowd around me. They come and touch my feet.' Kapil winced. 'I don't like it. It gives me goosepimples.'

CHAPTER THREE

The Cricket Box

Tense and perspiring, I took my seat in an upper tier of the Chinnaswamy Stadium. Reaching it had been a fight. But it was a fine February day in Bangalore and as I looked out over one of India's great cricket ovals, my spirits rose. Far below, green and perfect, the pitch was ready for the first big contest of the 2011 World Cup, India against England. In the azure sky above the stadium, long-winged raptors were wheeling in slow circles, surfing the thermals of a bright south Indian morning.

Play was not due for an hour but the stadium was already half-filled and in ferment. Bollywood songs blasted from a pair of giant speakers, half-drowning the background hubbub of drumming, laughter and chatter. The crowd was tuning up. Between songs, an official implored through the speakers, 'Please, no insulting of umpires or players. Let's have a friendly environment.' This drew a brief ripple of applause, and then the hubbub resumed.

A stream of new arrivals flowed past, many wearing the sky-blue India team shirt. Some looked as drained as I felt. Others took one look at the pitch and punched the air in elation. A group of young men with Indian flags painted on their cheeks burst into a war-cry, '*jeetega bhai, jeetega, India jeetega!*' ('We'll win, brother, India will win!')

Making it into the Chinnaswamy was alone worth celebrating. The game was originally to have been played in Kolkata. But Eden Gardens, to the embarrassment of its overseer, Jagmohan Dalmiya, had turned out to be a building site. The fixture was therefore switched to the smaller Chinnaswamy, which halved the number of tickets available to 40,000. And 33,000 of these were promptly gobbled by members of the state cricket association, local cricket clubs and Bangalore's great and good.

Local politicians, policemen, judges, civil servants and army officers – everyone who was anyone in Bangalore needed a ticket for the game. The remaining few thousand were to be made available online, but the website crashed within minutes. So they went on sale at the stadium, which caused a riot.

The night before the sale, a crowd of thousands had gathered outside the stadium, and when it became clear that most would leave empty-handed, they began to protest. The police beat them up with bamboo staves. It was the usual ticketing shambles, and grist to the mill of India's media. Every bungled detail was front-page news in the 330 million copies of newspapers that circulate in India every day, and headline news on India's 120-odd television news channels. As match-day approached, the fixture had received far more coverage in India than the British media gives to cricket in a year. And, despite my best efforts, I still had no ticket.

I had watched a fair amount of cricket in India in recent years, but mostly from the comfort of the press box or a hospitality suite. I wanted to watch this game, like the next man, from the general stand. But, like the next man, I couldn't get a ticket. In despair, the day before the game I called an influential friend. No problem, he said, and offered me a couple of VIP tickets for the pavilion. But when I said I'd prefer a cheap seat he sounded doubtful. No one elects to go downmarket in India these days. 'But get yourself down to Bangalore and we'll see,' he said and, sure enough, by the morning of the game he had found me a standard ticket (stamped 'strictly for exclusive use of the Karnataka Cricket Association').

Proceeding to the stadium, I found a prosperous-looking crowd gathered outside it, smartly dressed in bright-coloured polo or India team shirts. Many of those queueing for the stadium were chatting in English. At 1,000 rupees for even a cheap seat, the match was not for the poor. Having made it inside, I found two computer programmers, Ronak and Nishit, seated either side of me. They were not friends, though both were in their twenties, came from Baroda and worked for an IT firm in Hyderabad. They were not unfriendly, as I prodded them with questions. But they were reserved, perhaps shy, and neither said a word to the other. Both were convinced that India would win. And, of course, Sachin Tendulkar was their favourite player.

'Isn't that a bit unimaginative?' I asked Ronak, a slight figure in a blue polo shirt.

'But he's the god of cricket.'

'Oh, come on. Surely there are more exciting players than Sachin?'

'Don't get me started,' said Ronak. He did not look amused.

Tendulkar, or simply Sachin as Indians call him, means a lot to them. He means more than Nayudu, Pataudi, Bedi, Gavaskar and Kapil combined. Sachin started playing cricket for India as a curly-haired Bombay schoolboy, 5ft 2in tall, and 16 years old. That was in 1989. And more than two decades later he was still playing for India and had scored more international runs than any other cricketer ever has or probably ever will. But for Tendulkar's hundreds of millions of Indian devotees, he meant even more than this stupendous record would suggest.

'Cricket is like a religion in India and Sachin,' Indians like to say, 'is God.' Well, not quite. There is probably no Tendulkar temple in India, despite many rumours to the contrary. But the qualities Tendulkar cultists ascribe to their hero are truly superhuman. In India, Sachin is a paragon, not merely the best ever cricketer, but one of the best of all Indians. He is praised for his modesty, his patriotism, his devotion to his family and general high-mindedness. He is spotless and irreproachable, and anyone who dares challenge that view had better watch out. Sachin's fans will not have his perfections challenged. The minute Greg Chappell, India's former coach, fell out with him, who he appeared to find rather selfish and inflexible, his India days were numbered.

The crucial background to this Sachin adoration is an amazing surge in cricket's popularity over the course of his career. According to a survey conducted in 2007 by a Delhi-based think-tank, the Centre for the Study of Developing Societies, nearly 80 per cent of Indians under the age of 25 followed cricket either 'to a great extent' or 'somewhat'. Given India's youthful demography – over half the population are under 25 – that would suggest India has more than half a billion cricket fans. That represents an astonishing monopoly on India's sporting affections.

The explosive growth of Indian television ownership is chiefly responsible. India's 160 million – and rising – television households represent an eightfold increase over the course of Tendulkar's two-decade-long career. The India–England match in Bangalore was about to be watched by one of the biggest television audiences ever assembled for a live cricket match. Estimates of the Indian viewership alone started at 200 million.

Cricket is now ubiquitous on Indian telelvision. It is shown constantly on 16 sports channels and relentlessly discussed on over 100 news channels. Then there are ad breaks, and more cricketers appear, appearing in commercials for insurance, cement or mopeds, goods and services for a fast-emerging economy. Nalin Mehta, an expert on Indian media, describes this assault as the 'cricketisation' of Indian television.

It has made Indian cricketers as famous as film stars, and similarly rich. In 2011 Tendulkar earned an estimated $16.5 million from product endorsements alone. Yet unlike Bollywood stars, India's cricketers are additionally respected as national champions, on a footing with the Indian army. They are hybrid heroes – part soldier, part entertainer – and it is hard to describe the adulation this brings them.

I once happened to share a plane from Mumbai to Delhi with a sometime India cricketer, Mohammad Kaif, a hard-working middle-order batsman who was perhaps fortunate to play over 100 one-day internationals in the early to mid-2000s. Hardly any cricket fan outside Asia would have recognised him. Yet the effect he had on a crowded Kingfisher airliner cabin was incendiary.

When Kaif stepped aboard, his name was whispered up and down the aisle. Sitting behind me, a middle-aged man hissed the following commentary to his wife much of the way to Delhi: 'Oh my god, Mohammad Kaif!/Kaify!/Mohammad Kaif is sitting down/Kaif is reading/What is Kaif reading?'

The cricketer responded to the fevered murmuring with a mask of implacable benevolence, designed to radiate thanks and goodwill with minimum energy loss. As he left the plane, the purser seized one of his hands in both of his own and stooped low before him. 'Sir,' he said in a voice that was at once tender and respectful, 'We really miss you and we pray you are back in the team soon'. I suspect that wasn't true.

Multiply Kaif's appeal by 100 and you have some idea of the Tendulkar cult. He is India's best, most consistent and most enduring, and most internationally respected cricketer. He is also the richest; but in Tendulkar's case his commercial profile is more a counterpoint to his popularity than a cause of it. Tendulkar is not like David Beckham, a sportsman so reprocessed by celebrity it is hard to remember if he was ever any good. Sachin remains a slightly geekish cricketer, obsessed by the pursuit of batting excellence that, over the course of his long career, he has often delivered. 'Tendulkar never fails,' an Indian selector said of the 16-year-old prodigy he was then proposing for the national side. The wonder is that he so rarely has.

This explains the volume of Tendulkar's celebrity to millions of Indians. It still does not explain the tone of it, which is deeply personal. In a time of great change in India, Tendulkar, a modest, superstitious Hindu family-man, an Indian everyman, stands for continuity. For Indians over the age of 35, he conjures memories of a more modest, traditional India. When Tendulkar made his India debut, Rajiv Gandhi was prime minister and India had fewer than 850 million people. Now Rajiv is long dead and India's population is over 1.2 billion; yet Tendulkar goes on.

On that sunny day in the Chinnaswamy, we were blessed with an early look at him. India won the toss and chose to bat, bringing Sachin straight to the middle. As he walked out, looking as always slightly too small for his pads, the crowd welcomed him with a roar of 40,000 personal devotions.

'Sachin! Sachin-bhai!' the shouts rang out imploringly around the stadium as Sachin-themed banners and flags were unfurled. The television cameras picked them out and displayed them on a giant in-stadium screen. There was a row of middle-aged men, beaming and pointing to their paunches where their T-shirts bore the message, 'Until I see God I will settle for Sachin'. There were children, smiling shyly, with 'SACHIN' painted on their cheeks. One banner draped from an upper tier read: 'Commit all your sins when Sachin is batting. They will go unnoticed because even God is watching him bat.' It was a long banner.

In all this Tendulkar exultation, I noticed a small party of middle-aged British tourists a few rows behind me, laughing forcefully with their neighbours. I couldn't hear what was said but guessed they were bantering about England's chances in the game. You might come to regret that, I thought.

Tendulkar met his first ball with a solid forward prod and the crowd gave a burst of relieved all-in-this-together applause. The giant screen showed a line of celebrities in the VVIP seats, including the state's chief minister and Bangalore's playboy billionaire, Vijay Mallya, a liquor-to-airline baron and owner of the Royal Challengers Bangalore IPL side. They were clapping too.

What followed was the classic Tendulkarama that Ronak and millions of others had been hoping for. The little master – a nickname Tendulkar inherited from Gavaskar – was at first subdued while his partner, Virender Sehwag, blazed away as he does. But after Sehwag got out, with India on 45 for one, Tendulkar got moving. A graceful cut, a punch straight back for six, a couple of back-foot drives, and he had fifty, brought up with another punched six. The English bowlers, toiling on a flat pitch, were easy prey. The crowd was going berserk. 'Sachin-bhai!' people were screaming and laughing. 'Sachin-bhai, give me sixer!'

Tendulkar's batting is not (though millions would disagree) the most distinctive India has produced or even, to my amateur eye, especially memorable. He does not have an obvious signature shot: a fluid cover-drive or murderous pull to bookmark him in the mind. But that is partly because of his greatest asset, his versatility. Tendulkar is not representative of India's most beguiling tradition of batsmanship, the style of wristy artistry, of graceful cuts and drives, established by Ranjitsinhji. But he can play those shots. He is a product of the more coached and organised Bombay school of batting, as Gavaskar was. But he scores much faster and hits the ball harder than Gavaskar did.

He got his century with a flick off his hips for four, and the roar of the crowd was stadium-quaking. I turned to see Ronak with his mouth wide open in a drowned-out Munchian scream. 'Sachiiiiiiin!' he seemed to be shouting.

He leaned over and yelled jubilantly in my ear, 'Now do you see why Sachin is God?' Ronak's travel companion, a skinny young man wearing a blue Afro wig, was jumping up and down on his shoulders. High above the stadium, I noticed two kites collide and briefly lock on to one another.

Suddenly there was a different drama. As Tendulkar had approached his century, the flow of latecomers into the stadium, still pouring up the stairwell, began speeding up. I had spotted a few uniformed policemen among them, having presumably abandoned their posts for a glimpse of the final *coup de Sachin*. But the upper tier of the stadium was already packed: there was nowhere for the new arrivals to go.

A crowd of unwanted people started building at the head of the stairwell and, with hundreds more pushing up to join it, those in front were pushed, then suddenly surged forwards, tumbling down towards the precipitous edge of the upper tier in a mêlée of limbs and bodies. While the stadium was still in uproar, yelling for Tendulkar, these terrified people were screaming in terror.

A burly young Sikh, wearing an Indian team shirt and a baseball cap on top of his patka, heaved himself out of the scrimmage and grabbed my arm to steady himself. He stared at me, wide-eyed with fear. 'This country,' he said in a Cockney accent, 'is a fucking disgrace.'

Between innings, as I queued for a refreshing slice of cucumber sprinkled with chilli, the crowd burbled with delight. India had scored 338 – a huge total – of which Tendulkar had hit 120. Even the English supporters probably thought this was too much for their team, who had a poor reputation in one-day cricket. Indeed, no side had chased so many runs in Bangalore.

Yet England got off to a thumping start. They scored 63 in nine overs, before India made a fluky breakthrough. Kevin Pietersen, a thrilling long-limbed hitter, walloped a ball straight at the head of the Indian bowler Munaf Patel, who stuck out his hands to save his life. He then landed in a heap on the ground, followed by the ball, which landed almost in his lap.

But the other opener, the captain Andrew Strauss, was playing the innings of his one-day career. Pulling anything short for four and cutting fiercely, he raced to a run-a-ball century looking like the world's best batsman, which he was not. Batting was easy on this pitch, it was now clear. The crowd gave Strauss's hundred a brief, not ungenerous, burst of applause.

Yet as the evening sky darkened at a rush and the floodlights came on, the stadium hushed. Strauss and his partner, Ian Bell, looked untroubled by India's bowlers and were scoring freely. England's captain slapped a long-hop from the spinner Piyush Chawla for four – and that was his 150. England, with only two wickets down, now needed 67 to win at less than six an over. It looked to be all over.

The crowd started flooding from the stadium. I turned to say something to Nishik, but he had already gone. The VVIP pavilion was now almost empty. Ronak turned to me, as disgusted spectators flowed silently past to the stairs, with a look of embarrassment. 'You should know, we are very bad losers,' he said glumly.

'Why is that?'

'Because we make it more than a game.'

His friend in the blue wig sat hunched and disconsolate beside him. The floodlights shimmered off his plastic curls. The party was over.

India's captain Mahendra Singh Dhoni summoned his main fast bowler, Zaheer Khan, for a last try. The crowd gave a burst of hopeful applause; no one looked confident.

'We're just trying to get something good out of this terrible day,' said Ronak.

'Has it really been that bad?'

'Not for me,' he said, looking wretched. 'But I'm not a diehard.'

But then everything changed. Bell, looking to heave Zaheer for another six, looped a catch to mid-off. The crowd roared – and kept roaring as, next ball, Strauss fell lbw. A thunder of cheering rang out as the Indian fielders, like silent movie stars, started hopping up and down, clapping and encouraging the bowlers. No one was leaving now.

The new batsmen looked anxious, as anyone would. A deafening chant of 'Ind-i-a! Ind-i-a!' '*Jee-te-ga! Jee-te-ga!*' filled the stadium. Two more wickets fell.

The noise was now so loud it was possible to imagine, in the weird silver light, that the air was visibly pulsating because of it. The chanting got quicker, louder and more emotional. 'India! Indiaaa!' '*Jeetega! Jeetegaaa!*' The crowd was pleading for a wicket. A shower of shredded silver foil swirled down from the upper tiers across the pitch, sparkling like fireflies in the floodlights.

'Indiaaa!' '*Jeetega!*'

Another wicket fell. England were imploding. They were now way off the pace. They needed 29 off the last two overs, with their tailenders at the crease. They were being beaten by Zaheer, the pressure and the hostility of crowd.

The spectators around me were standing and, with one exception, yelling for India and victory. There was a furious urgency to their demands. When Tendulkar got his century the crowd had screamed with warmth and happiness; now its chanting was rhythmic and nasty. People were screaming – actually *screaming* – for India to win.

I looked from one snarling face to the next and wondered what I was seeing. It didn't feel threatening. It wasn't like being in a riot. It was like being in a dream riot, which had gone on so long it seemed almost real. Scanning the stand behind me, I briefly glimpsed the group of middle-aged English tourists. Standing rigid, staring at the pitch, they looked stunned.

But the England bowlers could bat. Graeme Swann, a cocky Nottinghamshire off-spinner, clouted a huge six over midwicket and three balls later his partner, Tim Bresnan, an unflappable Yorkshireman, did the same. A howl of anguish tore through the stadium, followed by louder and more urgent chanting, 'India! India!!' Next ball, Bresnan took another heave and was bowled. All around me families, friends and perfect strangers were jumping up and down and embracing each other.

This was the moment for which Ronak's friend had worn his blue wig. Leaping on to his seat, he arched himself backwards, cupped his mouth with both hands, opened his lungs and crowed, 'India!! Indiaaa!!' and then waited for the response. *'Jeetega!! Jeetega!!'*

Bending backwards again, he repeated the same jugular-popping scream: 'India!! Indiaaa!!' And again the crowd did as he demanded, shouting back, *'Jeetega! Jeetega!'*

The only Indian not screaming was Ronak. He stood silently next to me, in the thick of this mania, even when his friend in the blue wig almost fell on top of him. This was, I felt sure, meant as a courtesy to me and I was grateful for it; though I hoped I wasn't spoiling his fun.

England needed 14 off the last over, which Patel would bowl. Swann scrambled just three off the first two balls and the crowd screamed out, more confident now. Then the new batsman, Ajmal Shahzad (born in Yorkshire, just like Bresnan), hit another huge six back over Patel's head. The crowd groaned; then roared, as Shahzad missed the next ball and the batsmen muddled through for a bye.

England needed four off two balls to win, then two off the last, which Swann drove hard. He middled it, but straight to mid-off for a single. The scores were level and the match, momentously, a tie – the rarest result in cricket. And all at once the crowd was silent. There was suddenly no shouting at all, a contrast as dramatic as the tumult that had preceded it. Chatting calmly, or silently nursing their raw throats, the spectators filed peacefully out of the stadium and went home to bed.

India's television revolution started with a war. In 1990 Saddam Hussein's army rolled into Kuwait, imperilling, among others, a million and a half Indian migrants working in the Gulf. This created huge demand in India for news of the war, which Doordarshan, with its antique news bulletins, dominated by monsoon reports and the daily life of the prime minister, could not meet. But a new and rollicking sort of cable television entrepreneur could. In late 1990 and early 1991, as Operation Desert Storm was brewing, hundreds of small satellite dishes were set up in India to bring live coverage of the war to Indian homes via CNN.

Ajeet Kacker was one of these entrepreneurs. In January 1991 he was 24, the son of an army officer in Noida, a satellite city of Delhi, and ambitious to make money. While casting about for business ideas, a magazine article caught his eye. 'It was about how people in Bombay were watching movies at home from a wire coming into their house,' recalled Ajeet, now a very large middle-aged Punjabi, with a splendid moustache, waxed and curled upwards in salute to the family profession.

He had decided to give the new cable business a go. Ajeet therefore installed a video cassette recorder in the servant quarters of his parents' house and offered his neighbours a selection of Hindi and English movies for a small monthly fee. To those who took up his offer he ran a copper cable, slinging it over the rooftops and threading it through the branches of trees. His business took off. But then a rival cableman bought a satellite dish and started offering his customers CNN.

This was a popular offer in Ajeet's suburb, most of his neighbours being army men. To retain his customers Ajeet clubbed together with three friends and raised 115,000 rupees to buy his own dish, which allowed him to offer CNN too. His cable network started to grow rapidly. 'But even so I thought this was going to be quite a small business,' said Ajeet, chuckling at the naivety of that thought, as his tiny wife ushered in servants bearing trays loaded with ham sandwiches and cream cakes for a mid-afternoon snack.

Across India, thousands of miles of cable were being uncoiled: within a few months India's cityscapes became a tangle of copper wires. The new cable television business was unregulated, unpoliced and dangerous: many innocent pedestrians have been electrocuted by walking into cables carelessly slung around power lines.

The new industry was probably also illegal, being in contravention of the dusty Telegraph Act of 1885, under which the Indian state claimed a monopoly on broadcasting. Yet the government, with its mind on a bigger crisis at this time, let it grow, and the cablemen found their own ways to police the industry. When one or two of Ajeet's neighbours started freeloading on his network by hooking up to it on the sly, he put surveillance cameras on the rooftops to film them clambering around at night, then played the demeaning footage to all his subscribers.

The cablemen were making hundreds of dollars a month, even thousands. Many were local grocers who had started the business as a modest sideline, little guessing how it would grow. According to Ajeet, in and around Delhi the industry was run by Punjabis, who have a reputation in India for enjoying the good life. 'They were all Punjabis so it was all the vices,' he said, holding a tiny cup of syrupy coffee in his enormous hand. 'Most of them went mad, getting into bad habits, drinking all day, womanising. Even today, show me a cable operator and I'll know him instantly from his flashy clothes, his way of talking, his sunglasses, his holidays in Bangkok.'

Bigger entrepreneurs were impressed by this success. In 1992 a well-connected Marwari businessman, Subhash Chandra, launched the first Hindi satellite station, Zee TV. The son of a north-Indian wheat-trader, Chandra had made a vast fortune after briefly securing, under Indira Gandhi, an exclusive licence to manage India's rice exports to the Soviet Union. When Chandra launched Zee, with seed-money from the Anglo-French titan Sir James Goldsmith, he knew nothing about the media industry. But he had sensed a hunger for entertainment among India's swelling middle-class that Doordarshan could not sate.

Zee TV started out as a daily four-hour package of Hindi soaps and game shows. The shows were produced in India and recorded on to video cassettes which were then – to evade the Telegraph Act – flown to Hong Kong and bounced off a satellite back to India. Viewers loved them. 'Something modern was happening on television,' is how Ajeet remembered Zee's arrival. By 1993 India had an estimated 70,000 cable operators and over 3.5 million cable television households.

India was not known for such growth. It was known as an economic basket case. Four decades of utopian industrial policy, administered under the 'licence raj', had made Indian industry lumbering and uncompetitive. 'We have to industrialise India, and as rapidly as possible,' Nehru had declared in 1951. But by 1991 India's main exports included iron ore, cotton and artisanal goods, such as jewellery and leather-work, things India had been exporting for centuries. Because it made so little that anyone else wanted to buy, India was periodically on the edge of insolvency, with too little foreign exchange to pay for its essential imports, such as oil, which India has little of. In 1991, just as the satellite revolution was taking off, this led to the mother of all balance of payments crises, for which Saddam Hussein's invasion was also partly to blame.

The war sent the oil price soaring. It also sent thousands of Indian migrant workers scurrying home from the Middle East, which caused a steep fall in the dollars and dirhams they had been sending home. By the time India turned to the IMF for an emergency bailout, it was technically bankrupt, with less than a billion dollars in reserve – not enough to cover a fortnight's oil imports. Knowing the IMF would demand reforms in exchange for its money, Narasimha Rao, the Congress leader of a weak coalition government, appointed a respected technocrat, Manmohan Singh, as finance minister. He instructed Singh to do whatever was necessary to refloat the economy.

Little was expected of him. Singh was better known as an honest and biddable civil servant than for any bold thought or action. But, in that time of crisis, he announced the reforms demanded by the IMF and then went further, slashing tariffs, scrapping licences in some industries and dismantling barriers to foreign investment. The licence raj was largely dismantled. In July 1991 Singh announced many of these changes in his budget speech to parliament. As he drew to a close, in his whispery academic voice, the meek-mannered Sikh sounded a sudden bullish note. 'No power on Earth can stop an idea whose time has come,' he said, quoting Victor Hugo. He predicted a new course in Indian history, the rise of an economic giant.

For some investors, Indian and foreign, the cable revolution was an augury of that change. It was a glimpse of the enormous potential in India's hitherto constricted consumer market, and of the animal spirit of

Indian enterprise so evident among Indians abroad. Rupert Murdoch, who bought Asia's biggest satellite television network, Star TV, in 1993, derided India's cable operators as 'pirates'; but also 'splendid entrepreneurs ... pioneering the market'.

In one impudent spurt they had laid the foundations for India's modern media industry. They had also, in a spaghetti-mess of copper cable, provided much of its infrastructure. But this opening would not remain unchallenged for long. Within the state monopolist, Doordarshan, a jealous rage was brewing, which would boil over at the prospect of losing control over its richest prize, Indian cricket.

Until the late 1980s Doordarshan had actually charged the BCCI a fee to broadcast cricket. But Dalmiya was not slow to grasp the implications of competition in Indian broadcasting. In 1992, even before it was obvious who owned what on India's airwaves, the BCCI sold the rights to a forthcoming India–England cricket series to a private broadcaster, Trans World International (TWI), the television division of the sports marketing giant IMG. TWI paid $600,000 for the rights then flipped them to Doordarshan, to the state broadcaster's chagrin, for a million dollars.

A few months later another Dalmiya fiefdom, the Cricket Association of Bengal, attempted something similar. It invited Doordarshan to bid for the rights to a one-day tournament, the Hero Cup, which it was organising to commemorate its diamond jubilee. Unimpressed with Doordarshan's bid, the CAB sold the rights to TWI, for a minimum of $550,000.

As the sand slipped under their feet, Doordarshan's controllers hit back. Citing the Telegraph Act, the state broadcaster announced that only the government had the right to carry out live telecasts in India and, further, that allowing foreign companies to do so was a threat to national security. Doordarshan's spokesman labelled India's cricket authorities 'anti-national'.

In a hasty effort to appease the state broadcaster, Dalmiya offered it a share of the rights with TWI. But Doordarshan was not fighting for equality. Its director-general, Rathikant Basu, demanded the BCCI recognise the state broadcaster's exclusive right to film and broadcast the Hero Cup in India, and, what was more, pay a fee of 500,000 rupees per match for the service. Dalmiya refused, thereby sparking a protracted legal battle, which would show the Indian state at its most maddening and self-destructive.

On 7 November 1993 the Hero Cup opened in Kanpur, with a handsome Indian victory over Sri Lanka. Yet Indian cricket fans had to wait until the next day's newspapers for news of the game. With Doordarshan and the CAB still at each other's throats, TWI had been prevented from filming it, and the state broadcaster and All-India Radio were enforcing a blackout. Cricket lovers in the other participating countries were also deprived of coverage of a tournament that, in some cases, their local broadcasters had already paid for.

The farrago got worse. At the request of India's information ministry, TWI's production equipment was impounded by customs in Bombay, even though India's finance ministry had already cleared it for entry. Biting his lip, one of TWI's bosses, William D. Sinrich, told Indian journalists, 'At a time when your country is opening its economy, this act of the government is far from encouraging.' At Dalmiya's pleading, Calcutta's high court ordered Bombay's customs officials to release TWI's kit. But the customs men simply ignored the court's order.

Three Hero Cup games had now been played and TWI was facing mounting losses. Calcutta's cricket bosses appealed to a higher authority, the Indian Supreme Court: it ordered Bombay customs to release TWI's equipment but, dodging the bullet, called on the Indian government to resolve the more fundamental dispute over the status of Doordarshan's jaded monopoly. Within hours, the issue was back in the Supreme Court, and this time the bench ruled that TWI must be allowed to film and telecast the remaining games. Yet, in a typical Indian fudge, the judges granted this permission strictly and exclusively for the cricket. TWI was forbidden to point its cameras at anything off the field, including the spectators.

India had been made to look ridiculous. Foreign broadcasters had lost money because of its inability to enforce not merely a high-profile contract but the rule of law among its own feuding institutions. Many questioned what this would mean for the forthcoming 1996 World Cup, which was scheduled to be held on the subcontinent. Dalmiya had sold the TV rights to that tournament to another foreign company, an American sports media firm called WorldTel, for $10 million – ten times the fee for the previous World Cup, held in Australia and New Zealand. Yet would it, too, be forbidden to film the crowd? With foreign broadcasters breaking off negotiations, WorldTel's boss, Mark Mascarenhas, declared that 'irreversible damage has already been done' to India's reputation in sports media. Others foresaw an even worse outcome. *Business India* feared it might 'put the clock back on the entire reform process of the Narasimha Rao government'.

If that was an exaggerated fear, the mess certainly showed how hair-raising doing business in the new liberalised India could be, especially for naive foreigners. No politician could bring India's disputatious institutions to heel. Nor even, as the conflict between the finance and information ministries had shown, could the government be relied upon to pursue a single clear policy.

To prevent another damaging legal battle, Mascarenhas did a judicious deal with Doordarshan, giving it broadcast rights for the World Cup. But again the BCCI stirred the pot. It announced that it had sold five-year television rights to cricket in India to TWI and the American sports cable channel ESPN for $30 million. Doordarshan's boss, Basu, was incandescent: 'Who created Sunil Gavaskar and Kapil Dev?' he chuntered, as the dispute headed back to the Supreme Court. But this time its verdict, delivered in February 1995, was crushing. The court ruled that the Telegraph Act was 'intended for an altogether different purpose'. India's airwaves were public property and open to all under the right to freedom of speech enshrined in the constitution.

Indians often console themselves that, when every other branch of their state fails, their judges will save them. They often do, even if, as TWI had discovered, they can take their time over it. But this was a momentous reform, and it was no coincidence that cricket, because of its enormous advertising value, had helped drive it. The growth in India media that would follow, in the view of the historian Boria Majumdar, would 'forever remain a gift of Indian cricket to the Indian nation'.

In February 1996 the World Cup came to the subcontinent for the second time in less than a decade. But the contrast with the previous rendition, in 1987, was profound. That tournament, the first outside England, was praised for its careful organisation and good-spirited crowds. It was a fine advertisement for India's unique cricket culture. But the 1996 tournament was held in a different India – richer, more ambitious and belligerent – and the tournament reflected that.

It was blighted from the start, with Australia and West Indies both refusing to play qualifying matches in Sri Lanka for fear of Tamil Tiger terrorists. India's cricket bosses were livid.

There was further background to this ill will. The previous year three of the Australians, Mark Waugh, Shane Warne and Tim May, had accused the former Pakistani captain Salim Malik of trying to bribe them to throw a Test match in Karachi. This was the first big clue to something seriously wrong in cricket: a culture of match-fixing – of throwing matches in response to inducements from illegal Asian bookmakers, who were also finding rich pickings in cricket's growth.

Having received threats from Pakistan – where the World Cup final was to be played – some of the Australian players were reluctant to participate in the tournament. The Indian board, in flat denial over the match-rigging claims, accused them and their West Indian allies of nursing a vendetta against the Third World. It took Sir Clyde Walcott, the gracious Barbadian head of the ICC, to point out that the West Indian countries were also of the Third World.

The arrangements for the tournament were often shambolic. An ostentatious opening ceremony at Eden Gardens flopped after a gentle breeze disrupted its expensive laser show. The tournament's protracted early stages, designed to maximise advertising revenues, exhausted the players with arduous travel and viewers with too much meaningless cricket. Worst of all, the Indian crowds, so delightfully 'colourful' in 1987, were now bursting with belligerent nationalism.

When India met Pakistan in the quarter-finals at the Chinnaswamy Stadium, the Pakistanis were jeered by the Bangalore crowd, hitherto known as one of India's most informed and orderly. Many feared that if India lost the game there would be a riot. But India won, so passed through to the semi-finals against Sri Lanka at Eden Gardens. And there the feared riot ensued: as India struggled to 128 for eight, chasing a Sri Lankan score of 251, the crowd reacted with fury. Spectators rained plastic bottles on to the pitch and started fires in the stands. As smoke drifted across the outfield the game was called off, and awarded to Sri Lanka by default. Indian cricket was disgraced.

Dalmiya's plans for the tournament did not all go awry, however. The 1987 World Cup had been a commercial failure, with the BCCI losing $40,000 on it. But the 1996 rerun was a bonanza, reported to have returned a $50 million profit. Every facet of the tournament was flogged for advertising: the Indian tobacco company Wills paid $12 million for the naming rights.

This was a sign of how India was changing. Just as Manmohan Singh had predicted, opening India's economy had unleashed the dynamism exhibited by India's drunken cablemen. It had also brought foreign companies flooding into India, eager to claim terrain in one of the world's biggest and still largely untapped markets for consumer goods. The 1996 World Cup was a global advertisement for this change. It was perhaps most conspicuous in a row between two famous rivals, Coca Cola and PepsiCo, which was more memorable than almost any of the cricket.

Coke had fled India in 1977 after refusing a demand from the government to divulge its secret formula. It returned in 1993 as a result of the new foreign investment rules. Pepsi had arrived in 1988 but, under the old rules, was saddled with a local partner until 1994. As the World Cup approached, both companies were therefore thirsty for a share of a vast market for fizzy drinks and saw cricket, the biggest draw in Indian media, as the ideal means to promote themselves.

Pepsi moved first, signing up India's cricket captain, Mohammed Azharuddin, its boyish star Tendulkar and his childhood pal and team-mate Vinod Kambli for its ads. Though by no means the first campaign to use cricketers, this was by far the glitziest, awarding the cricketers a status previously reserved for film stars. According to Anuja Chauhan, who ran the campaign as creative head of the advertising agency JWT, the aim was to piggy-back on the India team's recent success. 'Cricket was the one thing in which we had done well internationally,' said Ms Chauhan (which goes to show what most Indians know about hockey). 'That's why cricket was cool. It was very tied up with our Indian self-esteem. Everyone stood taller, everyone walked with a bigger strut, when India played well.'

Pepsi also bid to be the 'official soft drink' of the World Cup. But Coke won that right with an offer of $3.6 million. 'Pepsi was devastated', said Ms Chauhan. 'We'd been investing in cricket for quite a while and now Coke had just swept us aside.' Her response, which has become a case study in ambush marketing, was to devise a campaign that poked fun at Coke for precisely the 'official' status that Pepsi had also sought. '*Officially*,' a plummy-voiced narrator said archly, as one advert opened with footage of Pepsi's paid-up stars flinging themselves around a cricket pitch, 'cricket is played in whites, at a leisurely pace. The *official* players are gentlemen, of restraint, who have to drink the *official* drink …' Pepsi's cricketers were then shown turning their noses up at a cup coloured Coca Cola red, in favour of an ice-encrusted bottle of Pepsi. 'Pepsi – nothing *official* about it,' the narrator concluded. 'Nothing official about it,' Tendulkar chimed in.

It was complete nonsense. Pepsi was not the cool outsider portrayed in the ad: it was the dominant foreign player in India's soft drinks market. But the campaign was subversive and very popular. 'It was about how the game had changed,' said Ms Chauhan. 'It had got faster, coloured clothing had come in, it had got cooler. The undercurrent was "official is boring", "official is the done thing".' It was also, as another popular subtext, about two of the world's most iconic firms fighting for Indians' favour. 'Everybody loved that, having these big guys, these big colas slugging it out,' recalled Ms Chauhan. 'It was just like America, just like abroad.'

Humiliated by Pepsi's coup, Coke started signing up its own stable of Indian cricketers shortly after the World Cup. This was the time at which the celebrity and wealth of Indian cricketers began to rocket. Shortly before the tournament Tendulkar had signed a deal with Mark Mascarenhas's management agency guaranteeing him $7.5 million in sponsorship deals over the next five years.

Indian cricket was suddenly suffused with commercialism and aggressive nationalism and some saw a link between the two. 'Perhaps,' ventured *Wisden*, 'we should not be too harsh on the individuals responsible for the riot in Calcutta. They were merely responding to the seductions created for them by the promoters of the Wills World Cup, an event that plainly, disastrously, put money making above all the fundamentals of organising a global sporting competition. As the glamorising of the Indian and Pakistani cricketers reached new and absurd heights, so too did the unshakeable belief of the masses in their invincibility.'

There may be some truth in this. Yet the association between cricket and nationalism predated the opening of India's economy to foreign fizzy drinks. The belligerent mood of Indian cricket crowds at this time also reflected what was happening in Indian politics. In the 1990s it was dominated by the rise of Hindu nationalism, a nasty and illogical ideology, which played to the worst Islamaphobic instincts of many Hindus.

Its march was fuelled by an act of vandalism. In 1992, whipped up by cynical politicians, a Hindu mob demolished the medieval Babri mosque in Ayodhya, in the northern state of Uttar Pradesh. The vandals believed it had been built over the birthplace of the Hindu god Ram. This led to the worst wave of Hindu–Muslim rioting in India since 1947 and, in turn, swelled the following of a small Hindu nationalist outfit, the Bharatiya Janata Party, whose leaders had played a lead role in the mosque's destruction. In India's 1984 general election the BJP won two seats. In the 1996 election – a few months after the World Cup – it won 161 and briefly formed India's government.

There were, of course, deeper reasons for Hindu nationalism's sudden surge. They included India's long years of economic failure. As a result, India had provided too little opportunity for its vast and fast-growing population, which in turn gave a dangerous primacy to political patronage, in the form of the government jobs, subsidies and free services with which politicians reward their supporters. The rise of Hindu nationalism was in part a symptom of this. It can be seen as a counterattack by high-caste Hindus, the BJP's core supporters, against a wave of new low-caste political parties, which were at this time threatening to deprive them of government jobs and other state favours.

The chauvinism displayed by Indian cricket crowds was, then, not merely a thuggish response to new wealth. It was also a product of India's dismal economic performance – which had forced India to open its economy with such dramatic consequences, including for Indian cricket. As the single main portal for advertising goods and services to a billion current or future consumers, it was being showered with cash. And this drenching would only intensify.

The 1996 World Cup marked the onset of a massive expansion in India's cricket economy. In a time of accelerating economic growth, no industry grew faster than cricket. In 1999 the BCCI again sold five-year rights to Indian cricket, this time to Doordarshan, for almost $60 million. Seven year later, ESPN Star Sports bought the rights to two ODI World Cups, the first two T20 World Cups and three renditions of a lesser tournament, the Champions Trophy, for $1.1 billion.

This was in line with a global trend. In 1992 Rupert Murdoch's Sky TV bought the rights to Premier League football and promptly rekindled its fortunes. 'Sport absolutely overpowers film and everything else in the entertainment genre,' the mogul declared, and spurred his executives to buy up as much of it as they could, not least in India, where Murdoch's company part-owned two sports channels – Star Sports and ESPN. In a 1996 speech to shareholders, Murdoch predicted, 'We will be doing in Asia what we intend to do elsewhere in the world, using sports as a battering ram and a lead offering in all our pay-television operations.'

Across America, Asia and Europe, sport was now being deluged with television bucks. Sky paid £304 million for its first lot of five-year Premier League rights; by 2012 they cost over £3 billion. In the process, English football has been transformed. Premier League clubs bought up the best foreign players, vastly improving the standard of the league, which in turn made it much more popular.

In India, this money-storm has been even more dramatic. Satellite television's discovery of sport has coincided in India with the opening of one of the world's biggest, fastest growing and least developed consumer markets. According to McKinsey, a management consultancy, the Indian middle-class is likely to grow from around 50 million in 2005 to 583 million in 2025. The size of the Indian consumer market will meanwhile quadruple. Capturing the affections of these future Indian shoppers is one of the biggest prizes in global advertising – and advertising on cricket is by far the best way to attempt this. In 2011 Indian advertisers spent $3 billion to buy airtime on televised cricket, representing 90 per cent of the total TV ad spend on sport in India, and a quarter of the total spent on television advertising. Cricket accounts for an estimated 60 per cent of Pepsi's entire Indian advertising budget.

Commercially and otherwise, cricket has indeed overpowered all other forms of Indian entertainment – including Indians' erstwhile favourite, film. 'Bollywood is very big, it has a very broad appeal in India,' Uday Shankar, the boss of Star India, told me. 'But it doesn't have the reach of cricket.' In fact Indians are not only turning on televisions to watch cricket – they are actually buying them for that purpose. 'Cricket has played a huge role in the growth of cable television, driving its penetration all over India,' explained Shankar. 'Because cricket is what people want to watch.'

Cricket's predominance in Indian media can also be seen by comparison with its other main rival for Indian eyeballs, Hindi soap operas. They are another oddity of Indian TV. Every evening, between seven and 11 o'clock, dozens of Hindi entertainment channels each show at least half a dozen of these family sagas, running consecutively in half-hour slots. The Zee network has more than 30 different soaps on its schedule. In those four soap-sudded hours Hindi entertainment channels generate more than half their profits.

The craze began in 2000, with the tearaway success of a soap shown on Star Plus, written and produced by a 22-year-old prodigy called Ekta Kapoor, a daughter of a veteran Bollywood star called Jitendra. It was called *Kyunki Saas Bhi Kabhi Bahu Thi*, or 'Because a Mother-in-Law Was Once a Daughter-in-Law', and followed the fictive fortunes of Tulsi Virani, a pious Gujarati woman married into an extended family of Gujarati industrialists.

I called on Kapoor in the Mumbai offices of her production company, Balaji Telefilms. She was wearing jeans and a tight white T-shirt embossed with a glittery union flag, and flicked her long black hair from her eyes theatrically as she spoke. *Kyunki*, she said, was her attempt to produce a more Indian-style plot than had previously existed on Indian TV. It was based on familiar Indian archetypes, a good housewife and her jealous, scheming harridan of a mother-in-law. It was also important to Kapoor that the show should air every evening, an innovation at that time.

'I said, "OK, in America they have weekly soaps, but India has a completely different mindset,"' Kapoor told me. 'We Indians love to have daily gossip about our neighbours. We believe in every day wanting to know what's happening in our neighbours' house. So what if those neighbours are a whole family that you see on TV every day? And what if we do this with the biggest issue there is in India, which is mother-in-law and daughter-in-law?'

Within a few months of its debut, *Kyunki* was drawing over 20 per cent of India's measurable television audience: roughly equivalent to the most popular cricket match. It would remain the top-rated show on Indian television for eight years. Kapoor was hailed as the 'queen of Indian television'. Yet the growth in TV-ownership that *Kyunki* drove also contributed to its demise. As television spread through India's smaller towns and countryside, the audience became increasingly diverse and less metropolitan in its tastes, and around 2005 Kapoor's soaps started to fizzle. 'People in small towns, they want simpler stories, they don't want a lot of complication,' she explained, looking rather tense. 'Our stories were more for the biggest 27 cities, sophisticated, and we had a lot of extramarital affairs, which were clearly not acceptable.'

No soap has since emulated *Kyunki*'s dominance of Indian viewers, nor does it seem likely that any could. 'It would be humongously inhuman to have one person catering to such a variety of tastes,' Kapoor said. 'It's such a vast range. There's Bihar who wants something, Gujarat who wants something else, there's some small town, Bhilai or somewhere like that, that wants something different altogether. So now you have very fractured programming.'

But in all these places Indians want cricket. This demand has had two main effects. First, it has driven a big increase in supply. In the 1980s India played 155 one-day internationals and 42 Tests, potentially adding up to 365 days of cricket. From 2000 to 2009 they played 257 one-day internationals, 47 Tests, plus (appropriately) 20 Twenty20 internationals – a possible 512 days of cricket. Second, this boom has made the BCCI, through its control of Indian cricket, spectacularly rich. In 2011 it generated revenues of over $180 million, which is a lot of money for a volunteer organisation with a legal status similar to that of a private club. Over 80 per cent of cricket's global revenues are now estimated to be generated in India.

It is not easy to see where this money gets spent. In 2006 the BCCI claimed to be spending $347 million on upgrading India's cricket grounds. It has spent much less on unfashionable things like cricket coaching in schools and clubs. According to a 2010 report by India's tax authority, the BCCI was spending just 8 per cent of its revenue on developing cricket.

This helps explain why India, despite its windfall, is still much less good at cricket than it should be. It has got better. The past two decades have been easily the most successful in the history of Indian cricket. Yet India still struggles to beat countries with a tiny fraction of its population and enthusiasm for cricket. Over this period it has played New Zealand in 19 Test matches, of which India has won four and lost three. That might sound respectable. But then consider that India has well over a billion people and effectively one sport. New Zealand has four million, and cricket is perhaps their third or fourth favourite game.

But off the pitch Indian cricket has been transformed. Once a cash-strapped supplicant, the Indian cricket board now more or less controls the political world of cricket. This was a power shift that also became apparent in the run-up to the fateful 1996 World Cup, which England had expected to host. It thought this had been settled by a gentlemen's agreement at the International Cricket Council – such agreements were the way the ICC had traditionally done business. But India, Pakistan and Sri Lanka challenged that assumption and on 2 February 1993, after an unprecedentedly long and fractious meeting at the ICC, England gave way 'in the best and wider interests of the world game'. This was the day that power in cricket shifted irrevocably to the east.

The governance of the game was already changing. Technically, as 'foundation members' of the ICC, England and Australia had vetoes, but it was not possible for these to be exercised against Asian opposition without risking complete break-up. Until this time, the ICC had been run under the aegis of the Marylebone Cricket Club. Yet the establishment of an independent secretariat was already imminent, and cricket's former masters recognised that the ICC must soon have an Indian head. Still, they hoped it would be someone more to their taste than the abrasive and controversial Dalmiya.

That was a forlorn hope. In 1997 Dalmiya became the ICC's first Asian leader, with the grand title of president, rather than old-style chairman. Playing to the Indian crowd, Dalmiya himself portrayed this logical shake-up as a continuation of India's momentous freedom struggle. 'They were a corrupt kind of a set-up,' he said of the unreformed ICC. 'Basically it was England, Australia and New Zealand ... It was more a colony or more a small kind of a club, and we felt it was necessary to change all that.' Yet Dalmiya was not content with a level playing field: India's struggle continued. Fuelled by a disorientating combination of postcolonial grudge and ruthless financial self-interest, the BCCI launched, in effect, a campaign for cricketing suzerainty.

It encountered little resistance. Because of the rocketing sums Indian broadcasters would pay for rights, a home series against India was suddenly the biggest windfall in cricket. This ensured that, by the turn of the century, the BCCI could count on enough votes at the ICC, especially from other Asian cricket boards, to get its way on almost any issue it cared about. Having huffed and puffed to remove from the ICC's statute the Anglo–Australian veto that was actually never wielded, the BCCI, through its financial stranglehold on the game, had since engineered one of its own. The result is that India can now cherry-pick opponents for its international calendar. It can more or less decide where and when international cricket tournaments are played. It can also demand India-sized exceptions to any ICC agreement, on disciplining players or introducing technology to assist umpires, for example, that it dislikes. As the Australian cricket writer Gideon Haigh has noted, 'this is more than a power shift. It is a change in the nature of power.'

Australia's cricketers felt the effects of this change early. By the late 1990s, they had been the world's best team for a decade, so India's cricket bosses – responding to pressure from Indian broadcasters and advertisers – wanted them to play India more and more. 'Suddenly we were going to India all the time,' Adam Gilchrist, Australia's star wicketkeeper-batsman, recalled. 'And not just us, the Australian development side, youth side, they were all coming to India.' During the 1990s, India played 26 one-day internationals against Australia; in the next decade it played 46.

At first, most Australian cricketers were, to put it gently, unhappy with this development. Tony Greig's enjoyment of the rock star status India afforded foreign cricketers was not widely shared among non-Asian players. 'You could say there was a negative perception of India in the team,' Gilchrist recalled. 'It was hot. You got sick.'

His team-mate Shane Warne was among the gripers. 'I don't like spicy food,' he told me, while in India to play in the IPL. 'Everything's spicy here, you know, so I struggled a lot when we played in India. And, of course, the Indians played the spinners really well, so I'd get a bit frustrated and a bit grumpy. They'd smash you all over the park and then you'd come back, it'd be boiling hot, the food was spicy and there were just people yelling and singing all night or whatever they were doing. And you'd just ... Aaaah! There was just no peace and quiet.'

Whether they liked it or not, the Australians started touring India every other year. This produced some wonderful games, including an Indian victory in Eden Gardens in 2001 which ranks among one of the finest in cricket. Having been dismissed for a paltry 171 in their first innings – 276 short of the Australians total – the Indians were forced to follow on. They then scored 657 for seven, including a glorious double-century by the wristy Hyderabadi V.V.S. Laxman. They proceeded to bowl the Australians out for 212 to record a famous victory. Henceforth Laxman would be known to the Australian cricket press as 'Very, Very Special' – not, as he was, Vangipurappu Venkata Sai. This Indian victory was immediately followed by another in Chennai that was almost as dramatic. The Indian media, showing little regard for the Ashes, the venerable rivalry between England and Australia, labelled the battle for the Border-Gavaskar Trophy the greatest in cricket.

The Aussies were also impressed. When they returned to India in 2004 under Gilchrist's leadership, they took India much more seriously. They rethought their approach to the country, on and off the pitch. This began, Gilchrist explained, with a decision to stop fighting India's peculiarities. Abandoning their usual aggressive game, the Australians reconciled themselves to lifeless wickets and the imperative of containing India's best batsmen. They also made a point of getting out of their hotel rooms more, to soak up a little more of India, and spit less of it back out. They dealt more courteously with the crowds that mobbed them. They kept their cool, and won the series 2-1. For Gilchrist, this was 'clearly the pinnacle' of his career.

In the course of this success, some of the Australian players discovered that India had rather more going for it than they had thought. 'We came here and saw some of the things that were happening,' Warne said. 'The sponsor deals and TV deals.' The fast bowler Brett Lee was one of the first to cash in. Having signed up as an India 'brand ambassador' for Timex watches, he went on to hoover up Indian advertising contracts, appeared in a Bollywood film and also released a self-penned duet with the Hindi singer Asha Bhosle that included the lines, 'I'm different, I'm not from here/I am just another guy, with blonde hair though.' He was, if not much of a song-writer, a wonderful fast bowler.

***

By the mid-2000s India's cricket bosses had become as powerful as most Indian politicians. And India's cricketers were among the world's richest sportsmen. Tendulkar, by one estimate, was earning nearly $30 a minute – four times what Amitabh Bachchan, India's most enduring Bollywood megastar, took home. But the third party in India's new cricket economy, television companies, was growing disaffected.

Alongside the vast potential rewards for broadcasting cricket, there were risks, which the rocketing cost of television rights had accentuated. First, the overarching focus on India's national team made cricket broadcasting more or less a zero-sum game. The winning bidder had the hottest property in Indian television; the runner-up had no compelling sports programming at all. Second, the television companies had to deal with the cantankerous and changeable BCCI.

Third, the Indian cricket broadcaster was, in effect, taking a costly gamble on the form of the Indian team. If they had a good tournament, as in the 2011 World Cup, which India went on to win, the rewards could be fabulous. ESPN Star Sports sold ten-second advertising slots for India's early games for a little under $10,000; it sold slots for the final in Mumbai, in which India triumphed over Sri Lanka, for almost $50,000. But when India got knocked out of a tournament early, Indian cricket fans switched channels and broadcasters could make enormous losses. After India failed to progress beyond the group stages of the 2007 World Cup, the tournament's Indian viewership slumped by almost 45 per cent.

These problems were especially irksome to that pioneer of Indian television, Subhash Chandra at Zee TV. Between 2000 and 2006, he bid in vain for televised cricket rights on five occasions. In 2000 Zee bid $650 million for rights to the 2003 and 2007 World Cups; the ICC rejected its bid on the basis that the company was too inexperienced at sports broadcasting. In 2003 Zee bid $307 million, in 2005 more than $340 million, for four-year rights to Indian cricket. On both occasions it lost out despite, it claimed, having made the biggest bids.

In 2006, after a change of leadership at the BCCI, Zee was confident its time had come. The cricket board's new boss, Sharad Pawar, a former chief minister of Maharashtra, was an old associate of Chandra. In anticipation of success, the company therefore launched a new sports channel, Zee Sports, and invested heavily in an existing one, Ten Sports.

It then bid $513 million for five-year India cricket rights – only to lose out to a sports marketing agency, Nimbus, which bid $630 million. A few months later Zee bid $800 million for rights for the next two World Cups, along with the new-fangled T20 version of the tournament. But ESPN Star Sports scooped them up with a bid of $1.1 billion.

This was getting out of hand. At such prices Chandra thought it would be impossible to turn a profit; he had been resigned to losing up to $100m on his own bids, so desperate was he to establish Zee's sports channels. 'What was happening in the marketplace was completely insane,' Zee's head of business, Himanshu Mody, told me. And Chandra was not the man to accept that. If he couldn't buy the board's cricket, he resolved to make his own.

'We said, "OK, if we're willing to lose over $100 million where we don't even own the intellectual property rights, why don't we invest that sort of money in something that we do own?"' said Mody. This made a lot of sense. A broadcaster that owned its own league could guarantee itself a good supply of cricket content and do away with the risks presented by the cricket board and India's misfiring national team.

The idea had been around for some time. Back in 1995 Lalit Modi, a Mumbai-based media entrepreneur, had pitched the notion of a new domestic contest, which he proposed calling the Indian Cricket League. It would be a 50-over tournament, launched in partnership with the BCCI, and contested by eight city-based franchises. But the board, fearing that this might devalue international cricket, its main cash cow, said no.

Then in 2003 the Indian division of Sony proposed another new tournament, to be called EMAX, which would also involve privately-owned teams and a crash-bang 15-over cricket format. Again the board said no. And so it did the following year, when Zee proposed yet another new tamasha, a 50-over joint venture with the board, as part of its latest bid for India team rights.

ESPN, similarly frustrated by the board's stranglehold on the cricket business, meanwhile tried to rekindle India's love for hockey. In partnership with the cash-strapped Indian Hockey Federation, it launched the Premier Hockey League, more or less along the lines of what its rivals wanted to do in cricket. The PHL was a city-based tournament, involved foreign hockey stars, dance music and flashing lights. Its first game, in Chandigarh in 2005, drew a crowd of 35,000.

But its television audience remained modest and, in 2008, when India's hockey board were expelled by the game's world governing body for failing to hold meaningful elections, the tournament was mothballed. The only sport that really mattered in India was cricket. Yet, for fear of being shut out of the bidding for India cricket rights, no television company was ready to challenge the BCCI's monopoly. After his run of losing bids for rights, however, Chandra was willing to give it a try.

On 3 April, he announced the launch of the Indian Cricket League at a press conference in Delhi. It would be a Twenty20 tournament, fully owned by Zee, which would consist of six city-based teams, playing for annual prize money of $1 million. The announcement was well timed. The board was both distracted by a contract dispute with its best-paid players and cowed by India's embarrassing exit from the 2007 World Cup in the West Indies. This allowed Chandra to present his new tournament as a patriotic effort to improve India's cricketing stock. As he said sanctimoniously, 'We feel that despite cricket being a passion, a religion in this country and despite it having great commercial players … there is need for some united effort to create a talent pool.'

The press were delighted. Here was a huge cricketing story – an assault on the board's monopoly by one of India's richest and best-connected men. It was also possible, in the generally enthusiastic coverage of Chandra's announcement, to detect an echo of a more profound struggle. This was between India's dysfunctional public sector, which the cricket board had come to resemble in the public mind, and the country's entrepreneurial private sector, whose billionaire tycoons were revered by members of India's ambitious middle class. To cricket fans, it also recalled the war between that other disgruntled media tycoon, Kerry Packer, and the Australian board in the late 1970s. 'Chandra does a Packer' was the headline in the *Business Standard*.

The comparison was imprecise, however. Packer was able to recruit most of the world's best players to his rebel World Series Cricket tournament by offering to pay them ten times more than they were getting from their impecunious national cricket boards. In 2007 the Indian board could pay India's stars as much as any private broadcaster. Moreover, their main income, from advertising, was largely dependent on their continued status as India team players. There was therefore no chance of Tendulkar and his team-mates forsaking the BCCI for Zee.

Unlike Packer, Chandra sensibly sought to avoid conflict with the board. He promised that Zee would continue to bid for the rights to broadcast India games. 'The initiative that we would launch is about a talent hunt and a talent-building process,' he said, and added hopefully, 'We are yet to get a reply from the BCCI. But the feedback so far is positive. While the previous regime was a control freak, things have changed now.'

It was audacious; but Chandra reckoned he might just get away with it. Private cricket leagues were nothing new in India. There were hundreds of them, run by companies and clubs, albeit on a much more modest scale than Zee was planning. He had also taken the trouble to brief Pawar about his plans and, at the time, the BCCI's ruler had shown no sign of opposing them. But it was not long before the BCCI hit back, through the man who had tried a similar cricketing venture himself, Lalit Modi, who was now a vice-president of the cricket board. 'The board does not give private parties permission to do anything like this,' he said.

Undeterred, Zee recruited an 'ICL board'. It was led by Kapil Dev, and included a clutch of other former international cricketers, such as India's Kiran More, Australia's Dean Jones and Tony Greig, a South African who had captained England but is best remembered for having abandoned it for Packer. Kapil's home town, Chandigarh, said it would provide the ICL with a stadium. Many foreign stars were rumoured to be prepared to sign up for the new league. Brian Lara, a retired West Indian genius, did so, for around half a million dollars a year. Australia's Glenn McGrath and Shane Warne admitted to mulling similar offers.

Tangled up in the excitement this caused was a sense that cricket, for good or bad, was about to be profoundly changed. Zee and its cheerleaders promised to globalise their tournament further – even to crack North America, a longstanding ambition of cricket impresarios. 'This game is fast, it's exciting,' Kapil told me at the time, 'It can go to America, it can go to China!'

In August, at the ICL's official launch, Zee unrolled an impressive cast of players. They included 44 Indian first-class players and four Pakistani internationals – including a pair of aging great batsmen, Inzamam-ul-Haq and Muhammad Yousuf. Addressing them for the cameras, Kapil Dev was at his impassioned best. 'I will back you till the last day I live,' he swore.

CHAPTER FOUR

The Pawar and the Glory

To see the ruler of world cricket, I naturally headed for Krishi Bhavan, the home of India's agriculture ministry. A big cuboid building, mixing Mughal red-stone colours with 1950s brutalism, it was, like most New Delhi ministry buildings, hard to enter and harder to navigate. After leaving my details in three ledgers, passing through two metal detectors and wandering the building's mazy corridors I arrived, a minute before my appointment was due to begin, at room 120. It was from here that Sharad Pawar ruled over the agricultural livelihood of 750 million Indians and the affairs of the International Cricket Council.

It was not a very hot day, one of the last of spring. But as I was flunkeyed into the minister's presence, I felt a trickle of sweat under my armpits. Pawar would not be the first Indian minister I had interviewed. Yet he was unusually imposing. He was a pachyderm of Indian politics, one of the biggest of the regional satraps who, over the past two decades, have come to dominate it. Few Indian politicians could match his reputation for ruthlessness in the exercise of power.

Pawar was the unrivalled boss of Mumbai, from where he had ruled his native state of Maharashtra during three separate terms as chief minister. He was a master of Indian elections. In a 44-year career, he had won 14 consecutive votes to India's and Maharashtra's parliaments. In recent years, he had not even bothered to campaign. He had been India's defence minister, agriculture minister and, in 1991, had nearly become prime minister in one of only two Congress Party governments not ruled, directly or behind the scenes, by a member of the Nehru–Gandhi family. Pawar had served under Indira, Rajiv and Sonia Gandhi, either as a member of Congress or, more recently, as the head of his own

Nationalist Congress Party, a coalition partner of Congress in both Maharashtra and Delhi.

He was a far more effective and clever politician than any of the latter-day Gandhis. If he had a weakness, it was only his reluctance to prostrate himself before them in the manner Congress required of its acolytes. He had twice been forced out of the party, most recently in 1999, when he was expelled after expressing a view that, having been born in Italy, Sonia Gandhi should not be India's prime minister. But even after this outrage Congress needed Pawar.

There was no more formidable or enduring Indian politician. It was also said none was richer. He was rumoured to own stakes in many companies and a vast land bank in his home city of Pune. Almost any new tower block that went up on Mumbai's coastline was said to be his. He strongly refuted these rumours.

As I entered his office, Pawar was sitting behind an austere desk wearing a grey safari suit. He pointed me to a chair, unsmiling but courteous, and asked if I would take tea and how he could help. He was hard to understand. This was partly because his English was accident-prone, but mainly because cancer had left half his face paralysed. He had therefore to squeeze his speech out of the right side of his mouth. (When he said 'Test matches' I at first thought he was saying 'chess matches'.) He was also the first Indian politician I had ever heard say 'thank you' to the peon who brought his tea.

'Mr Pawar, what brought you to cricket?'

He cogitated, sipping his tea, then said softly, 'I like game.'

'Anything else?'

Pawar appeared to reflect. 'It keeps my association with younger generation.'

'And I suppose that helps you politically?'

'No,' Pawar said firmly, with a look of benevolence on his semi-frozen features. 'We don't bring party and political there, but we get happiness. You see, person who is continuously in the political field also wants some changes, no?'

'You find cricket relaxing, then?'

'Yes. Away from your day-to-day political things if you spend some time on ground with sports players, you forget about other things.'

I saw his point. Cricket is relaxing. No doubt kabaddi and kho kho, traditional Indian games that Pawar also presided over, are relaxing too. But I still didn't see why Pawar needed to control them.

After a long pause he concentrated his features into a frown. Something important was coming. 'I'll tell you frankly, sir. There are three kinds of section in the society which I have observed being ICC president. First take the English. An Englishman prefers Tests. He doesn't like Twenty20 or one-dayers so much as Tests. I personally come into the category of an Englishman. An Englishman gives a lot of attention, gives a lot of time, to Tests because that is the real game, where you can see the calibre, the capacity of the players. So Englishmen like Tests. Me too.

'But there are other sections of the society. Some like one-dayers. Others like Twenty20 for some evening entertainment. In India all three classes are there. To watch five days of cricket is one thing and to watch three hours is another.'

I thought I probably agreed with this. But surely there was no need for such an exceptionally busy Indian politician to take charge of world cricket in order to discover it.

In fact, Pawar's interest in cricket was in line with a trend. In the past two decades dozens of Indian politicians have piled into the game. Arun Jaitley, a leader of Bharatiya Janata party, took over cricket in Delhi, assisted by Rajeev Shukla, a Congress politician closely attached to the Gandhi family. Shukla also presided over cricket in Uttar Pradesh; another Congressman, C.P. Joshi, India's rural development minister, was the boss of cricket in Rajasthan. Gujarat's cricket association answered to the state's BJP chief minister, Narendra Modi. Another regional leader, Lalu Prasad Yadav, a former Indian railways minister, moonlighted as Bihar's cricket boss. In all, about two-thirds of India's 27 state cricket associations were being run by politicians, drawn from all the main political parties.

This was remarkable. Imagine if British MPs took over the running of the Football Association? Or if American politicians surged into basketball? There would be uproar. In India, the takeover was not unnoticed, but there had been little resistance to it. A recent public interest suit, filed in the high court, was a rare exception. It singled out Pawar for having 'failed to manage his agriculture ministry due to his heading three premier cricket bodies ... resulting in excess or inadequate harvesting of variety of crops like vegetables, onions, garlic, grains, pulses, groundnuts, cotton and so on.' Yet, by and large, the political capture of Indian cricket elicited little negative comment.

This reflects the outsized role that politicians occupy in India. Cricket is not the only sport they dominate. Praful Patel, India's minister of heavy industry and Pawar's main henchman, ran Indian football. The Congress MP Suresh Kalmadi was head of the Olympic Association – even after being briefly jailed over corruption allegations related to the 2010 Commonwealth Games in Delhi. Indian theatre and academia were also often run by politicians, especially in Kolkata, where the arts are unusually popular. The political scientist Yogendra Yadav attributes this ubiquity of politicians in Indian society to the abiding influence of the freedom struggle, in which political leaders displaced princes and religious leaders in importance. He calls politics India's *yuga dharma*, or 'power of the age'.

Yet Indian politicians' annexation of cricket is a comparatively recent phenomenon, as sudden as the entry of the native princes into the game in the early 20th century. The princes were attracted to the prestige the Raj gave to cricket. Contemporary politicians are drawn by its modern equivalents, money and fame, the keys to electoral success. By 2010 India's state cricket associations were each receiving over $5 million a year in cash handouts from the BCCI. It would be remarkable if some of this cash did not end up in campaign war chests. Yet this is probably not the main reason Indian politicians love cricket. Rather, it is the stupendous opportunity it provides for showing off.

There is no surer way to be seen by millions of Indians than at a televised cricket match. And to be seen ruling over the proceedings, enthroned in the VVIP gallery alongside celebrity tycoons, Bollywood stars and revered cricketers, is power itself. Indians refer to this sort of high-rolling attention-seeking as 'visibility politics', and it is especially useful for politicians, such as Jaitley and Shukla, who are not directly elected to parliament, but rather nominated to its upper house, the Rajya Sabha. In such cases, prominence in Indian cricket is almost an alternative to electoral prowess.

Another illustration of cricket's political potency is an increasing traffic in the opposite direction – star players heading into politics. In 2012 Sachin Tendulkar was nominated for the Rajya Sabha by Congress (many Indians considered his willingness to enter India's corrupt polity the first ever stain on his reputation). At that time the elected lower house, the Lok Sabha, included a dozen former international cricketers, including India's former captain Mohammed Azharuddin, for Congress, and Navjot Sidhu, a former hard-hitting opening batsman, for the BJP. They are appropriate representatives of a house in which a third of the members have been charged with criminal offences. Azharuddin was banned from cricket in 2000 for match-fixing, though he was later exonerated by India's high court. Sidhu was convicted in 2006 of beating a man to death in a row over a parking space; though he, too, won a reprieve after India's Supreme Court stayed his three-year prison sentence to allow him to contest an election.

None of India's politician-cricketers has obviously distinguished himself in politics. Yet they have at least greatly improved the quality of the parliamentary cricket team – as I discovered, humiliatingly, when I played against them for a scratch foreign press side. On a sizzling day in Delhi, Chetan Chauhan, Sunil Gavaskar's former opening partner and now a BJP politician, hit our lollipop bowling for a century.

But why would Pawar bother himself with cricket? I still didn't get it. He had no obvious shortage of money or fame.

'How do you find time for cricket?' I asked him.

Pawar replied patiently. 'I take half an hour a day on telephone or internet for ICC work. That's easy enough. And when I was BCCI president, one full day in a month, mostly on telephone, giving instructions.'

For most of his political career Pawar had shown little interest in the game, despite being the son-in-law of a former Test player, Sadu Shinde. But in 2001, his interest in the game freshly awakened, he defeated India's former captain Ajit Wadekar in a leadership election for the Mumbai Cricket Association. He then set his sights on the BCCI, which was at the time ruled by Jagmohan Dalmiya.

Dalmiya had finished his term at the ICC in 2000 and returned to India to resume control of the BCCI. He was president from 2000 to 2004, and when his term was up he sought to install a loyal proxy, a Congress politician called Ranbir Singh Mahendra, to preside on his behalf. Pawar – who, like Dalmiya, was well known for never having lost an election – stood against Mahendra.

It was one of India's more controversial polls. To ensure his man won, Dalmiya voted for him three times, once on behalf of each of the cricket associations over which he presided. Yet the vote was tied, whereupon Dalmiya voted a fourth time, having claimed a presidential right to a casting vote. Mahendra was thereby declared president of the BCCI; Pawar was livid. With backroom assistance from Lalit Modi, who had recently emerged as the boss of Rajasthan cricket, Pawar forced another leadership election the following year, and this time won a crushing victory.

His rule over Indian cricket began with the release of a stirring document entitled: 'The Cricket Board in the 21st Century – A Vision Paper'. It promised to make the board, in all its dealings, open, fair and efficient: 'The buzzword should be transparency,' it read. 'There can't be a better start to the new-look board than resolve that everything we do from here on will be transparent and in the game's and public interest, be it election or allotting television rights or the team selection.' It was an impressive message. And then Pawar went after Dalmiya.

The board accused Indian cricket's former strongman of embezzling funds from the 1996 World Cup, although the allegations were later withdrawn. He was also forced, under pressure from West Bengal's communist rulers, to relinquish his main fiefdom, the Cricket Association of Bengal. After yet another legal battle, Dalmiya nonetheless stood for re-election there, and won easily. The state's chief minister called this a 'victory of evil over good'.

Having achieved almost everything he had set his mind to, Pawar told me he was almost through with politics, cricket and otherwise. 'This year, as of today, I will complete 44 years without single day's break,' he said. 'How long should one work? I don't want to work. I am trying to disassociate myself from these political things and concentrate on sports, cultural activities, reading.'

Yet Pawar was – that very day – rumoured on the Delhi grapevine to be plotting to bring down the government (of which he was, of course, a member) in a final bid to become prime minister. I wondered how Mumbai's big man felt about having such a spicy reputation.

'In retirement, will you, er, also be spending much time on your business activities?'

Pawar hardly moderated his kindly tone. 'I have no business interests at all, except some agriculture,' he said. 'My family, yes. My younger brother now he is retired but his son is looking after one major newspaper, with 1.8 million circulation ... so my family also is there ... but I am only person in the family who doesn't have association with business ...'

'You are often said to be the richest politician in India.'

'I also read and I enjoy that,' said Pawar, just perceptibly smiling on the unfrozen side of his face.

'You don't deny it?'

'Why should I challenge anyone making foolish statement? Why challenge? Let's enjoy.'

'You mean it's not true?'

'I said it's a foolish statement. Let's just enjoy.'

'You are said to own most of Pune, for example. Is that true? Do you have large real estate interests in Pune and Mumbai?'

'Not even one ... in Pune, in one company, I have small interest, and that for many years, but except that, no.'

Even after this impertinence, Pawar betrayed not a twitch of impatience. He was calm, his voice untroubled, soothing, like a kindly grandfather, even though the interview had already stretched to an hour, which was twice the time the ruler of world cricket would be devoting to the game that day. So I thanked him and left the ministry.

India's democracy is justly praised. While neighbouring Pakistan and Bangladesh have had coups and dictators, India has maintained the democratic rituals except during a brief pause, Mrs Gandhi's two-year state of emergency in 1977. It is the great achievement of modern India, a source of stability in a vast and diverse country, and a dramatic break with an autocratic past. But take a closer look at the way power is actually wielded in India and that break becomes less obvious. Indian politics remain, as they always have been, feudal, vindictive and corrupt. And India's pseudo-democratic cricket politics exemplify this.

As India's princely patrons withdrew from cricket in the 1960s and 70s, they were typically replaced by ambitious local businessmen, such as Dalmiya, who could afford to play cricket politics as an unpaid hobby. Niranjan Shah, the boss of cricket in Saurashtra, a state formed out of Nawanagar and other former principalities, was another example. The Saurashtra cricket association was at first run by princes including, during the 1960s, our old friend Shatrusalyasinhji. But in 1972 the pet-loving Jam

Sahib was deposed by an uprising of local students and businessmen, led by Shah. A resident of Rajkot, where Ranji was schooled, Shah was an undistinguished first-class cricketer from a wealthy Jain business family, which owned a newspaper in the city. He vowed to make the cricket association democratic. But four decades later he was still in charge of it.

I arranged to meet Shah at his suite in a luxury Mumbai hotel, where he was staying while on a business trip from Rajkot. He was a short 66-year-old, dressed in surprisingly blue denim jeans and a dapper Oxford shirt. He greeted me with a wide amphibian smile and ushered me to a chair.

His longevity had made Shah one of the most powerful men in Indian cricket. He was a vice-president of the BCCI, its former secretary, chairman of the umpiring subcommittee and a former IPL vice-chairman. At the time of our meeting he was also in the running to be the BCCI treasurer, overseeing the finances of an organisation estimated to be worth around $1.5 billion. No wonder people called him the *badshah* – the king – of Indian cricket.

I started by asking Shah about his long-ago freedom struggle. He nodded gravely. 'At that time all the ruling class were controlling cricket, the maharajas, just because they were the ruling class. You have heard the name of Shatrusalyasinhji?'

I nodded. 'Well, he was a good player,' Shah said. 'But some other good players, who were not princes, were not being chosen for the team, so we thought the time has come for us to be given equal opportunity. The maharajas, they were decent players, but maybe we were better, if we had a chance. So I gathered some industrialists and said, "We must fight the system! There is no proper thing going on and this is how we must change the whole thing!" And because I had a newspaper I had a voice.'

'It was a democratic uprising?'

'I was wanting more democracy, that's right,' Shah said cautiously. 'But people might say today I have been controlling since 38 years, and whether that is democratic or not I don't know.'

I agreed they might say that. Shah was by my reckoning India's longest-reigning cricket boss. He had recently beaten the previous record set by the Rungta family that had ruled over Rajasthan's cricket until Lalit Modi seized control of it in 2005.

'Yes, they might say that. I don't know,' Shah continued. 'But before that there were five or six people controlling Saurashtra cricket. Now there are two or three hundred members of the association, and as long as my members want me, as long as I have a majority, I am ruling. And I feel my members are happy.'

Shah was good at keeping his members happy. Membership of the Saurashtra cricket association conferred high status in Rajkot, and a regular supply of international match tickets. The association was a closed shop – no new member had, by Shah's admission, been admitted for over two decades. In a semblance of democracy, one of the association's senior officers once told me, elections were held every six years, at which a third of the members were voted out. But most were then voted back in again.

Many of the association's lucky members were rumoured to be Shah's friends, relatives and employees. I asked him if this was true.

'No, no,' he said. '... maybe 15 or 20 only. I don't know. And employees, hardly, I don't think there are many.'

It would be hard to check: the association's membership list is not publicly available. Neither are its annual accounts. But Shah was good enough to give me several issues of these – stamped 'private and for members only'. They revealed that Shah presided over six of the association's nine committees, including those concerned with selection, discipline and finance. 'We do have a governing council,' he admitted. 'But generally people depend upon me.'

The accounts also included several gushing profiles of Saurashtra's captain, Jaydev Shah, who happened to be the badshah's son. Naturally, the father was very proud. 'I don't want to boast,' Shah said. 'But my son as a captain is a totally independent persona and he has no liking or disliking of any player and I think the players and selectors respect him.' No doubt this was true and to his credit. But the seasonal averages printed in the association's accounts also suggested that Jaydev was consistently Saurashtra's worst batsman.

His career batting average was 28, about half what the best batsmen expect to average on the flat pitches and against the mediocre bowling common in domestic Indian cricket. Sachin Tendulkar and Vinod Kambli both averaged over 60. Yet Jaydev nonetheless had a knack of picking up contracts in the IPL, having at various times been on the books of the Mumbai, Jaipur and Hyderabad teams, even though he had not actually played a game for any of them.

Whatever his merits as a captain, it is inconceivable that Jaydev would have enjoyed such a fine career if his father hadn't, in effect, owned the shop. Such nepotism is a common feature of Indian cricket, which also recalls its princely past. Another beneficiary is Tejashwi Prasad Yadav, son of Bihar's cricket boss, Lalu. At the age of 12 Tejashwi, who was said to be an all-rounder, was honoured with Bihar's highest award for sporting merit. It was bestowed upon him by his mother, Rabri Devi, who was at that time chief minister of the state (she was holding the fort for Lalu, who was in prison on corruption charges at the time).

In 2008 Tejashwi's skills were further recognised when he was signed up by the Delhi Daredevils. He remained on their playing staff for five years – making him the longest-serving Daredevil – though he never actually made the team. In fact, he has only played a single first-class game, for Jharkhand, Bihar's neighbouring state, in which he scored 19 in the second innings and took no wickets. 'Lalu had no interest in cricket except to promote his own son,' another senior cricket-politician told me. 'He was always pestering Sharad Pawar to get him picked for India. He thought cricket was like politics – that just as you can get a ticket to fight an election, so you can get a place in the team.'

The politics of Saurashtrian cricket are time-worn – but the economics have changed a great deal in recent times. At the start of his reign the badshah had to beg money from local businessmen to pay his side's travel expenses. 'Team would go by train. Not have nice hotel. There was hardly any money from board,' he told me.

But during the 1990s the television lucre started to flow. In 2000, according to its annual accounts, the association received $470,000 from the BCCI as its annual share of television and other revenues. By 2010 this annual dividend had risen to $6.6 million.

Shah was using this money to build a new 30,000-seater cricket stadium outside Rajkot. He referred to this construction as the 'Dream Project', and the webpage of the Saurashtra Cricket Association described it thus:

> It was a dream, it was an ambition and it was an irresistible urge and aspiration of Niranjan Shah to give to the city of Rajkot, and in turn, to the cricket fans and sports loving people of Saurashtra region an ultra-modern and state-of-the-art cricket stadium.

The dreamer Niranjan Shah firmly believes what is stated by Karen Stevens:

'You can be all of the things you dream of being, if you're willing to work at them and if you'll believe in yourself more. Be the person you were meant to be. Everything else will follow; your dreams will come true.'

With such belief in dreaming and realising the dream, Niranjan Shah and all at SCA have been endeavouring very hard, persistently and devotedly to realise, to achieve what is dreamt and aspired.

'So are you going to name it after yourself then?' I asked. 'Will it be the Niranjan Shah Stadium?'

Shah smiled and shook his head. 'No, no,' he said, and then added, 'Let's see, I am not very keen on these things.'

In fact Shah wanted to leave more than a poxy stadium as his legacy. He wanted to change cricket – specifically by ending the primacy of international contests, one of the game's most distinctive and attractive features.

'At the moment we are getting money only when there is an international game,' he said, sounding almost resentful. 'So I think IPL is the first step on this issue. Like in baseball, America is not worried whether other country is playing or not. Because cricket is a major game here, so we should not depend on whether England or South Africa come to India to get money. Why not play between two states? Maybe we call ourselves Saurashtra Lions or something. We can get 40,000 people to that game and bring revenue from TV. That's what I want to see – cricket has to go to the level of baseball of America. We are one billion people, three times bigger than America. We should not be dependent on whether this or that country comes.'

'And international cricket?'

'International cricket, that is OK.' Shah said dismissively. 'As long as people like it. But it should not be our core thing because at the moment all earning is through international cricket only. No earning is through our local competition. That's why we are losing a lot of money.'

Losing money? That was madness. The BCCI was as rich as a Mughal emperor. It was building new cricket stadiums by the dozen. Yet what Shah was proposing made perfect sense to him: it was *swadeshi* in cricket, a continuation of India's great struggle. 'ICC is trying to control us. That's my feeling,' Shah explained. 'Most of the other boards do not like that we make so much money and that their revenue depends on whether our team goes to play them. So the whole thing has been reversed. For cricket the only market in the world is India. The market is here. So we will control cricket, naturally.'

I hoped this was the badshah's personal opinion. But it probably was not. He was not known for original thinking or for sticking his head above the parapet. In Saurashtra, he was a feudal lord, but at the BCCI headquarters in Mumbai Shah had for decades played the part of a loyal retainer to bigger men, flitting between Dalmiya, Bindra and Pawar, ingratiating himself to each in turn. The badshah was not an outlier at the BCCI. He represented its majority view.

The Dream Project is a couple of miles outside Rajkot, next to a railway line running south to the Indian Ocean. When I showed up there one sunny weekday morning, it was, though still under construction, hosting a 50-over friendly between Saurashtra and Baroda. The stadium was almost empty. There were just a few workers in yellow crash helmets sitting in one stand and some officers of the cricket association in the pavilion. A freight train rattled by, bound for a large oil refinery outside Jamnagar; the clanking of its carriages echoed around the empty stands.

The Project is a smooth concrete bowl, not unattractive as concrete stadiums go. It carries, too, the stamp of its dreamer's ambition – in the form of a perfect replica of the spaceship-like press box at Lord's. I made for the pavilion, where I found, sitting alone, a middle-aged spectator with thick spectacles and a mop of lightly hennaed hair. This was Haresh Pandya, one of Rajkot's few English-language journalists. He had kindly agreed to be my guide to Saurashtra.

We sat together for a while, watching the play. Baroda were batting second and struggling, several wickets down, chasing an impossible target. The sound of mistimed thwacks resounded around the ground.

'You are interested in cricket,' Haresh said. 'Very good. And I will help you however I can. But I have to tell you something. My passion for the game is dead.'

'Oh. Why's that?'

'Match-fixing,' said Haresh urgently. 'It has killed my passion. I could never have believed that my heroes would do such a thing.'

We sat on, drinking tea together and enjoying the sunshine and the sound of bat on ball. A grey pi-dog ambled across the outfield, ignored by the fielders.

It became obvious why Haresh, who described himself as a specialist in 'politics, crime, obituaries and cricket', was so stricken by the corruption in cricket. He was a serious fan, who had devoted much of his life to reading, thinking and talking about the game. No sort of a cricketer himself, Haresh had spent much of his youth writing fan mail to famous players all around the world. He had received over 100 replies, he said – including ten letters from the great Donald Bradman. 'I will never part with them,' he said. 'Nor will I ever reveal what Sir Don wrote to me …' I wondered, briefly, what he meant by that.

Haresh's favourite player was Gundappa Viswanath, a wristy Bangalorean batsman of the 1970s. Vishy, as he was known, is the Indian aficionado's favourite. He scored fewer runs than his brother-in-law Sunil Gavaskar, yet was especially revered by many who watched them playing together in the 1970s. Gavaskar was a genius, yet restrained himself, husbanding his talent, in ruthless pursuit of runs. Vishy was an artist, who played in a style that was beautiful and carefree. He was also, unlike Gavaskar, loved by opponents for his graciousness in victory or defeat.

I told Haresh that my own hero was David Gower, an English batsman not dissimilar to Vishy. Haresh sighed. 'Gower, yes, he was a beautiful player. But he was also lucky to be English and written about by English writers. Vishy's misfortune was to be born Indian, which meant he never got the recognition he deserved. You know, sometimes I think you need a great writer to make a great cricketer.'

'You don't sound like a man out of love with cricket …'

'I didn't say I was!' said Haresh, looking shocked. 'I said I had lost my passion for the game. But it is still cricket, so of course I still love it.'

The last Baroda wicket fell and the players began trooping in. The groundstaff, women wearing salwar kameez and long dupatta scarves, walked out to sweep the pitch with bundles of twigs. Haresh and I then drained our tea and set off for Rajkot, and the office of the cricket association.

Shah was there, chatting with some of his officers. He was wearing an India team tracksuit and was nowhere near as friendly as he had been in Mumbai.

'Well,' he said, 'what is it?'

I congratulated him on the Project. But Shah frowned. 'Hmm. It is quite good. But what we need there is an integrated hotel. That is very essential now. Because we spend lots of money on hotels so we need our own.'

There was not much else the Project would lack. It would soon have an indoor cricket school, a swimming pool, several restaurants and a health club. It would be one of the smartest stadiums in India. This was in sharp contrast to the rest of Shah's domain. Rajkot, a city of 1.5 million people, in one of India's historic cricket regions, had only five other turf pitches. They included those at the Rajkumar College and at the city's Madhavrao Scindia stadium, which had hosted 12 one-day internationals. Outside Rajkot, in the seven districts of Gujarat that comprise Saurashtra, the situation was much worse. By Shah's reckoning, only three or four had a cricket pitch worthy of the description.

'We are running cricket in Rajkot, basically,' he conceded. 'Next I will start spending in the districts. I will see if I can find six or seven acres of ground, then we can have a pitch.'

I asked why he had not done this already. It seemed odd that he had chosen instead to build a wonderful modern stadium, at a cost of around £15 million, in a city that already had a perfectly serviceable one. The Project looked to me like a temple of concrete to Shah's enormous personal ambition.

The badshah glowered across his desk. But Haresh, as a local cricket reporter, could not afford a row with him. 'Niranjan-ji, who is your favourite cricketer?' he asked soothingly.

Shah grinned. 'Well everyone has to say Sachin, don't they?' he replied, then chuckled in self-delight, as if he was about to say something daring. 'But I have to say it – Sehwag!'

Now it was Haresh's turn to fall silent. He wore a look of mild disdain, and I felt sure I could imagine his thoughts. 'Sehwag indeed! What of Vinoo Mankad? What of our Vishy?'

We left Shah soon after. But I called him again a couple of days later, with a question I had forgotten to ask. 'Mr Shah, who is Karen Stevens?'

The big man of Saurashtra cricket wasn't sure. 'She's from quote book,' he said. 'Maybe poet.'

***

At 7am the next day, I left my hotel to find Haresh waiting for me. Rajkot was already bustling with the morning rituals of provincial India. Barrow boys in grubby slacks and shirts were rearranging piles of bananas, potatoes and papaya on the narrow pavements. Cows moved slowly among them, flicking their tails at the clouds of flies that were rising with the warming sun. A clanging of temple bells could be heard above the buzzing of scooters and auto-rickshaws that were already choking the city's streets.

We made our way to another of Rajkot's cricket grounds, this one owned by Indian Railways. It was a more modest ground, flat at least, but with no facilities to speak of, and surrounded by scruffy concrete apartment blocks for railway workers. In a corner of the ground, a pair of tattered nets had been erected around two practice pitches, one of dirt, the other made of concrete.

A broad-shouldered man, dressed in an old tracksuit, was standing halfway down the concrete strip, lobbing cricket balls at an adolescent boy. Behind him, half a dozen teenagers were standing in a silent huddle, waiting to be invited to bowl.

The man, whose name was Arvind Pujara, was delivering the balls in a ten-pin bowling style, with a fast underarm action. Striding forward confidently, the young batsman drove them off the middle of his bat into the tattered netting. He looked a good young player. But Arvind was unhappy. 'He has talent, that is not the problem,' he said as I approached, barely looking up. 'But he's so late. At the age of 13 my son had already scored a triple-century. He needs a lot of practice but because he lives far away he cannot come here often. Look at that! He's standing right but he's not watching the ball on to the bat. He's a good boy but it will be very difficult for him to succeed.'

Arvind, now a grey-haired 50-year-old, had been a cricketer himself. He was a good enough wicketkeeper-batsman to play half a dozen games for Saurashtra and Indian Railways. But, unlike the badshah, who made frequent reference to his own inglorious career, Arvind hardly referred to it. He wasn't a bad player, he had told me, when we met the evening before. But he was poor, so had been unable to practise much, and had left the game early. Arvind's contribution to cricket came later.

For nearly two decades he had provided daily coaching on the
railways ground, free of charge, to the sons of poor railway workers.
That described most of the teenage bowlers lining up behind us, most
of whom lived in the adjoining flats. The batsman, Kalpesh, was the son
of a woman who cleaned Arvind's house.

Arvind had spent most of the little money he had ever saved on this
hobby. Having worked as a clerk on the railways, he was not charged
for using the ground. But he had to buy the cricket balls – 'season balls'
as Indians call them – and as they were quickly shredded on the rough
concrete surface this was a considerable expense. The balls cost 80
rupees each, which had been about half Arvind's daily wage as a clerk.
Even before his recent retirement, he had therefore been dipping into
his pension fund to pay for them.

But now consider the return on this investment. Arvind had coached
around 20 seriously committed boys at the railways ground. He was
not especially selective, he said. 'Sometimes, when a boy has no talent,
I tell him to go away and concentrate on his schoolwork instead. But
this has not happened very often. Most boys can learn. Hard work,
that is what is required.' Of Arvind's 20 pupils, four had played for
Saurashtra. Another four were currently playing for Saurashtra's junior
teams. And one, his own son Cheteshwar, a tall 23-year-old batsman
with a fine, classical technique, had done rather better. A few months
earlier 'Chintu', as he was called, had played his first Test for India.

Haresh had taken me to meet Arvind at the small concrete house he
shared with his son. I was immediately struck by the force of his manner,
which was not usual in a poor man. Arvind seemed not remotely fazed
to see a foreigner on his doorstep late in the evening. Courteously, he
had ushered us inside.

'When did you realise that your son was talented?' I asked.

Without answering, Arvind got up off the floor where he was sitting
and left the room. He returned with a small, faded photograph, which
he handed to me. It showed a small boy swiping at a bouncing rubber
ball with a toy bat.

'Do you see it?' Arvind said eagerly. I looked hard, wanting to see
what he had seen. The ball was in reach of Chintu's flailing bat, about
two feet off the ground. I looked harder.

'He's really watching the ball. Is that right?'

Arvind nodded approvingly. 'When this photograph came back from the shop, I showed it to his mother, who was very intelligent,' he said. And he gestured to a black-and-white picture of a woman's face, garlanded with marigolds, on the wall behind him. It was a portrait of Chintu's mother, Reena.

'I said to her, "I think this boy may learn cricket easily,"' Arvind continued. 'She said to me, "Then you must teach him."'

The family was living in a flat in the Railways colony at the time. So every morning before work Arvind started taking his four-year-old son to the ground. There he set him in front of a tree and lobbed a rubber ball at him, underarm, 50 or 100 throws at a time.

'Let me show you my method,' he said, leaping up. He grabbed a newspaper and, in the urgent, muscular way that he had, rolled it up and began brandishing it like a cricket bat.

'A boy must learn to play straight,' he said, assuming a batting stance. 'Like this and like this,' said Arvind, moving his front leg forward into a drive, then back to his stance, then forward again. 'And, see, this is my method,' he said, now miming bowling a ball with his ten-pin bowler's stride.

'A boy cannot play straight, as he must, if the ball bounces up – here – above his knees. That is why it must be pitched underarm … like this … and he must come forwards … like this … to hit the ball on this side and – see – on that side. This is my method.'

After only a few months, Arvind introduced a 'season ball' to Chintu's practice sessions.

'But he was tiny!' I said. 'Surely he was too young?'

'No,' said Arvind firmly. 'I wanted him to get used to it. I didn't want to put fear in his heart by avoiding it.'

Facing a hard leather ball, Chintu needed batting pads but there were none small enough. So his father cut an old foam mattress into strips and tied them around the boy's legs. And the practice sessions continued, every morning and every evening, 50 or 100 balls at a time.

The sons of other railway workers gathered to watch. Arvind started coaching them too. He didn't look for help from the Saurashtra Cricket Association. As a student he had played cricket with Shah, supported his putsch against Shatrusalyasinhji, and he had later worked as a proofreader on his newspaper. But the two men had since fallen out badly.

Arvind accused Shah of mishandling the affairs of the cricket association and launched a one-man campaign against him. He did not get far. No one wanted to hear a penniless Railways clerk criticise such a powerful local figure; it was partly in an effort to make him drop this campaign that Reena encouraged him to devote his restless energies to coaching their son.

I asked him if he had considered this as an investment for the family's future prosperity.

'Not at all!' cried Arvind. 'There was no money in cricket back then. We were just doing our work, trying to do something good. That was enough.'

Arvind's mobile phone rang. It was Chintu calling from Baroda, where he was playing for another Saurashtra side. Switching to Gujarati, Arvind shot urgent questions down the phone. Then he listened gravely to his son's answers, nodding his head in silence.

He put down the phone and apologised for the interruption. 'We have got into this habit since Cheteshwar was a boy,' he said. 'Whenever he is away from home he always calls about 9pm, before he goes to sleep.'

I asked what they talked about. 'Generally we talk about cricket,' said Arvind. 'Nearly always we talk about cricket. We talk about how he has played that day, what happened in the game, how many runs he scored, what mistakes he made. This is our routine.

'As a father, I have no complaints. My son's character was built by my wife. He is a good boy, a very religious boy who has a good relationship with God. If he scores runs, he thanks God. If he fails to score runs, he says it is God's will.'

When Chintu was 12 he started playing for Saurashtra's junior sides. His results were dramatic. Arvind handed me a piece of paper on which he had recorded his son's first run of scores: 79 not out, 77, 77, 72, 52, 138, 302 not out. These were some of the first innings Chintu had ever played, Arvind having discouraged him from playing even games of street cricket previously. 'We had worked so hard,' he said. 'I did not want his technique to be messed up.' In his first two seasons of cricket, Cheteshwar scored a century on average every four innings, and it was often a double or even a triple.

It was everything Arvind had dreamt of. But then, when Chintu was 16, the family suffered a catastrophe. Reena was diagnosed with terminal cancer. Arvind and Chintu were devastated. Like so many strong men, Arvind had relied on his calm, understated wife far more than almost anyone knew. As she lay dying, she tried to console him. 'She told me, "I assure you our son will play for India and nobody can stop him,"' Arvind said, and abruptly flicked a tear from his eye as if it was a fly. 'Her guru had told her that this was so and she knew that he was right.'

C.A. Pujara made his first-class debut for Saurashtra against Vidarbha in December 2005, two months after his mother's death. He scored 145 in his second match, and was picked for India Under-19s the following year. In 2007–08, his second full season of first-class cricket, he scored more runs in the Ranji Trophy than any other player: 807 at an average of 73.36. He was easily Saurashtra's best batsman. By the end of 2009–10, his first-class average was above 60 – more than twice that of Saurashtra's captain, Jaydev Shah.

His India debut came the following year. In October 2010, in the middle of a two-match series against Australia, India's selectors announced that Yuvraj Singh had been dropped for the forthcoming game in Bangalore. Chintu would take his place, thereby fulfilling his mother's prediction. But Arvind, asked for his delighted response by many journalists, refused to celebrate. 'This is a very good chance given to Chintu,' he said grimly. 'Now he has to prove himself.'

The first Test of the series, held in Mohali, had been won by India by a single wicket. India's hero, as often against Australia, was V.V.S. Laxman. Half-crippled by back pain, he had scored 73 not out off 79 balls to deliver India's closest ever Test victory.

It was a wonder the game was played at all. The BCCI had planned the series as four lucrative one-day internationals. But because India was then on top of the ICC's Test rankings, the board had been persuaded to revert to cricket's traditional format. The match was a reminder of how wonderful it can be. And the second Test, Chintu's debut, was almost as gripping.

It started on 9 October 2010 – the fifth anniversary of his mother's death. Arvind, unusually for a proud Indian cricket parent, did not attend the game, instead preferring to watch it on television in Rajkot. 'I had done my best for Cheteshwar,' he told me. 'Now it was time for him to do what he could. He did not need me to be around him.'

The Australians, a great team on the way down, scored 474 in the first innings. India replied with 495, of which Tendulkar scored 214. Pujara, batting at No. 5, came in when the Indian score was 346 for three. He had spent six hours watching his team-mates bat. But his long-awaited innings only lasted three balls. He blocked the first, drove the second for four and the third was a shooter from the fast bowler Mitchell Johnson that barely bounced above ankle height. He was out lbw for 4. It was desperately unlucky.

In the fourth innings of the game, India needed 207 to win, almost the same as in the previous Test. Chintu, promoted to No. 3 in the order, walked in to bat in the third over of the innings, after Sehwag got out. It was a daunting position for a 21-year-old debutant. He was effectively playing his first Test innings all over again, against the fastest bowling he had ever faced, and charged with winning the game for India. Yet he set about the Australian bowling, calmly and viciously. He reached his fifty off only 64 balls, with a pull for four. Not many Indian debutants have scored fifty in the fourth innings of a Test match: Gavaskar had been the last. Tendulkar, batting sedately at the other end, watched approvingly.

Chintu was out for 72, bowled by a straight ball from the off-spinner Nathan Hauritz. But India, at 146 for three, were now comfortably on their way to victory. Tendulkar and Rahul Dravid knocked off the remaining runs, but Chintu was the hero of the day. When the match was over, he shrewdly praised Tendulkar for his support, reporting that Sachin had told him, 'God has given you this chance to play, he will help you score runs. Don't worry.' Then he flew home to Rajkot.

Several thousand people were waiting outside the city's small airport. As Chintu emerged, they surged forwards to place garlands around his neck and shower him with rose petals. He then drove, at the head of a long convoy of well-wishers, directly to seek the blessings of his mother's guru. Yet at 7 o'clock the next morning Chintu and Arvind went to the Railways pitch, to resume their practice, just as they always did.

It was almost midnight by the time Arvind finished the story. He had told it thoroughly, as if every detail was an important part of the record. But he did not seem remotely boastful: for himself, he made no claims whatsoever. He was imposingly self-assured, yet modest. He had often broken off, more in frustration than embarrassment, to apologise for his self-taught English – though it was in fact very fluent.

As I was thanking him, Arvind suddenly interrupted me. He needed to be sure I had appreciated the crucial point. 'What you have to understand is this,' he said. 'My son had the worst facilities in India, but the best record in India.'

If democratising Saurashtrian cricket was the badshah's objective, he had made a poor fist of it. He ruled the association in Rajkot more obviously like a feudal lord. In this it resembled most Indian political parties. The Congress party, which may soon have its fifth Gandhi–Nehru ruler, in the diffident form of Rahul Gandhi, son of Sonia and Rajiv, is only the most prominent of India's dynasties. Most political parties are family-run businesses, passed from father to son or daughter – as perhaps the Saurashtra cricket association will also be.

Feudal politics, in cricket or otherwise, might not be fair or efficient, but it is not without merit. In the right circumstances, it imposes a certain stability: the ruler rules and his acolytes benefit. But where power is contested, the flaws of India's patronage politics become much more obvious. This takes us to India's capital, one of the world's great power centres.

Delhi is littered with the Ozymandian debris of empires. (There were the monuments of at least four – Lodi, Sayyid, Moghul and British – within a short walk of our flat.) It is an historic city of politics and contestation – and its cricket reflects this. Cricket in Delhi is run by the Delhi District Cricket Association, also known as the Delhi Daddies Cricket Association, or the Delhi District Crooks Association. You get the idea. No Indian cricket administration is so notorious for nepotism and misrule.

This often arises in the matter of team selection. In 2006 the DDCA's boss, the Hindu nationalist Arun Jaitley, sacked the association's selectors after they allegedly picked a player because his friends had threatened to beat them up if they did not. Jaitley said he was 'trying to immunise the selection process from any kind of associational activities'. He is one of the more admired cricket politicians, with an impressive knowledge of Indian cricket history. But his explanation didn't say much for his association. Nor did this stop the rot. Delhi's best players, including Virender Sehwag, have repeatedly threatened to quit the state in protest at its biased and inconsistent selections.

The problem is greatest at youth level. In 2007 one of the DDCA selectors was alleged to be demanding sex from mothers in return for picking their sons for his age-group side. On learning that this was a sure-fire route to getting his son picked for Delhi, one ambitious father was reported to have fixed up the selector with a 5,000-rupee-a-trick prostitute, masquerading as his wife. If this happened, commented Kadambari Murali of the *Hindustan Times*, it was 'far less than what some parents have allegedly paid to get their sons to play for Delhi'.

Such capers have not improved Delhi's results. Though it is not one of India's traditional cricket centres, Delhi has contributed a dozen players to the national side over the past two decades, more than any other city except Chennai. They include some of India's biggest recent stars, such as Sehwag, Gautam Gambhir, Virat Kohli and Ishant Sharma. This success reflects the Indian capital's size and prosperity – Greater Delhi has a population of 25 million and is one of India's richest regions. But over the same period Delhi has won the Ranji Trophy only once.

Rotten coaching is also to blame. In 1999 the association spent only 20,700 rupees on coaching – less than the 24,606 rupees it made that year by selling empty bottles from the members' bar for recycling. As so often in India, Delhi's star cricketers rise in spite of the system not because of it. According to Tarak Sinha, a disenchanted former head coach of the DDCA (who was coaching the Rajasthan side when I met him), if there were 50 Delhi boys sufficiently talented, motivated and tough enough to play cricket for India, no more than five would have a hope of making it. The rest would get ignored or ruined by the DDCA.

Jaitley has tried to improve matters. But his influence is limited. India's former law minister wields nothing like the same power in Delhi cricket as he does in the BJP. He presides over it at the grudging behest of two mutually loathing factions, each dominated by a local businessman whose power derives from the number of DDCA members he claims to represent. Those claims are also controversial and contested – owing to the association's arcane system of voting by proxy. Under its rules, DDCA officers claim, for years on end, to represent the votes of thousands of silent members, some of whom are almost certainly deceased. Like feudal lords measuring their battle strength, Delhi's cricket bosses refer to themselves and their rivals in terms of the number of proxy votes they wield. The leader of one of the biggest factions, C.K. Khanna, is said to command over 1,000. He is known as the 'Proxy King'.

Understanding Delhi's cricket politics is not easy. The voting system is opaque and most DDCA bosses are reluctant to illuminate it. But one of them, Sunil Dev, agreed to explain matters to me.

We met in the dowdy south Delhi office where Dev runs the family fertiliser business. It was cluttered with the usual paraphernalia of the Indian cricket administrator: Hindu icons, autographed cricket bats and pictures with self and Sachin. Dev, a squarely built and prosperous man, was head of the DDCA's sports committee – a powerful post.

Across his office desk, he studied me in silence. Then he emitted a long sigh, rubbed his face with a meaty hand, sucked in his cheeks, and started shouting.

'Today you see before you a pained man!' he exclaimed. 'Appalled by what THEY are doing in the name of cricket. Shall I tell you of the secret wars, the OFFENCES they are committing in cricket? I may tell you. Yes I may. But what of me?

Dev paused.

'How will you use what I say? How will they harm me?' He was grimacing in mock torment. Bollywood had clearly lost a bright talent to the fertiliser business. Then with a mighty thwack he slapped his hand down on the desk. 'But now I recall what Lord Krishna said to Arjuna: "YOU'RE RUNNING AWAY FROM YOUR FUCKING DUTY!"'

Dev jabbed himself in the chest. 'They have called me a "loose cannon". Oh, have they? I say, GOOD! In today's society a man has to be a loose cannon to speak the truth!'

Dev bowed his head. He put his hands on the desk between us, clenched his fists and then looked up, snarling with ham ferocity.

In the DDCA, there are 25 men who matter, Dev explained, each elected on the basis of his strength in proxies. These officers are known as the directors, and he is one of them – having, Dev reckoned, somewhere between 300 and 400 proxies.

The directors secure their proxy votes either by wooing existing members or, more often, by sponsoring new ones, whose votes they will then command. There were thought to be around 4,500 members in all. But this was a rough estimate.

'Who keeps the membership list?' I asked.

Dev raising his eyes to heaven. 'That is a very great question and I will give you enormous respect and many great parties if you can find out and explain to me how it works.'

Like almost all positions in Indian cricket, the DDCA's directors are 'honorary', which means voluntary and unpaid. But Dev suggested they were not always uncompensated for their efforts.

'Are any corrupt?' I asked.

'Many!' he hissed.

Even for the scrupulously honest administrator, the benefits of being a Delhi cricket boss are substantial. The Feroz Shah Kotla Stadium in Delhi is one of India's top cricket grounds. This makes a man with access to a regular supply of match-tickets a powerful fellow. Tiger Pataudi, who played for Delhi in the early 1960s, before shifting in disgust to Hyderabad, once told me how this works. 'If you can get hold of 200 spare tickets for an India game, you can organise yourself pretty well,' he said laconically. 'You give some to the income tax people, to the police, to anyone whose good offices you might need in the future. It's been like this at least since the late 1950s or early 1960s, which is how far I go back.'

This is serious influence in India. But according to Dev, it is easily lost. I had asked him what, for an ambitious Delhi cricket boss, were the main threats. Dev shot a suspicious glance towards the closed door, leant forward in his chair, and hissed: 'He must, must, must keep his members obliged. Or else he may LOSE THEM!'

'And how is that done?'

Dev froze, as if bludgeoned by the question. Then he exploded: 'HE MUST KEEP GIVING PASSES AWAY!'

Dev slumped back in his chair like a spent oracle. And suddenly he looked up, flashed me a wild glance and lunged at the drawers of his desk, tugging them open with melodramatic abandon while saying, 'Here, I will show you, yes, yes, I will show you!'

Reaching into the drawers, he started heaving out brick-sized wads of unused match tickets and piling them on to the desk. I noted a stack from a recent World Cup match, West Indies v the Netherlands. I sensed that Dev didn't want me to inspect them too closely.

He appeared extremely agitated and was chuntering manically to himself. 'I will not do it, no, no, I will not and I cannot!' he rambled, while flinging more multi-coloured slabs on to the desk. Then he looked up and said gravely, 'I am keeping these for the courts.'

The South African cricket administrator Ali Bacher once asked one of his Indian counterparts an uncomfortable question. 'Why is India so much less good at cricket than it should be? Producing a top cricket side is not rocket-science,' Bacher said. It requires three things: money, talent and popular support, all of which India has in unrivalled abundance. 'So if you're not far and away the best in the world,' Bacher said, 'there's something wrong.'

There is a lot wrong with how Indian cricket is run. Yet India is run even worse. The BCCI – for all its caprice, bombast and nasty politics – is actually one of India's better-run institutions. It has hosted three World Cups, not without trauma, but much better than India handles most public events.

The 2010 Commonwealth Games in Delhi, organised by the Indian Olympic Association, provides a bleak comparison. It was a decade in the planning. Yet a few days before the event, despite massive cost overruns, almost none of the venues was ready. A road bridge outside the stadium collapsed. The athletes' village was 'filthy and uninhabitable' according to the Commonwealth Games Federation – there was dog excrement on the beds and human excrement in the sinks. The Federation was anticipating a fiasco: 'If the minister tells me one more time, "Don't worry. Haven't you seen *Monsoon Wedding*? It'll all come good in the end," I'll go mad,' one of its despairing officials told me at the time.

In the event, the games went OK, but it was a close-run thing. As a vaunted display of the new India, it was a humiliating episode. And this was not for want of cash. India spent at least $4.6 billion on building facilities and upgrading Delhi for the event – having estimated that this would cost no more than $500 million. At least part of the problem was that the organising committee was as sullied as the sinks. There was evidence of massive over-invoicing on procurement contracts: soap dispensers costing $1.97 were invoiced at $61 and toilet paper at $80 a roll. The boss of the Olympic Association, the Congress MP Suresh Kalmadi, was sacked and jailed over the allegations. Yet after ten months, he was released on bail, returned to parliament, and reinstated in his Olympics post. At the time of writing his case was pending.

India's cricket administration is better than that. It is also improving, partly thanks to investments – especially in infrastructure – brought about by Pawar. The BCCI has had, since 2006, smart new offices outside the Wankhede Stadium in Mumbai and a dozen full-time employees. It previously operated out of a basement office in the stadium, with concrete floors and a lavatory that required key access. The New Zealander John Wright, India's national coach from 2000 to 2005, reckoned these ramshackle surroundings were the 'greatest feat of camouflage since a wolf put on sheep's clothing'.

India's national side is now as professionally run as any other. There are also few allegations of the regional bias that once plagued its selections. Television, by giving stark exposure to cricketing talent, has made that unsustainable. Some of the state associations are also better run these days, especially in India's richer and better-governed southern states: including Karnataka, where, uniquely in India, cricket is now run by two former India cricketers, Anil Kumble and Javagal Srinath.

This is promising. Yet a much greater force for improvement is the effect that cricket's boom has had on the game's image. Indian cricket, once elite and exclusive, has come to be seen as a route from poverty to riches. Across India, poor boys are now thronging to play it, hoping to emulate their heroes' earning power as well as their hitting.

Even Saurashtra's complacent badshah has noticed the change. 'Before, parents said to their sons, "you study, you don't go, you must take care of your family,"' he told me. 'But now people know players can go by plane and stay in good hotels. Now parents will send their boys to cricket because there is a hope that he will be good at cricket and earn money.'

This change is manifest in an increasing number of cricket stars hailing from humble backgrounds. Sehwag learned batting by studying Tendulkar on his neighbour's colour television in Najafgarh, a suburb of Delhi. Mahendra Singh Dhoni, India's captain, is the son of a humble engineer from Ranchi, in the poor eastern state of Jharkhand. Such players are typically self-taught, introduced to the game by television, and hungry for its riches. They are also emerging from India's furthest-flung towns. In the first decade of this century, Uttar Pradesh, India's most populous state and traditionally a cricketing backwater, has supplied seven international players, more than any other state.

This democratisation of the game, as one commentator has termed it, promises a huge expansion in Indian cricket's talent pool. It might also be seen to represent the wider burgeoning of opportunity that has come with India's growth spurt. This is one of the world's great developments – the raising of millions from poverty to middle-class status. Yet India's recent progress is still fragile. Its rags-to-riches success stories, in cricket and otherwise, are still exceptional, and highlight just how hard it remains for most people to get on in India. For every Sehwag or Dhoni that emerges to the light, hundreds of talented players remain mired in poverty and obscurity.

India's north-eastern state of Bihar was once one of the glories of Asia. It is where, sometime around 400 BC, Gautama Buddha achieved enlightenment under a pipal tree. In medieval times Bihar's main city, Patna, was a centre of scholarship, a wellspring of mathematics, astrology and Hindu philosophy.

But Bihar now struggles for any memory of its former greatness. It is India's poorest state, overcrowded, lawless and wretched. Bihar's average income is a quarter of the national average. Almost half its 100 million people live below the poverty line. Bihar is India's last redoubt of polio.

This makes it a tough place to govern, and Lalu and his wife, in power from 1990 to 2005, hardly seemed to try. Under their rule, law and order in the state broke down. It was known as the Goonda Raj: Rule by Gangster. Now matters are improving. Their successor, Nitish Kumar, has locked up many of the gangsters, cleaned up the streets and deployed thousands of teachers in Bihar's schools. India's least hopeful state now has a fighting chance. But this cannot yet be said of its cricket, which Lalu still controls.

The Bihar Cricket Association was formed in 1935 and, until a decade ago, was run from Jamshedpur, a company town of Tata Steel. It is by far the biggest employer in Jamshedpur. It also runs much of the city, managing its hospital, schools, academies for football, archery and athletics, golf courses, a zoo, and Jamshedpur's international cricket stadium. It also used to run the state cricket association. But in 2000 a chunk of southern Bihar, including Jamshedpur, was hived off to form the new state of Jharkhand. This partition – or 'bifurcation' as it is called – cost Bihar over 20 million people and most of its mineral wealth and industry.

Most of Bihar's cricket estate, including its main stadium, administration, pitches and $1 million in the cricket association's kitty, were located in Jamshedpur, within the breakaway state. So was its best player – India's future captain, Dhoni. Yet this development was not uncontested: power rarely changes hands in India without a fight.

The members of the old Tata-run cricket association, based in Jamshedpur, renamed themselves the Jharkhand Cricket Association (JCA). Yet their right to run cricket in the new state was challenged by another group, formed by local clubs, which called itself the Cricket Association of Jharkhand (CAJ).

In Patna, a group of Bihari businessmen formed a new Bihar Cricket Association (BCA), and unanimously elected Lalu their leader. 'Even though I was least interested, I took up the responsibility,' the politician declared. 'I will contribute my share to prop up Bihar on the world sporting map.' All three new organisations claimed the right to the erstwhile Bihar association's lucrative BCCI membership and cash reserves. It fell to the Indian cricket board to decide which of the rival claimants to recognise. And, lo, this local wrangle became enmeshed in loftier politics.

The outgoing BCCI president, a Tamil industrialist called A.C. Muthiah, recognised Lalu and his BCA Patna. But soon afterwards Dalmiya, newly returned from running the ICC, rescinded that decision, and recognised the JCA. The issue went to court, and as the writs and counter-writs proliferated, so did the outfits claiming to represent Bihari cricket. In 2002 Kirti Azad – the World Cup-winning all-rounder who lost his trousers at Lord's – formed the Association of Bihar Cricket.

Azad, a BJP politician, held a parliamentary seat in Bihar. Hence his claim to run its cricket. 'I'd already said to Lalu, if you do something for cricket in Bihar, I will support you. But he was doing nothing,' Azad told me. He and his followers organised some district competitions in his constituency and, naturally, also ended up in court against Lalu's BCA. An outspoken man, Azad took a poor view of Indian cricket politics. 'We learned from you English,' he guffawed. 'We corrupt really well.'

Cricket in Patna, so lovingly described by Sujit Mukherjee in his *Autobiography of An Unknown Cricketer*, a memoir of his playing days in the 1940s and 50s, was dying. To advertise this fact, in 2004 representatives of Lalu's Bihar Cricket Association staged a hunger strike outside the BCCI's annual general meeting in Kolkata. Unless the board recognised their association, they further threatened to launch a 'fast unto death' outside the home of India's president. But the board was unmoved.

Then Pawar got hold of the BCCI in 2005 and appointed a commission, headed by Arun Jaitley, to review the issue. Its recommendations were due to be voted on by the board the following year. In the run-up to this event the Bihari cricketers renewed their lobbying. They wrote to India's president threatening that 25 first-class cricketers would immolate themselves outside his house unless their cry was heard.

In a way, it was: the Indian board decided to leave things as they were. It vowed to merge the BCA and the JCA and keep Bihari cricket in its former undivided state. Lalu welcomed the plan with the proviso that his body would be in charge of the merger.

But the JCA took that decision to court and soon enough the Bihari cricketers were back on hunger strike outside the BCCI's office in Mumbai. 'All we want is to play cricket,' their leader Mrityunjay Tewari implored.

More than a decade after Bihar's bifurcation, the issue remained unresolved. Yet a solution was quietly emerging. The JCA would retain, de facto, Bihar's first-class status (which is why Lalu's boy, Tejashwi, had played for it). The BCA was meanwhile vying to be accepted by the Indian board as an associate member, a status that would in due course lead to full membership.

That was probably the best Bihari cricketers could hope for. But it was far from clear when, if ever, it would happen. Lalu's organisation was meanwhile impoverished and largely inactive. Its leader's political influence had collapsed. At a state election in 2010 Lalu's party won just 22 of the 243 seats. Having lined up behind a powerful politician, the BCA was now saddled with a leader uninterested in cricket, who lived in Delhi and was reviled in Bihar.

On a dark night in Patna – as most nights are, there being few street lights – I called on Lalu's point-man in the city. His name was Abdul Bari Siddiqui. A sturdy Muslim, built like a boxer, Siddiqui ruled over Lalu's party and the BCA in his leader's absence. He was sitting outside his bungalow, in a cloud of mosquitoes, chatting with some friends.

'I ask you,' Siddiqui said tragically, as a skinny servant brought the tea. 'Is it right that everyone should harass us terribly only because Lalu Prasad Yadav is our leader and president of our cricket association?' Siddiqui shook his head. 'No, I say, this is unsporting! Whenever politicians enter sport, the politician prospers and the sport suffers.'

This was a bit rich, I suggested. Besides his cricket duties, Siddiqui was also the deputy head of India's national badminton association. 'Ah, yes!' said Siddiqui, perking up. 'Only I, Siddiqui, am different. I am a politician, yes. But actually I am a sports person. As a boy I played badminton, I also played cricket.' His cronies nodded approvingly.

Well, in that case, I suggested, perhaps he had better take over the BCA from Lalu?

Siddiqui looked delighted. 'Aha!' he said. 'Why not?'

At 7.30am the next day I turned up to the Sanjay Gandhi Stadium in Patna. I wanted to see what cricket had survived in the city, and had been directed to what was, I was told, the second-best cricket ground in Bihar. But it was not much of a stadium or ground. It was a rectangular patch of wasteland, strewn with bricks and sparse patches of grass, with a collapsing brick wall running along one side. Opposite was a small concrete stand, with space for a few hundred people. Arvind Pujara, it turned out, had exaggerated: the Railways ground in Rajkot was not the worst in India. Compared to the Sanjay Gandhi Stadium, it was Lord's.

Yet the stadium was packed on that early morning, with over 100 youths playing noisy games of cricket. Most were using piled-up bricks for wickets. They did not appear to be especially poor, not by Bihari standards. Most of the cricketers wore shirts and jeans, not *kurta* pyjamas, and looked well fed – in a state where more than half of children are stunted by undernourishment. Their shouts included a lot of English words: 'Bowling, bowling – Shabash!' 'Hit it!' 'Keeper! Keeper!' 'Out!' This was the middle class of Patna at play.

In the centre of the action, I spotted a teenaged youth, fielding in the covers, who was leaning on a bamboo stick to stop himself toppling over. He was a cripple, with skinny and twisted legs, obviously wrecked by polio.

I walked over to introduce myself. The fielder's name was Gyan Prakah and he looked a lot less pitiful up close. Above his ravaged legs, Gyan's torso ballooned into muscular arms and shoulders, hugely developed by the effort of dragging himself around with the stick. As I had walked up to him, with my friend and translator, Utpal Pathak, a Patna-based journalist, I had worried that he might feel patronised by our attention. Not a bit of it. Gyan, who was aged 18, seemed at ease with the world and keen to discuss his cricket.

He and his friends played at the Sanjay Gandhi ground almost every day, he said, apart from when it was flooded during the monsoon. They took it in turns to arrive early – often by 4am – to claim a good pitch. Then he nodded at the crevassed patch of mud on which they were playing. Apparently it was a good pitch.

I asked Gyan if he could bat. 'Of course I can bat!' he exclaimed. 'I'm mainly a batsman.' With his strong shoulders, Gyan could support himself on his stick with one hand and wield the bat with the other. 'I'm very good at hitting ones and twos,' he said and, to his friends' delight, mimed neat dabs and cuts with one hand in the air. His friend Dharmendra acted as Gyan's runner and also did the calling. Gyan was a baby when polio wrecked his legs: having no memory of walking, he was a poor judge of a single.

'But sometimes when Dharmendra-bhai is about to run, I shout, "No! No! Stop!"' said Gyan and his friends fell about laughing, for this was obviously a standing joke. Gyan also bowled leg-spin, but not too well, he admitted.

As the sun climbed and the working day approached, the cricketers began drifting away. Gyan, hopping along on his stick, turned to wave as he went. Then a more serious-looking group of cricketers, young men wearing whites, walked out to inspect the potholes in the middle of the pitch. After this inspection they summoned the groundsman – a tiny old man nicknamed Gabbar Singh, after Bollywood's most celebrated villain – to heave out a roll of thick coconut matting. Once pegged down, this provided the surface on which most first-class, and even Test, cricket was once played in India.

These young men were some of Bihar's best cricketers and chief victims of the ongoing fight over control of cricket in the state. Utpal had got in touch with one of them, an off-spinning all-rounder called Kundan Kumar, ahead of my visit and asked if he would meet us for a chat. 'No problem, but we can do better than that,' he had said. 'We'll organise a game for you.'

Kundan was a short 21-year-old who divided his time between studying at Patna University and working on his father's fruit stall. He was also a handy cricketer. He had represented both Bihar and Jharkhand at several age-group levels and had recently helped Bihar Under-22s to victory in a 40-over tournament. But that had been a rare event. 'Right now my career is over,' he said. 'There's no good cricket in Bihar.'

Earlier in the season Kundan and two friends had travelled to Jharkhand and played a few games for a district side there. Their hope was to get picked for the state side in Jamshedpur. 'Jharkhand is the key,' he said. 'If you can make it into the state side, your career can take off.' But none had managed this and Kundan said he didn't have the money to give it another go next season.

The game was ready to begin, with Kundan and his team-mates due to bat first. I left him lounging on the boundary and walked out to observe the action from mid-on. Kundan had not exaggerated about his friends' skills. The opening bowler, a muscular teenager, slung the ball hard into the matting, whence it skidded through fast. And the batsmen were even better. Both came quickly on to the front foot to drive the ball hard, sending it racing over the wasteland through extra cover. The fielding was also good: the returns came in low and fast to the stumps. Most of these players, I guessed, would walk into a good English club side; but no English side would play on their pitch.

Returning to the boundary, I asked Kundan and his friends who their best player was. As soon as Utpal translated the question, they started laughing. The best player, they said, was Pintu Kumar – he was easily the best player on either side. An older man, aged 28, Pintu was sitting a few yards away. He was poor, rather hapless and a well-liked figure of fun. Yet Pintu, an off-spinning all-rounder, was apparently well known in Patna as the best Bihari cricketer never to have been given a fair chance.

'How good is he really?' I asked, unsure whether the joke was on him or me.

'No, no, we're not kidding,' Kundan assured me. 'Pintu is brilliant, that's the whole point. He's never been coached but he's a natural. He's much better than the rest of us. You have to see him play.'

I asked if Pintu was better than Tejaswi Yadav, Lalu's son – and Kundan and his friends fell about.

'Most of us are better than that guy!' he said. 'But Pintu's much, much better. You can't even compare them.'

Playing for Patna a few years before, Pintu had hit two centuries and five fifties in seven innings. He batted like a street-cricketer, trying to hit almost every ball, and when he was on the go there was no one who could bowl to him. Fast bowling, spin bowling, it was all the same to Pintu – he just stepped forwards and walloped it. But he had never been picked for Bihar or Jharkhand. He was penniless, entirely without influence, and the selectors had always found one reason or another to ignore him.

'Hey Pintu!' Kundan called over to his team-mate. 'Come here and tell this white guy what the selectors said about your teeth!'

Wearing a shy smile, Pintu came over, hunkered on the grass, and did as he was asked. After he was inexplicably left out of Bihar's Under-15 side, Pintu explained, he had asked one of the selectors why. He was told he had too many teeth for a 14-year-old, and had therefore been ruled as over-age.

'So what did you do next, Pintu?' Kundan said, smirking, because he knew the answer.

Pintu grinned. 'I went to a dentist and asked him to take some of my teeth out,' he said. Thankfully, the dentist refused. 'The big men didn't want me because I was much better than their sons and I didn't have a godfather of my own,' said Pintu. 'That's why I was never picked.'

Denied opportunity in Bihar, Pintu went off to play cricket for Sikkim, the tiny Himalayan state next door. But, as an associate member of the BCCI, it does not contest the Ranji Trophy; and Sikkim's cricket association is almost as penniless as the BCA. So Pintu moved on to Kolkata, where he was hired by a club and paid 22,000 rupees for a four-month season. He considered that pretty good money. But he was homesick for Patna and soon returned there. Now he had no job and no regular cricket. He didn't even have any kit.

Out on the matting, the first wicket fell, and Kundan sent in Pintu (wearing borrowed pads and gloves) to show what he could do. I walked back out to mid-on to watch, as Pintu defended the first two balls he faced. Then he charged forwards at the third, and took an extravagant, point-proving swipe. He missed the ball by a foot and was stumped, yards out of his crease. Shoulders slumped, Pintu trudged back towards the boundary. And laughter rang out around the ground.

CHAPTER FIVE

Boundaries of Belief

In the heart of south Delhi is a crowded Muslim village called Nizamuddin. Built around the shrine of a 13th-century Sufi saint, it is a honeycomb of winding alleys and small bazaars selling meat, votary scarves and sticky heaps of dates. It is malodorous, wonderful and I often wandered there – especially on Thursday evenings, when Nizamuddin's streets swelled with pilgrims from across India. Evensong in the shrine, after the custom of the Chisti order of Sufism, is one of the cultural highlights of Delhi. Yet one hot afternoon in March 2011, I went to Nizamuddin to watch cricket.

India were playing Pakistan in the World Cup semi-final, in Mohali. Even by the standards of a great sporting rivalry, this was a big game. The winner would be through to the final of the tournament in Mumbai. The losers would face the fury of their millions of disappointed fans. It was also the first cricketing encounter between India and Pakistan in either country since an attack on Mumbai by Pakistani terrorists, carried out in November 2008.

The jihadists had landed in the city in an inflatable dinghy, having originally set sail from Karachi. During a three-day rampage, which was covered live on Indian television, they shot up a railway station, a restaurant, a Jewish centre and a couple of five-star hotels. By the time the last terrorist was cornered and killed, 175 people were dead, including nine of the attackers. The surviving jihadist, Ajmal Kasab, a brainwashed Punjabi, was sentenced to hang by an Indian court (he was executed in November 2012).

Bilateral cricket ties between India and Pakistan were frozen after the attack, and Pakistani players banished from the IPL. This was a familiar occurrence in India–Pakistan cricket. Between 1952 and 1977 cricket's most bitter rivals did not meet on the field of play, owing to the animosity arising from two of their four wars. Yet in the modern age of international tournaments, this complete estrangement was no longer possible.

Tensions were running high ahead of the game in Mohali. If the Pakistanis won, they would contest the final in Mumbai – a prospect most Indian media considered intolerable. Almost every pre-match report included excited descriptions of the no-fly zone and other security arrangements in place at 'Fortress Mohali'. According to the *Times of India*, 'Commandos armed with Heckler & Koch 9mm MP-5 sub-machine guns, corner shot guns, Glock 17 or Sig Sauer pistols and poison-tipped knives, would take charge of the outer field'.

Around two o'clock on a fiercely hot afternoon, I strolled through deserted streets to Nizamuddin. An impromptu national holiday had been called to allow public-sector workers to stay home and watch the game. Many private companies had followed suit, including Mukesh Ambani's Reliance Industries, which had given its workers a half-day off 'to cheer the Indian team to victory'. It was typical of India's biggest private-sector company to make its gift performance-based.

Turning into Nizamuddin, I made for the main bazaar, hoping to find a crowd. It felt slightly dishonourable, but I wanted to perform a small experiment – a version of the 'cricket test' once meanly proposed by the British Conservative politician Norman Tebbit, to ascertain the national loyalties of British Asians. I wanted to see whose side the Nizamuddin crowd was really on.

In the bazaar, a couple of hundred men and boys crowded around a television set placed under a spindly thorn tree. Most wore prayer caps and beards, but their features and hues were from all over India. Dark-skinned Bengalis and lighter Keralites, pudgy Punjabis and slight Biharis were crowded together, watching the cricket. They were pilgrims and Koranic students, who were staying in a large madrassa that fronted onto the bazaar. Evidently it had no television set.

As I shuffled into the crowd, feeling rather clean-shaven, India were batting and Sehwag in full flow. With his usual chutzpah, he smacked anything too straight to the leg-side boundary and, with lavish drives, anything wide through the covers. He hit nine fours off his first 23 balls. After each blow, the television cameras swept around the ground, showing the wildly celebrating Punjabi crowd. This Muslim gathering was more restrained.

'Who do you want to win?' I said to the rather fat young man I was squeezed against. He turned to me with a look of surprise. 'What?' he said. He was a Tamil from Chennai, it turned out, and could speak some English.

'Er, who do you think is going to win?' I asked, embarrassed now.

'India!' he shot back. 'India!' his companions joined in.

A few minutes later, Wahab Riaz, a young fast bowler who was bowling beautifully, trapped Sehwag on the back foot and appealed for his wicket. The Nizamuddin crowd tensed. Dozens of hands clutched prayer caps. The umpire's finger began its slow ascent to send Sehwag on his way, and an excited hubbub filled the bazaar – though whether of delight or dismay, it was hard to tell.

In the early years of India–Pakistan cricket ties, it was only natural that some Indian Muslims would have conflicted loyalties. Before India's bloody partition, the community had been very prominent in Indian cricket. The Muslims won the Bombay Pentangular in six of its last ten renditions, between 1934 and 1946. Muslims were also well represented in India's national side – 13 of India's 52 pre-independence Test players, a quarter of the total, were Muslim. They included some of the great names of the era, players such as Mohammad Nisar, the burly Punjabi who led the attack in India's inaugural Test match in 1932, and Syed Wazir Ali, who top-scored in both Indian innings of that game and scored six centuries on the tour. Immaculately turned out, in pressed flannels and a natty cravat, Wazir was known as the best-dressed cricketer in Asia.

Then, in 1947, India lost some of its best Muslim cricketers and cricketing terrain to Pakistan. When the first India–Pakistan Test series was played in 1952, the Pakistanis fielded two men who had previously played for All-India, including their captain, Abdul Hafeez Kardar. They also included a 17-year-old refugee from Junagadh, Hanif Mohammed, who would go on to become Pakistan's first great batsman. Hanif was the original 'little master' – the moniker later given to both Sunil Gavaskar and Sachin Tendulkar. Mohammad Nissar and Wazir Ali also migrated to Pakistan, though neither played for their adopted country.

India also lost most of its Muslim intelligentsia to Pakistan: civil servants, academics and lawyers. The Muslims who remained in India were mostly poor, illiterate and congregated in poverty-stricken parts of the north and east. If they played cricket at all, they were ill-equipped to take advantage of the changing system of cricket patronage, which favoured educated, middle-class players. In the 1950s and 60s, only four of India's 72 Test players were Muslims. That was much less than the remaining Muslim portion of India's population, which was around 14 per cent. The next three decades were worse: only three Muslim Test players out of 99 in all.

Indian Muslims still had role models, mostly drawn from the rump of the community's elite. Many were in Bollywood, which was, as it remains today, dominated by Muslim directors, composers and actors. Artists such as Mumtaz and Dilip Kumar (né Muhammad Yousuf Khan) kept alive a Muslim courtly tradition of music and dance. And India's early Muslim cricket stars were similarly charismatic.

Ghulam Ahmed, an off-spinner from Hyderabad, was the mainstay of India's bowling in the 1950s and briefly India's captain. Tall and elegant, he was nicknamed the 'Nawab of Hyderabad'. Salim Durani, a spin-bowling all-rounder of the 1960s and early 1970s – and the only Test cricketer born in Kabul – was even more of a crowd-pleaser. Handsome, debonair and capable of unpredictable brilliance, he was one of the most popular cricketers of his day. When he was dropped ahead of a Test against England in 1973, the crowd in Kanpur agitated for his reinstatement with placards that read, 'No Durani, no Test'. He was also the first Indian cricketer to appear in a Bollywood film.

But if such cricketers inspired poor Indian Muslims, they were hardly representative of them. Two of the four picked to play for India in the 1950s and 60s also played for Oxford together. They were Tiger Pataudi and Abbas Ali Baig, alias 'Buggy', the son of an engineer in the service of the (actual) Nizam of Hyderabad.

Like his university captain, Baig was marked for greatness from boyhood. He had made his debut for Hyderabad aged 15. At Oxford he secured his blue as a freshman in 1959 and was then rushed into India's touring side against England. The series was already lost: England were 3-0 up when Baig was picked for the fourth Test at Old Trafford. India lost that game, too. But Baig scored a glorious 112, an innings filled with elegant off-side strokes.

The Indian press went wild for him. 'One thought one had become a big celebrity – comparisons with Ranji, all that sort of thing,' a 73-year-old Buggy recalled languidly, when we met for coffee one rainy monsoon day in Delhi. He was another natty Muslim dresser, with a silk handkerchief flowing from the breast pocket of his blazer.

Fifty years earlier, after his century on debut, Baig had returned to India a hero and a heart-throb. In India's next series, he hit two fifties against Australia in Bombay. After the second of these innings, a match-saving knock of 58, he was trudging back to the pavilion when a pretty young woman dashed on to the outfield and planted kisses on Buggy's cheeks. The crowd was scandalised and delighted. The historian Mihir Bose considers those kisses a signal moment in cricket's transition from popular sport to Bollywood-style tamasha.

Yet Baig never scored another fifty for India. Early in 1961 he was dropped after scoring just 34 runs in five innings, during three home Tests against Pakistan. It was subsequently revealed that he had received hate mail accusing him of deliberately underperforming against his fellow Muslims. 'I was flabbergasted,' Baig recalled. 'I mean, it hadn't even occurred to one that anyone could connect my poor form to my being a Muslim.'

It was a bitter calumny, which went to the heart of Pakistan's vexed creation. The Muslim homeland had been founded on the strength of two claims made by Muhammad Ali Jinnah's Muslim League, a small political party dominated by north Indian landowners. First, that the League represented India's Muslims, though clearly it did not. In India's first provincial elections, in 1937, it failed to win even in provinces with strong Muslim majorities. Its second claim was that Muslims could never expect fair treatment in a Hindu-dominated India. Congress rejected both arguments, which its leaders considered a cover for the League's real concern, its leaders' desire for power. 'What is really the religious or the communal problem,' said Nehru, 'is really a dispute among upper-class people for a division of the spoils of office.'

There is evidence to suggest he was right. Ignoring Jinnah's summons to Pakistan, most Indian Muslims stayed put in the mainly Hindu villages they had occupied for centuries. There, Indian Muslim and Hindu rubbed along pretty well, as they usually have done. And soon the migrant flood into Pakistan turned into a trickle, then dried up altogether. Very few Indian Muslims moved to Pakistan after 1947. Most were content to be Indian.

Within a year or two of Partition – despite all the massacres that had attended it – Hindu–Muslim relations appeared, almost miraculously, to have returned to normal in India. This was highlighted by Pakistan's maiden Test tour of India, in 1952.

It was by far the most prominent interaction between the two countries since their bloody separation. It was also less than five years since their inaugural war, over the former princely state of Kashmir, which was divided in the process. Yet the visiting Pakistanis were feted by India's government in Delhi (where they also visited the shrine in Nizamuddin) and by rapturous crowds. On a 36-hour train-journey across India, between Lucknow and Nagpur, Kardar, the Pakistani captain, wondered at the 'hearty crowds' that greeted his team at almost every passing station.

The governments of both countries talked of cricket healing their terrible hurt. 'We hope,' advised the government-owned *Pakistan Times*, 'that on the cricket field will be forged new friendly ties that will help to bring two estranged neighbours closer together.' The same hope has since been expressed almost every time the countries have met to play cricket. And it is easy to see why. The deep kinship between India and Pakistan is never more evident than on the cricket field.

Their players speak the same language, play cricket in a similar way, in the same conditions and before the same impassioned crowds. They are prey to the same team-wrecking rivalries. They also understand each other's dreadful burden in carrying the fragile hopes of millions of cricket fans. It is not surprising that Indian and Pakistani players have traditionally got along well. Sunil Gavaskar and the Pakistani batsman Zaheer Abbas roomed together in Australia during the 1971 Indo-Pakistani war, while playing together for a Rest of the World side. They were said to have 'shared the tension by consoling each other'.

As cricket fans, Indians and Pakistanis also have a great deal in common. They like the same feverish tamasha cricket and understand how it is played in Asian conditions. They have an instinctive grasp of each other's cricket politics: an Indian cricket fan has an above-average chance of guessing not only what shot Muhammad Yousuf is about to play to the off-spinner, but also why his batting-partner is not speaking to him. Cricket has been by far the most prominent arena for Indians and Pakistanis to meet and rediscover their shared history and culture. Yet, blighted by politics, it has not led them to peace.

The uplifting 1952 Test series was won by India 2-1. The next two series, in 1954 and 1960, were held against a backdrop of rising tensions over Kashmir, and this was sadly reflected in the cricket. Terrified of losing, both teams played very defensively, producing ten consecutive and extremely boring draws.

The slandering of Buggy occurred during the second of those series, which was again held in India. It illustrated that for some Hindus, perhaps many, the loyalties of Indian Muslims were still deeply suspect. And India–Pakistan cricket contests now seemed to exacerbate their suspicions – because of a fundamental confusion over what they were. They were not, as chauvinists on both sides of the border thought, a continuation of the Pentangular in international form. Pakistan had scooped up only a little over half the Muslims of British India. And the Indian side were emphatically not the Hindus. In 1952 they included two Muslims, a Christian and a Parsi. Yet, despite this triumph for Indian secularism, the old habit of seeing cricket in communal terms persisted. 'Unless we can bury once and for all the idea that the Pakistan–India sporting contests are as between Muslims and Hindus,' warned the Parsi journalist A.F.S. Talyarkhan, who revealed the allegations against Baig, 'we had better put an end to rubbing against each other.'

As it turned out, the 1960–61 India–Pakistan series was the last for 17 years. India and Pakistan returned to war in 1965 and again in 1971, and bilateral cricket ties were frozen meanwhile. They were resumed in 1978, when an Indian side led by Bishan Bedi toured Pakistan.

The three-Test series that resulted, which Pakistan won 2-0, was also notable for the demolition of India's famous spin attack. Bedi and his partners, Prasanna and Chandrasekhar, took 16 wickets between them at an average of nearly 68. Their chief tormenters were Javed Miandad and Zaheer Abbas, batsmen for whom spin held no mysteries. The new masters of subcontinental wickets were Pakistan's fast bowlers: Imran Khan and Sarfraz Nawaz took 31 Indian wickets during the series at less than 28 apiece.

Between 1978 and 1989, India and Pakistan played 29 Tests. Pakistan won six and India just two. The rest were drawn, in the worst subcontinental fashion. They also played 38 one-day games, of which the Pakistanis won 24 and India 12. Regular cricket contests were a sign of a wider improvement in Indo-Pakistani relations – most obviously because Pakistan's belligerent generals were too busy fighting the Soviet army in Afghanistan to worry much about India. Pakistan's cricketing superiority was a huge confidence boost to the Islamic republic. It was chiefly due to the brilliance of Pakistan's fast bowlers, who had made their side one of the world's best and were creating an enduring tradition. Sarfraz and Imran would give way to Wasim Akram and Waqar Younis, then to Shoaib Akhtar, Mohammad Asif and many more. Armed with pace, Pakistan's teams, although notoriously inconsistent, are almost invariably aggressive and exciting. Unlike the Indians, who have always been poor travellers, they can also be formidable in any conditions.

India has produced hardly any fast bowlers at all. This irks Indians a good deal, and the reason why is not obvious. One possibility, ventured by Vijay Merchant as early as 1952, is that Pakistanis tend to be bigger and stronger. The Australian scholar Richard Cashman lends support to that thesis: he found that the average height of Indian Test cricketers diminished significantly after 1947.

To this day, Indians continue to denigrate their cricketers' physiques. According to Zaheer Khan, one of India's few successful recent fast bowlers, 'Indian bodies are not designed to bowl fast.' This is a popular theory. When, in the 1990s, the south Indian Javagal Srinath – one of India's few genuine pacers – proved to be an exception to it, the reaction was wryly self-deprecating. Srinath was hailed in India as 'the world's fastest vegetarian'. That sounds close to an admission that the problem lies, in fact, with Hindu bodies or at least with the Hindu diet. Zaheer Khan, after all, is a strapping Muslim.

This recalls an age-old Hindu bogey – the hulking meat-eating Muslim. During the Raj, the British encouraged that caricature. They labelled well-built Muslim Punjabis and Pushtuns as 'martial races' and recruited them into their armies. Tragically, the martial race theory lives on in Pakistan, where it has encouraged the generals to start three wars against their much bigger neighbour, none of which they have won. And theories of Hindus' physical inability to bowl fast are on similarly shaky ground. The best explanation for India's shortage of fast bowlers is not religious or physiological: India has 30 million Punjabis of its own and an awful lot of tall people. It is cultural. India's biggest cricketing heroes have been batsmen, from Nayudu to Gavaskar and Tendulkar. Some see in this a continuation of the old British snobbery favouring gentleman-batsmen over working-class bowlers. But, at any rate, it is clear that Pakistan is different.

Pakistanis love cricket as fervently as Indians – maybe even more. Geoff Lawson, the former Australia fast bowler and Pakistan national team coach, told me he thought Pakistanis cared more about cricket 'because there's not a whole lot else for them to do. It's either cricket or the mosque'. Above all, tearing in with their salwar kameez flapping behind them, Pakistani boys love to bowl fast.

An indication of this is a crucial innovation known as 'tape-ball', which is ubiquitous in Pakistani street games. It involves wrapping a tennis ball in masking tape to make it heavy enough to bowl fast, but not so heavy that it requires batsmen to wear gloves or pads. By loading one side of the ball with more tape than the other, a tape-ball can be made to swing. This makes tape-ball cricket a superb proxy for the real thing, and I have seen it played (and played it) across Pakistan, from the slums of Karachi to the battlefields of Waziristan. Yet I have hardly ever seen a tape-ball used in India.

Regular India–Pakistan cricket during the 1980s made life uncomfortable, once again, for Indian Muslims. Whenever India played Pakistan there were reports, from the small towns of north India and the slums of Bombay, of Muslims flying the Pakistani flag. Such displays caused outrage in the Indian press; though they were hardly treasonous. Indian Muslims remained as pacific and, by and large, uncomplaining as ever. Yet in cricket many let their imaginations wander.

Under its third dictator, General Zia ul-Haq, Pakistan was prospering and also becoming increasingly Islamicised. In 1956 Pakistan was declared an Islamic Republic; under Zia, sharia law became an important part of its legal system. Conservative Indian Muslims liked the sound of these changes. They had no wish to move to Pakistan. Yet they idolised it, in the words of the historian M.J. Akbar, as a 'psychological refuge' from their daily cares. Some also attributed this feeling to a shortage of appropriate Indian Muslim role models.

This was explained to me by Javed Akhtar, a Muslim tailor well known in Delhi expatriate circles for stitching ill-fitting suits for gullible foreigners, such as myself. Javed, who was cricket-mad, wore his beard to his chest, his salwar trousers hoisted up around his ankles and had a shiny patch of dead black skin on his forehead recording his thousands of repetitions of Muslim prayer. He was also a thoroughly loyal Indian. A lifelong Congress voter, he had no relatives in Pakistan, no desire to visit that country and strongly disapproved of mixing Islam and politics. Yet since he had first started listening to cricket on the radio in the 1960s, Javed admitted that he had found it impossible not to support Pakistan's team. 'In my heart,' he said, 'I have to support my Muslim brothers.' But what of Tiger and Baig and Salim? I asked. Javed shook his head. 'Nawabs, filmy people – these are not Muslims.'

After a decade of relative cordiality during the 1980s, Indo-Pakistani relations dived. The cause, as so often, was Kashmir. In 1987 India's intelligence agencies rigged an election in India's richer portion of the divided region, to keep Kashmiri secessionists from power. This triggered an insurgency, which Pakistan's generals, triumphant after thwarting the Soviets in Afghanistan, surreptitiously backed. By the early 1990s over 1,000 people were being killed in Indian Kashmir every year. I spent a few days there, in Srinagar, its lakeside capital, during this time. I vividly recall watching, from the veranda of the houseboat where I stayed, the nightly pyrotechnics, of gunfire and explosions, lighting up the dark sky across the lake.

Later that same year, in December 1992, Hindu zealots demolished the Babri mosque in Ayodhya, and Hindu–Muslim rioting ripped through north India. About 2,000 people were killed. Most were Muslims, the violence having been organised in many places by Hindu nationalist gangs, including a thuggish outfit in Mumbai called Shiv Sena.

The two crises – the fighting in Kashmir and the Hindu–Muslim riots – were unrelated. Hardly any non-Kashmiri Indian Muslims joined the insurgency. Yet Hindu nationalist politicians connected the two conflicts, and fed off them. And the violence proliferated. In March 1993, 13 bombs exploded in Mumbai, killing 257 people. The attack was perpetrated by Muslims as a reprisal for the Babri mosque's destruction and its bloody aftermath, allegedly on the orders of one of the city's Muslim dons,

Dawood Ibrahim. Henceforth Hinduist demagogues openly questioned the loyalties of every Indian Muslim, especially ahead of India–Pakistan cricket ties. 'It is the duty of Muslims to prove they are not Pakistani,' declared Shiv Sena's leader, Bal Thackeray, ahead of a big match. 'I want them with tears in their eyes every time India loses to Pakistan.'

That happened rather often, because India–Pakistan cricket could no longer be mothballed when political tension arose. The growth of televised one-day cricket had made it too lucrative. During the ill-tempered 1990s there were only three India–Pakistan Test matches. But India played Pakistan in 45 one-day internationals, of which it lost 26 and won 17.

All but seven of those games – including the 1996 World Cup quarter-final in Bangalore – were staged on neutral ground. The venues included Singapore, Toronto and the Arab emirate of Sharjah, where the glitterati of both countries, socialites, tycoons and Bollywood stars, put aside their differences and partied. Mumbai's Muslim mobsters, including Dawood, often joined them. A drug-dealer, gunrunner, bookmaker and Bollywood financier, Dawood loved his cricket. Sharjah was also only a short hop from his adopted home in Karachi. As a symbol of the gangster's deep attachment to the game, Dawood's daughter Mahrukh would later marry Junaid Miandad, the son of one of Pakistan's greatest batsmen, Javed Miandad.

In the summer of 1998 the BJP formed a coalition government in Delhi and celebrated, just a few weeks later, by testing a nuclear bomb. Pakistan followed suit – albeit with a heavy heart, according to Prime Minister Nawaz Sharif (a former first-class cricketer of no distinction). This was the unpropitious backdrop to the first India–Pakistan Test series for a decade, which was scheduled to commence in January 1999.

Thackeray, Shiv Sena's leader, said the Pakistanis 'should not be allowed to set foot on Indian soil'. Only a decade before, he had been an irrelevant Maharashtrian oddball, a former cartoonist. Now his party was in coalition government with the BJP in Maharashtra and Delhi. It was also influential in cricket – the Sena chief minister of Maharashtra, Manohar Joshi, was a vice-president of the BCCI. The prospect of crowd violence, of the kind that had blighted the 1996 World Cup, loomed.

Because of Thackeray, there could be no Test in Mumbai, the spiritual home of Indian cricket. His supporters also tried to prevent the match in Delhi, by digging up the Feroz Shah Kotla pitch and threatening to release snakes into the crowd. Yet the series went ahead, and produced wonderful cricket.

Pakistan won the first Test in Chennai by 12 runs, due largely to a century of reckless brilliance by its young Pushtun all-rounder, Shahid Afridi. And if the game was superb, what followed was better. As India's last wicket fell, the Chennai crowd rose to applaud the victorious Pakistanis. It was a reminder that some Indian fans could still appreciate a good game, whatever the result. Barely believing what they were witnessing, the Pakistani cricketers went on a slow victory lap of the stadium. Audibly moved, the Indian television commentator Harsha Bhogle intoned, 'If you ever wanted to see a victory for sport, here it is in your television screens, in your drawing rooms.'

India won the second Test, in Delhi, with ease. So there was no crowd trouble there. Anil Kumble, a tall Bangalorean leg-spinner who bowled faster than some Indian seamers, made history in the second innings by taking all ten wickets, a feat achieved only once before in a Test. But during the final match in Kolkata, there was trouble. Chasing 279 in the fourth innings, India were going well at 145 for two. Then Tendulkar was run out controversially, while leaping to evade a Pakistani fieldsman. Outraged, the Bengali crowd began raining water bottles on to the outfield and lighting fires in the stands. There was an overnight pause. But early on the next day after the local Bengali hero Sourav Ganguly got out, reducing India to 219 for seven, the rioting began again. The match was stopped while the police herded the crowd out of Eden Gardens. It was resumed, in an empty stadium, to allow the Pakistanis to complete their win.

By the end of the 1990s, a casual Islamaphobia had percolated Indian society. I caught a glimpse of this in June 1999, on a visit to Delhi from Tokyo, where I was living at the time. I had come to see the girlfriend who would become my wife. My visit was also strategically timed: the World Cup was being held in England and was unavailable on Japanese television.

It was, despite the fiery summer heat, a pleasant week. In the early mornings, when there was just a breath of dewy cool, Mian and I escaped her flat, which had no air conditioning, to walk among Delhi's Mughal and Lodi ruins. Then she went off to work and I went home to read the newspapers and await the first cricket match of the day. The papers were filled with reports of a new war, in Kargil, a district of Indian-controlled Kashmir that Pakistani militants had invaded earlier in the year. India had struck back, battling for the heights where the Pakistanis were dug in. As the World Cup was being played, dozens of Indian and Pakistani fighters were being killed in Kargil every day.

On the eve of my return to Tokyo, we went to watch India play Australia at the home of some friends. Our hosts were three unmarried sisters, all of whom claimed to be cricket-mad. Yet their enthusiasm soon began to wane. The Australians scored a formidable 282. And the Indian reply was inept. Tendulkar went for a first-over duck and Rahul Dravid and Sourav Ganguly swiftly followed, reducing India to 12 for three. By this point our hosts had almost given up on the game, and the sight of India's captain, Mohammed Azharuddin, walking to the wicket did not encourage them. Azharuddin was one of India's best players. Yet he often struggled on fast overseas pitches and he was currently in wretched form. He lasted only eight balls, before edging a catch to point. As he trudged off, one of the sisters screamed, 'Bloody Azharuddin, we should have got rid of you and your family at Partition!' I remember this very clearly. I don't remember having been shocked by it. I thought such views were normal in India.

Azharuddin, a Muslim from Hyderabad, had been India's captain for almost a decade. For liberal Indians, he was a sign that India's secular underpinnings were still in place. To millions of poor Muslims, including my friend Javed the tailor, he was inspirational. Azhar was not Oxbridge-educated or filmy. He was from a religious, lower-middle-class family, and had learned cricket in the street. 'Azharuddin was different,' Javed told me. 'He was like us.'

On form, he was wonderful to watch. Azhar was relaxed at the crease, with slumped shoulders and no wasted effort, with little but balance and timing in his shots. When he drove the ball at the top of its bounce through the covers, standing back and on tiptoe, he seemed to hover over the pitch. 'It's no use asking an Englishman to bat like Mohammad Azharuddin,' commented John Woodcock of *The Times*. 'It would be like expecting a greyhound to win the Epsom Derby.'

It was the sort of encomium Cardus had once heaped on Ranji. And that was fitting, because Azhar's early achievements recalled the genius prince. He scored centuries, against an England touring side in 1984, in each of his first three Tests – a feat no one has ever matched.

Yet Azhar also had it tough. When India played Pakistan, the pressure on him to perform was enormous. Indian Muslims needed his runs for inspiration; Hindu nationalists needed them to be convinced of his loyalty. When Azhar once scored a match-winning century, Thackeray declared him a 'nationalist Muslim', a phrase that was doubly insidious. It carried a suggestion that, by contrast, many or most Indian Muslims were unpatriotic; also that, should Azhar fail, his allegiances might require further review.

The inference was not lost on Azhar. 'I don't deny that people look upon me as a Muslim,' he told his biographer, Harsha Bhogle. 'But whenever I have gone out to bat, or to field, I have done so as an Indian and so it shouldn't matter what religion I follow ... I guess I will have to learn to live with it. But that can never prevent me from giving 100 per cent for India every time I walk out.'

Only that wasn't true – for reasons that had nothing to do with his religion. In April 2000, the police in Delhi announced they had taped phone conversations between South Africa's captain Hansie Cronje and an Indian bookmaker, Sanjeev Chawla, during a recent South African tour of India. They allegedly recorded the pair discussing arrangements to fix two forthcoming one-day games. This led to one of the biggest corruption scandals in sport, and Azhar's disgrace.

Further investigations by detectives, journalists and, lagging far behind, the national cricket boards revealed a rottenness in cricket that had long been rumoured. It turned out to go deeper than almost anyone had feared. For years, some of the game's biggest stars had been taking money from bookmakers in return for privileged team and other match-day information, and sometimes for wilfully under-performing in games. Cricketers from every major country were implicated in the scandal. The Australians Mark Waugh and Shane Warne became whistleblowers after admitting taking money from a bookie two years previously. But most of the fixers, on the evidence produced, were Indians and Pakistanis, and so were the bookies, based mostly in India and the Gulf. Some worked for Mumbai's mostly Muslim gangsters, including Dawood. By one estimate this mafia were responsible for a quarter of India's illegal gambling industry and much of the fixing.

Those accused included some of India's most revered modern cricketers. Kapil Dev was among them. A former team-mate, Manoj

Prabhakar, accused Kapil of offering him 2.5 million rupees to throw a game against Pakistan. Kapil was forced to resign as India's national team coach, though he denied the charge, and was subsequently exonerated.

That left Azhar, whom Cronje had referred to in the tapes as an accomplice, as the biggest Indian villain. He was accused of taking millions of rupees from bookies, since 1996 or earlier, in return for team information and attempting to fix one-day internationals. At first he suggested he was being victimised because he was Muslim. Then Azhar allegedly admitted 'doing' three one-day games and was banned for life. Three other Indian players, Manoj Prabhakar, Ajay Sharma and Ajay Jadeja, also received bans. Though Jadeja – an old boy of Rajkumar College in Rajkot who had been accused of associating with bookmakers – succeeded in having his five-year ban overturned by the high court in Delhi.

Azhar the modest, god-fearing Hyderabadi was now a distant memory. The portrait that emerged from the match-fixing investigations was of a venal cynic, greedy for expensive cars and watches. It was a transformation that had been evident for some time; many dated its onset to when, five years earlier, Azhar had ditched the mother of his two sons and shacked up with a minor Bollywood actress, Sangeeta Bijlani.

His fall was dramatic. But for the BCCI it should be temporary. In 2006 Azhar appealed against his life-ban and the board suggested it would overturn it. One BCCI official, Ratnakar Shetty, described the ban as having been a 'knee-jerk reaction' which the BCCI regretted: 'In retrospect, they feel the board had been too harsh on its players considering the way the other boards went about protecting the guilty.'

Yet Azhar remained banned, and also shunned by his former teammates. Though still revered by many Indians, he was *persona non grata* in Indian cricket. In 2008 he therefore followed a path trodden by many alleged miscreants and entered Indian politics. He stood for Congress in India's 2009 general election, in the poor and Muslim-heavy constituency of Moradabad; and won election by more than 50,000 votes. Three years later, to the surprise of many cricket fans, the Indian high court overturned his ban – the judges having found no evidence that Azhar was guilty of match-fixing.

As the 21st century dawned, Indo-Pakistani relations were dire. In 2001 more than 4,500 people were killed in Kashmir, making it the deadliest year of the conflict. In December of that year, five jihadist terrorists attacked India's parliament – the most potent symbol of Indian democracy. They breached its outer perimeter, killed seven people in a shootout and, but for the quick thinking of a police constable, might have made it into the main chamber. Most Indian MPs were inside at the time.

Both countries rushed their armies to the border, amid fears of a nuclear exchange. War, thankfully, was averted. But it surely would not have been if another planned jihadist plot had come to fruition. In February 2002 three Kashmiri militants, under arrest in Delhi, confessed that they had been hatching a plan to kidnap Tendulkar and India's then-captain, Sourav Ganguly.

Yet in late 2003, there was a surprising lurch for peace. India's Hindu nationalist prime minister, Atal Behari Vajpayee, and Pakistan's latest dictator, General Pervez Musharraf, called a ceasefire in Kashmir. Two months later, they reactivated air and rail links. In January 2004 Vajpayee visited Islamabad, where I had recently set up shop, as the Pakistan correspondent of the *Guardian*. His visit led to two important announcements. The countries would embark on a new 'Composite Dialogue' to settle all their outstanding differences. And, despite a wave of terrorist violence in Pakistan, as the overspill from the war in Afghanistan between NATO and the Taliban, the first Indian Test tour of Pakistan for nearly 15 years would go ahead, as planned, in March. It would include five one-day internationals, followed by three Tests. This was the most ambitious 'cricket diplomacy', as the effort to improve neighbourly relations through cricket was known, ever attempted.

Vajpayee, a Hindi poet and wit, underlined its significance at a farewell party for the Indian players in Delhi. '*Khel hi nahi, dil bhi jeetiye!*' he instructed them. 'Win not only matches, but also hearts!' Even Musharraf, who was more of a tennis man, sought to capture the importance of the occasion. 'It's not the question of win or lose, the good performance should be appreciated,' he declared on the eve of the first ODI, in his home town of Karachi. Then the General added: 'We must show that we are a disciplined nation.'

This is not a quality for which Pakistanis are well known. And the crowd in Karachi, Pakistan's biggest and most lawless city, was notoriously riotous. In 1997 it had stoned the Indian team during a one-day game. And the jihadist blowback from the 9/11 attacks – whose plotter Khalid Sheikh Muhammad was then hiding in Karachi – had introduced new dangers. New Zealand's cricketers fled the city in 2002 after seeing a busload of French engineers blown up outside their hotel.

I was in the press box at Karachi for the game. As the Pakistan captain, Inzamam-ul-Haq, led his team out on to the turf in their Muslim-green costumes, the crowd roared. When they were joined by India's opening batsmen, Sehwag and Tendulkar, the volume rose. I had never heard such thunderous cheering – this was the first India–Pakistan game I had seen. But the crowd was only warming up.

The first over was to be bowled by Shoaib Akhtar, the 'Rawalpindi Express'. This would be a significant event, because it was the series in a nutshell: great Indian batsmen against searing Pakistani pace. As he began his run-up, from almost beneath the press box, Akhtar was a fearsome sight. Most fast bowlers accelerate to the wicket, husbanding their energies for their delivery stride. Akhtar just charged in like a Celtic psychopath joining battle. He ran with his mighty torso inclined forwards and his bowling-arm half-extended, less like a limb than a weapon, a javelin to be hurled.

As he reached the crease and unleashed his first missile, the roaring of the crowd was tremendous. The ball bulleted wide down the leg-side, but at such thrilling velocity that the crowd kept on yelling – '*Zindabad Shoaib!*' 'Long live Shoaib!' – as the Express hiked back to the end of his run-up. This was proper Pakistani fast bowling, the real 90mph terror.

But the Indian openers survived the opening salvo from Akhtar and his willowy new-ball partner, Mohammad Sami. And as they started laying about the bowling, the crowd started shouting appreciation for them too: '*Sachin Zindabad!*' and '*Sehwag Zindabad!*' And suddenly thousands were shouting '*India Zindabad!*' A group of youths were tearing around the boundary line holding the Indian tricolour and green flag of Pakistan knotted together. '*India Zindabad! Pakistan Zindabad!*' the crowd thundered. Had I not heard it, I would not have believed it was possible. In mad, murderous Karachi, the crowd was working itself into raptures over these Indians who, despite everything they knew about the city, had trusted to come to it to play cricket.

I left the press box and wandered through the stands. 'This cricket series is our greatest and happiest Eid, for which we have been waiting for 15 years,' one spectator told me. 'This game is not just about cricket.

Musharraf and Vajpayee are brothers and that is what we are celebrating. And cricket will win. Whether we win or lose is nothing to us,' he said as his friends laughed and tousled his hair.

I went looking for some Indian spectators. There were only a couple of hundred in the stadium, sent to test the waters ahead of the much bigger Indian influx expected for the later games in Lahore. Most of this forward party worked for Samsung, the series sponsor, and were sitting together. They were easy to spot: a square of blue India team shirts in a stormy sea of white salwar kameez.

Yet the Indian spectators could not have sounded more relaxed. They enthused about Pakistani hospitality, one of the glories of Asia. Whenever the Indians took a taxi, the driver-wallahs waived the fare, when they ate in a restaurant, strangers demanded to pay their bill. What's more, gushed one Samsung man, 'The women! How pretty the women are here, with wonderful grace!' He had not expected even to see any. 'But it's really very like India.'

Then the Karachi crowd upped the ante. India's foremost political celebrities, Rahul and Priyanka Gandhi, son and daughter of the murdered Rajiv, were ushered into the stand to greet the Indian spectators, surrounded by a phalanx of bodyguards. Their grandmother, Indira Gandhi, had ordered Karachi to be shelled during the 1971 war. Yet no sooner had the Pakistani spectators cottoned on to the Gandhis' presence than they were cheering for them too. *'Priyanka Zindabad!'* they shouted as Priyanka, who resembles her grandmother, beamed with delight. Rahul looked more awkward, as he usually does.

Back in the press box I bumped into Pakistan's greatest cricketer, Imran Khan. He was not at this time contemplating the motivations of a suicide bomber. He appeared deeply contented. 'I've never seen an India–Pakistan game with an atmosphere like this,' he said. 'There's such a feeling of friendship. It's as if we're saying: "War is no longer an option, we need something new."' Outside a sudden roar signalled that an Indian wicket had fallen. The match was turning out to be worthy of the mood.

India scored 349 for seven, including a wonderfully paced 99 by Dravid. It was India's highest 50-over score against Pakistan. In reply, the Pakistanis started disastrously, with both openers going cheaply. But this put together their two best batsmen, Inzamam and Yousuf Youhana, and they changed the game.

Inzamam was one of my favourite players. He was from Multan, Pakistan's ancient 'city of saints', and there was something appropriately medieval about him. He was a round-shouldered giant, rather fat, enormously strong and comically idle. Besides batting, Inzy mainly liked eating and sleeping. Like most Pakistani cricketers, he was pious and uncomfortable speaking English and his batting was largely uncoached. On occasion his manners let him down. As when, fielding on the boundary in a hilariously misnamed 'Friendship Cup' game against India in Toronto, an Indian heckler had insulted him, calling him 'mota aloo', or fat potato. Inzy then called for a bat and leapt into the crowd with it to try to brain the heckler. But Inzy's batting was not unpolished. It was a vision of unlikely elegance. And that day in Karachi, Inzamam played one of the great one-day innings.

He and Youhana put on 135 together. Youhana then got out, attempting yet another six, but Inzy rumbled on, putting on another century partnership with Younis Khan, the best Pushtun cricketer since Imran. India's captain, Ganguly, who looked anxious at the best of times, started switching his bowlers around frantically. The deficit was now less than 100 and he needed a breakthrough.

Inzy had by now scored 122 off only 100 balls, half of them in seemingly effortless boundaries. But there his innings ended. He was caught behind, attempting a delicate late cut. I walked out to the boundary to watch Inzy come in: as he trudged past, vast and saturated in sweat, his pudgy face betrayed no emotion.

The match was by no means over. After a flurry of lower-order hitting, Pakistan needed only nine off the last over to win. But they were seven wickets down and one of their poorest batsmen, Naved-ul-Hasan, was on strike. The Indian seamer Ashish Nehra bowled beautifully. Naved and his partner, the wicketkeeper Moin Khan, could scramble only four off his first five balls.

This left Moin needing to hit a six off the last ball to win. The crowd was boiling over, everyone remembering the time in Sharjah in 1986 when Javed Miandad had done just that. But Moin, a much lesser player, heaved and was caught. India had won. But the game had been magnificent.

Pakistan's score of 344 was the highest by a team batting second in a one-day game; and the 693 runs scored that day the highest combined total in one-day international cricket. Enraptured by the drama, the emotion, the deafening expressions of goodwill, I foolishly wondered whether I had just witnessed, played out on the cricket field, a turning point in one of the world's deadliest rivalries.

The thought persisted as the series progressed. It never regained the emotional heights of Karachi, but the Indians were received warmly everywhere. They went next to Rawalpindi and Peshawar, where Pakistan went 2-1 up in the one-day series.

More than 50 Indian journalists accompanied the team on the 'cricket visas' that Pakistan had made easily available. Every day they filed back to India reams of heart-warming stories, of intense cricket and warm welcomes. Most of the rest of the time they spent in Pakistan's bazaars, looking for carpets, dried fruits and spices, things that had once flowed freely down the Grand Trunk Road, from Kabul to Chittagong. 'Huge, huge, huge shopping in Pakistan!' laughed Sharda Ugra, then of *India Today*. 'It was wonderful. I remember going from Delhi to Lahore for the first time, and thinking "My God! So this is how people in Delhi must have been like once." You know, well mannered, courteous, helpful and all that. Only the vegetarians suffered.'

The two concluding one-day games were held in Lahore, in the city's 60,000-seater Gaddafi Stadium, the biggest in Pakistan. It got its name in 1974 to thank Libya's dictator, Muammar al-Gaddafi, for a speech he gave supporting Pakistan's right to nuclear weapons. But if that was an illustration of General Zia's efforts to orientate Pakistan away from South Asia and towards the Middle East, the Lahore one-dayers represented a counter-tug, signalled by the presence of 8,000 rambunctious Indian fans.

The usual suspects of India's cricketerati were among them, including film stars and politicians. So was a more beguiling presence: Dina Wadia, the 85-year-old daughter of Pakistan's founding father, Muhammad Ali Jinnah. Estranged from her father even before Pakistan was created, on account of her marriage to a Parsi industrialist, she had visited the country only once before, for her father's funeral in 1948. She now returned with her son Nusli and grandsons Ness and Jehangir to watch the cricket and visit Jinnah's mausoleum.

It was in many ways an appropriate visit, for the Wadias, Jinnah's unwanted relations, were among the original Parsi patrons of Indian cricket. They would soon maintain that tradition by buying a stake in the Punjab IPL side, though it is hard to think Jinnah would have approved of the IPL any more than he approved of the Wadias. He was a man of conservative tastes. Then again, as a liberal democrat, he would not have approved of a military dictator naming Pakistan's biggest stadium after an Arab despot either.

India won the first of the Lahore games, brilliantly chasing down 293. That put the series at 2-2 with one game left. I drove down from Islamabad to watch, but it was a disappointing game. The Indians batted first and also scored 293, which the Pakistanis never looked remotely like getting. They lost early wickets, including three to Irfan Pathan, a 19-year-old Gujarati fast bowler, who radiated boyish delight in the game. When Inzy got out, caught on the boundary by Tendulkar, Pakistan were 87 for five, and the series was all but over.

I remember little more of the game, but I will never forget the crowd. It was less euphoric than in Karachi, but memorable for a different sort of entente. This time the Indian and Pakistani fans were not segregated. Scanning one of the smarter stands, I watched as Punjabis from either side of the border laughed, screamed and harangued each other. The men, middle-class Pakistanis and Indians, wore the same sports shirts over the same ample paunches and servant-ironed jeans. Their Punjabi wives wore the same costume of salwar kameez and showy jewellery. It was hard to tell Pakistani from Indian.

I also remember Musharraf, who was watching the game from the VVIP gallery, rising to salute the crowd. It cheered raucously as the dictator snapped to attention – because all Punjabis, whether Indian or Pakistani, like a man in uniform. But I thought this was a strange sight at a cricket match.

The Test series, which India won 2-1, attracted less attention. None of the games was close or drew much of a crowd. Pakistanis are even more out of love with Test cricket than Indians. As a result, the cricket series slipped down the Pakistani news agenda, for which there was great deal of competition at this time. On the eve of the cricket tour, the father of Pakistan's nuclear programme, Abdul Qadir Khan, was revealed to have been hawking bombs to North Korea. Meanwhile Musharraf, having recently survived two jihadist assassination attempts, had declared a crackdown on the Islamist militant groups his army had previously nurtured. A new war in the tribal region of Waziristan, where Pakistan's army were battling jihadist fugitives from Afghanistan, was at the same time going disastrously.

In an echo of the 1980s, the mounting troubles on Pakistan's north-west border underlay Musharraf's sudden enthusiasm for making peace with India. Flagging Pakistani support for the insurgency in Kashmir was another sign of that change. In 2004 around 1,800 people were killed there, less than half the record toll of three years before. By 2012 the death toll was down to 117.

Quite how earnestly Musharraf wanted peace, future historians will decide. Yet there was clearly more than political expediency to Pakistan's warm welcome for the Indian players. It was a sign that many Pakistanis had had enough of the old antagonism. After a decade of political upheaval, Pakistan was enjoying a period of stability under its fourth army dictator. The economy was buoyant. Despite the bad news from the north-west frontier, there was a new optimism among middle-class Pakistanis, including many recently returned from Dubai, Britain and America. They were in no mood for war with India.

Pakistanis had also, unbeknown to most Indians, started seeing a lot more of India. Musharraf – in what remains the single lasting achievement of his rule – had liberalised Pakistan's media in 2002. This led to a flood of Indian news programmes and Hindi dramas and films appearing on Pakistani television. And many Pakistanis were impressed by the new Indian affluence they revealed. Middle-class Pakistanis spoke wistfully of the opportunities to be had in Mumbai and Bangalore. Reports on India's perfidy in Kashmir, hitherto a staple of Pakistani news, became increasingly rare.

Hence the enormous goodwill shown towards the Indian cricketers. It was more than starry-eyed fandom. In fact India-style celebrity worship scarcely exists in Pakistan: though its people love cricket as Indians do, they make much less of their cricketers. Even the most revered Pakistani players can be seen out and about in the shops and restaurants of Islamabad and Karachi. Indian players cannot live anything like so freely in Mumbai and Kolkata. They would get mobbed by sobbing fans. Pakistanis, by contrast, would consider such behaviour absurd.

On a flight from Lahore to Islamabad, I once bumped into the all-rounder Shahid Afridi. He is not a great cricketer, but he can be a thrilling one. 'Boom Boom', as Pakistanis call him, has hit three of the seven fastest one-day centuries, including the fastest, a crazy thrash of 102 runs off 37 balls against Sri Lanka in 1996. He was a teenager at the time. With the exception of Imran Khan, who holds an exalted place in Pakistan (and may one day be its prime minister), there is no more popular Pakistani cricketer. Yet in the intimate confines of a small Pakistan International Airlines plane, no one gave Afridi a third glance. As he disembarked, the purser showed no hint of recognising him. As Shahid waited for his bag to appear on the carousel at Islamabad airport, only one slavish cricket fan went up to shake his hand, and that slavish fan was me.

By contrast, when four Indian cricketers paid a visit to one of Pakistan's best private universities, the Lahore University of Management Studies, they must have felt at home. A crowd of well-heeled students, representatives of Pakistan's small English-speaking elite, screamed like Beatle-maniacs when the cricketers appeared. The Indian party included Lakshmipathy Balaji, a journeyman Tamil medium-pacer who the Pakistani crowds had, for some reason that no one quite understood, taken to their hearts. 'Balaji! Balaji! Balaji!' the students chanted as the Indians made their entry. It was an echo of Indian-style celebrity kerfuffle – an augury, perhaps, of how Pakistan's media revolution was changing the country.

The question-and-answer session that followed was also revealing. Rahul Dravid, another in the Indian party, sounded a diplomatic note: 'I did not come with preconceived notions. I told myself I would come with an open mind and I have liked what I have seen and experienced.' Then Balaji brought the house down. Asked what he liked about Pakistan, he grinned and said, 'the girls here are really pretty.' A more interesting question was asked by a small boy, who had been brought along by his elder sister: 'You're a Muslim,' he said to the fast bowler Irfan Pathan, 'so why aren't you playing for Pakistan?'

Seven years later, Irfan was sitting on the bed in his Delhi hotel room, wearing his Delhi Daredevils practice kit. The room was neatly filled with running shoes and brightly coloured breathable fabrics, the luggage of the peripatetic sports star. It was his home for the duration of the fourth IPL season.

We had been reminiscing about the 2004 tour. Leaving aside the cricket, Irfan had two vivid memories. One was of the crowd in Karachi.

The other was of the question he was asked by that impudent boy in Lahore. 'He was very young, very innocent, probably 12 or 14,' said Irfan, in his smooth, Bollywood-accented English. 'He didn't know what it was he was asking.'

Yet it was a question that went to the heart of Pakistan's troubled identity. It was one that Indian Muslims had been asked too many times. And whether the boy knew it or not, it also had a special significance for Irfan, which no Indian could miss.

Just over two years before that now-famous tour, in February 2002, Irfan's home state of Gujarat had suffered one of the worst bouts of communal killing since India's partition. It began on a Wednesday at 7.43am, when a train called the Sabarmati Express stopped in Godhra in eastern Gujarat. It was bound for Ahmedabad, Gujarat's biggest city, and was laden with Hindu pilgrims returning from Ayodhya, where they had been campaigning for the government to raise a temple to Ram over the rubble of the Babri mosque. Much of what followed is contested. Yet it is certain the train was stoned by a Muslim mob and that a fire broke out on it, in which 58 of the passengers, including women and children, were incinerated.

Gujarat's recently elected BJP government called an official day of mourning the next day, which allowed the bodies of the dead pilgrims to be carried in slow funeral processions through the streets of Ahmedabad. In the state of India most roiled by Hindu–Muslim violence, this was tantamount to inciting the violence that duly ensued.

Mobs of livid Hindus attacked Muslim areas in almost every Gujarat town, including Ahmedabad, Baroda and Rajkot. Muslim women were raped, forced to drink kerosene and set alight; their children were hacked to pieces with swords. The police failed to stop the violence. There were reports that in some places they were leading it. Members of the government were also involved. A BJP member of Gujarat's state assembly handed out swords to the rioters, urging them to 'kill those bastards'. Her boss, Gujarat's BJP chief minister Narendra Modi, was reported to have insisted on the Hindus' right to 'vent their anger'. In many places, Muslims retaliated; but they accounted for most of the dead. In all, perhaps 2,000 were killed.

Irfan was 17 at the time and living in a small mosque on the edge of Baroda. He had grown up there, along with his elder half-brother, Yusuf, who would follow him into the Indian team. Their father, Mehboob Pathan, was employed to look after the mosque and deliver the Muslim call to prayer five times a day through its crackling loudspeakers. If any Muslim cricketers can be said to have had their allegiance to India seriously tested, it was the Pathan brothers.

Irfan did not like talking about the violence, certainly not to a journalist. 'Obviously, a lot of people created a bad name for Gujarat in 2002,' he told me, 'you know, what with what happened and everything … I would rather not go into it because it was just a bad phase, which is gone past now. And even then I really don't think there was an issue with the people who lived around us, in the temple behind our mosque. We were all together, we never had any issue.

'The trouble came from … I don't know where it came from … it's very unfair to say those people, I mean those our friends and those our neighbours who were from different religion … We never had any trouble from them.'

It was a shame. For fear of courting controversy, Irfan wouldn't say what his family had endured during the riots, in which more than 500 mosques and Sufi shrines were destroyed or damaged. Therefore he couldn't tell me about the kindness of his Hindu neighbours either.

Yet just as Azharuddin's captaincy had been an important consolation for put-upon Indian secularism, so would Irfan be. Less than two years after the massacres in Gujarat, in December 2003, he made his Test debut for India in Adelaide. His left-arm swingers were raw but fast and hugely promising. It was not long before informed pundits were calling him India's best seam-bowling prospect since Kapil Dev. According to Irfan's father, Gujarat's tainted chief minister telephoned to congratulate him on having such a fine son. '*Irfan aapka hi nahin, hamara hain!*' he said: 'Irfan is not yours, but all of ours!'

Given Modi's reputation for Muslim-baiting (he once referred to relief camps for the Muslims made destitute by the riots as 'baby-producing factories'), this was remarkable. It might also recall the rabble-rousing Thackeray's double-edged accolade to Azharuddin, that other 'nationalist Muslim'. Yet Irfan, a strikingly modest Indian celebrity cricketer, is not Azhar. And India, despite what many feared in the aftermath of the riots, is not Gujarat.

With the BJP also in power in Delhi at that dreadful time, many Indians looked into the future and saw a saffron haze. The prospects for Hindu nationalism looked excellent. The BJP's core supporters were anxious middle-class Hindus, a constituency that was growing rapidly with India's economy. Many feared that India's secular foundations were crumbling, with perhaps grim repercussions for Indian Muslims.

But those fears now look exaggerated. Soon after the 2004 India–Pakistan series, India held a general election, which the BJP was expected to win. But it lost to Congress, which formed a coalition government under the premiership of its old economic reformer, Manmohan Singh. The reasons for the result were complicated, as Indian electoral outcomes always are. They included the disgruntlement of millions of poor villagers who had seen little benefit from India's recent growth. But this was also a reminder that die-hard support for Hindu nationalism was much smaller than many had suspected, perhaps representing only a tenth of the electorate. And India's rising middle class was not, after all, flocking to increase that number. The doom-mongers had underestimated India's accommodative traditions. They also overlooked the condition most associated with middle classes the world over, which is stability. The BJP has remained out of power ever since and, though it may soon return – so corrupt and ineffective have Congress's subsequent governments been – it will not be by attacking Muslims. That, it is now clear, puts off more Indians than it pleases.

Meanwhile the fortunes of India's 180 million Muslims have started looking up a bit. The community is still wretchedly poor. In 2006, according to a high-level commission, only 4 per cent of Muslims above the age of 20 were graduates or diploma holders, compared to 7 per cent for the population as a whole. Their share of public-sector jobs was 'abysmally low', including just 4 per cent in the police. Yet poor Muslims have, like all Indians, benefited from the increased opportunities that India's growth has delivered. Labour migration from eastern India, which has a high proportion of poor Muslims, to the flourishing cities of Maharashtra and Gujarat is running at a record high.

Indian Muslims also have useful new role models, following an encouraging rise in the number of Muslims playing cricket for India. During the first decade of the 21st century, seven of India's 43 Test players were Muslim. Most, like Irfan and Yusuf, were lower-middle-class strivers. And more such Muslim stars will rise, ensuring that Indian Muslims will be even less likely to support Pakistan, which these days far fewer do. In January 2011 the Pathan brothers, no longer resident in the family mosque, were given three-year contracts to play in the IPL, together worth $4 million a year. That sort of money is a powerful incentive for all poor Indian cricketers, whether Muslim or Hindu.

'This is such a great country,' Irfan said, 'that if you are good at something, no matter your religion, you will get there. I'm proud to be an Indian and I'm proud to be a Muslim and I'm proud of the way I've been brought up in the mosque. And I can say that in the seven years I've been in the limelight not a single fan has come up to me and said something about me being a Muslim. Not once. Abusive, yes, that can happen when you play badly. But that is just a fan getting upset with a cricketer. It has nothing to do with religion. I've never had a fan come up and make me realise I'm anything other than a cricketer.'

'Would you ever want to talk in public about Islam?' I asked. Irfan seemed intrigued by the idea.

'If the time comes, yes, I'd definitely like to tell the world, not just the media: "Read the Koran, do what it says and teaches." My belief in Allah is always there. You know, I want to make sure before I die that I tell the world this is such a beautiful religion and what's happening around the world is not right. Because Allah has said it – only He is going to give life, take life, as well as only He is going to control the world. We only come here to the world to pray, to do the right things.'

'Do you pray much yourself?'

Irfan looked slightly sheepish. 'I do pray, but I would like to be a bit more prayer-friendly.' He said. 'But definitely, me and my whole family, we believe in Allah big time.'

Between 2004 and 2007 India and Pakistan came closer to making peace than ever before. Their leaders and officials met regularly, to discuss differences and forge agreements. Telephone hotlines were created, rail, road and air connections expanded, and visa regimes relaxed. Thousands of Indians and Pakistanis visited each other's countries for the first time.

Draft agreements were reached on the countries' outstanding territorial disputes: including over the Siachen glacier and even Kashmir. The latter would have involved, more or less, settling on the status quo,

Bhupinder Singh, Maharaja of Patiala (*turbaned, front row*) and A.E.R. Gilligan (*on his right*), captain of the MCC, with their teams around them in Lahore in November 1926. Two weeks later, in Bombay, the MCC side would face the Hindus of India: tougher Indian opponents than they had believed possible.

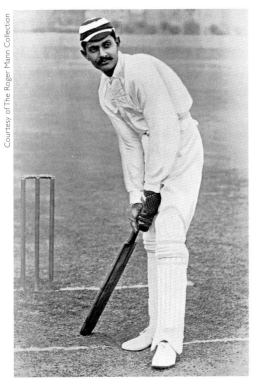

Two cricketing princes: Kumar Shri Ranjitsinhji (*left*) and Bhupinder Singh (*right*).

India's first batting star,
C.K. Nayudu (*left*); and
Palwankar Baloo (*below*),
the great 'untouchable'
spin-bowler.

Wearing solar topees, after the colonial fashion, Syed Wazir Ali (*left*) and Phiroze Palia walk out to bat against the MCC in Benares in January 1934.

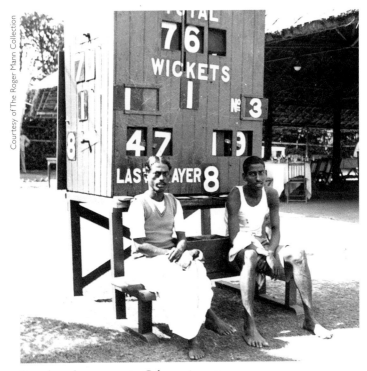

Scoreboard operators in Calcutta in 1933.

The Maharajkumar of Vizianagram – 'Vizzy' – with the All-India team mascot in 1936 (*left*) and having unaccountably missed a straight one in Gravesend (*right*).

India's captain: Jawaharlal Nehru walking out to bat for the Prime Minister's XI against the President's XI

The queen is introduced to the Indian side at Lord's in 1952. She is shaking hands with Sadu Shinde.

Tiger Pataudi (*in raincoat*) arriving in England with his India side in May 1967.

The crowd riots at Eden Gardens, Calcutta, in January 1967, interrupting the second day of a Test match between India and West Indies.

Cricket on Oval Maidan in Mumbai, a surviving fragment of the 19th century Esplanade – where it all began.

Kapil Dev, India's captain, lifts the World Cup at Lord's in 1983. India's shock victory unleashed enormous demand for the one-day game in India.

The progress of a megastar:
Sachin Tendulkar as a diffident
schoolboy prodigy, alongside his
friend and batting partner Vinod
Kambli (*above*); as a teenage
India star (*right*) and, over two
decades later, as India's most-
revered celebrity (*below*).

Wrestling at Nawab Ganj, eastern Uttar Pradesh, in 2010. Tournaments like this one, held to commemorate Gandhi's birthday, draw big crowds in northern India. But they are becoming rarer, as cricket fever sweeps the countryside.

Men and boys gather in a Karachi street to watch a one-day game between Pakistan and India, held in Dhaka in March 2012. Pakistan would win this one.

Scenes from the National Stadium in Karachi during the first game of the 2004 India tour of Pakistan. Making a nonsense of pre-match fears, the Karachi crowd gave the Indian team a wonderfully warm welcome (*above*) and was rewarded with one of the finest one-day games ever played. The Pakistani attack was led by Shoaib Akhtar (*below*), who bowled ferociously that day.

Heavyweights from Indian business, politics and film were all drawn to the IPL. Here Mukesh Ambani (*wearing a check shirt*), India's richest man and owner of the Mumbai Indians, talks to BCCI president Sharad Pawar (*wearing a white shirt*), Lalit Modi (*wearing glasses*) and Niranjan Shah.

Vijay Mallya (here chatting with Modi), added the Royal Challengers Bangalore team to his airlines and liquor empire.

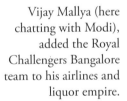

Preity Zinta, Bollywood star and co-owner of the Kings XI Punjab team, watches with Ness Wadia, her sometime boyfriend and business partner, as Irfan Pathan is greeted by the Dalai Lama in Dharamsala.

IPL cheerleaders represent a big cultural change to a conservative country. They are disapproved of by Hindu nationalist politicians and lusted after by millions of spectators.

Cricket in Dharavi, a giant slum in Mumbai. These are the sorts of conditions in which most Indian cricket is played.

which is what India has wanted all along. By the time I moved to Delhi with *The Economist*, in early 2007, commentators in both countries were predicting peace by the end of the year.

But then the diplomatic wheels fell off. Protests against Musharraf broke out in Pakistan, causing a year of political turmoil, during which the bilateral process stalled. By the end of it, Musharraf was in exile in London, Benazir Bhutto, Pakistan's most popular leader, had returned from exile in Dubai and been assassinated by jihadists, and Nawaz Sharif, her long-time opponent, was also back home. Completing this round of Pakistani musical chairs, after an election in February 2008, Bhutto's widower Asif Ali Zardari, a louche Sindhi feudal lord tarnished by allegations of gross corruption, was installed as president.

He at least wanted to make peace with India. But that hope died in November 2008, with the three-day rampage through Mumbai by Pakistani terrorists. The peace process was ended – and so, for the time being, was India–Pakistan cricket. Since India's dramatic tour of Pakistan in 2004 there had been three more closely fought series, played in both countries, including nine Test matches of which India had won two, lost two and drawn five. These fixtures were also lucrative; advertisers had spent nearly $70 million on the 2004 series, roughly three times the usual figure for a bilateral India series. But, after the terrorist attack, India's next tour of Pakistan, planned for the spring of 2009, was cancelled. 'You can't have one team coming from Pakistan to kill people in our country, and another team going from India to play cricket there,' said India's sports minister M.S. Gill.

Most Indians assumed Pakistan's army was behind the Mumbai attack. It was carried out by Lashkar-e-Taiba, a jihadist group with strong ties to Pakistan's generals. But the government of Manmohan Singh showed restraint. It did not threaten war. Nor was there a backlash against Indian Muslims. Days after the attack the BJP took out front-page newspaper advertisements in Mumbai and Delhi that depicted a blood-spattered backdrop and the words: 'Brutal terror strikes at will. Weak government unwilling and incapable to fight terror ...Vote for the BJP.' Four state elections were looming. But the Hindu nationalists won only one, in Madhya Pradesh, and for reasons that had nothing to do with Islamaphobia or Pakistan.

It was just possible that Pakistan's army was not to blame for the attack: because its former jihadist proxies were now running wild. By 2007 Pakistan's main cities had become battlegrounds. Islamabad, a Himalayan refuge for rich Pakistanis and foreign diplomats, was seeing bomb blasts every few weeks. The Marriott hotel, where I stayed during frequent visits from Delhi, was blown up by suicide bombers, killing 54. A grenade was tossed over the wall of a nearby Italian restaurant where I often ate, killing a Turkish woman and wounding a dozen others. The terrorists were probably from Waziristan, from which an Islamist insurgency had now spread across Pakistan's north-west frontier. By 2010 almost 40,000 Pakistanis had been killed in a decade of terrorism and insurgency. Many wondered how long the country could even hold together.

The national cricket team, for so long a source of Pakistani pride, was also having difficulties. In 2006 Inzamam's Pakistanis were penalised for allegedly scratching the ball to make it swing during a Test match in England, and were so angry they walked off the pitch and conceded the match, leading to a huge international rumpus. Inzamam was later cleared of deliberately altering the condition of the ball, but penalised for bringing the game into disrepute by his protest. Ball-tampering was an old problem in cricket. Yet the tour was also notable for a newer one, as signalled by the head of the Pakistani cricket board, Dr Nasim Ashraf.

'There should be balance between religion and cricket,' he said, after the team had returned home. He referred to reports that Inzy's religiosity was getting out of hand. The captain and most of his team had started celebrating runs and wickets by dropping to the wicket in prayer. Net practices were turning into prayer sessions, which continued late into the night before a big game. There were allegations that the team's younger players were being pressurised to join in. 'There should be no pressure on players who don't pray regularly or any compulsion on them to do it,' said Ashraf.

The Islamisation of Pakistani cricket reflected how Pakistani society was changing. Yet it is said to have started with a tragedy. In 2001 the infant daughter of the Pakistani opening batsman Saeed Anwar died after a long illness. Saeed was distraught. He sought comfort in a stringent, missionary school of Islam, Tablighi Jamaat. Impressed by his example, several of his team-mates, including Inzamam, Saqlain Mushtaq and

Mushtaq Ahmed, also grew their beards and began attending Tablighi gatherings in Raiwind, a town outside Lahore.

This injection of piety into the team led to controversy. In September 2005 it was announced that Yousuf Youhana, a rare Pakistani Christian cricketer, had converted to Islam and would henceforth be known as Mohammad Yousuf. Pakistani Christians, members of a small and much put-upon minority, were devastated. Yousuf's family disowned him. Unabashed, and now sporting the longest beard in cricket, Yousuf scored nine centuries in 11 Test matches the following year. For many Pakistanis, this was a high-level endorsement of his decision.

But providence did not prevent further scandals, often involving the Rawalpindi Express. There was no danger of him turning fundamentalist. Shoaib, a poor boy from Rawalpindi, was an incorrigible larrikin who liked bowling fast, fast cars and, yes, fast women. He had been in and out of trouble his entire career, for almost every imaginable misdemeanour: for calling an umpire a 'twat', for throwing a bottle into a crowd, for ball-tampering, for attending a fashion show on a Muslim holiday. Shoaib seemed to resist authority as a matter of principle.

That was often apparent during the momentous 2004 series against India, which saw clashes between Shoaib and his captain. After he had turned in several poor performances, Inzy more or less accused his star bowler of not trying. Shoaib also got into hot water for fighting a policeman at the Gaddafi Stadium. The legality of his bowling action was meanwhile questioned by newspapers.

That led me to an interesting assignment, one sunny mid-April morning at the Rawalpindi Cricket Stadium. The last Test of the series was due to begin there the next day. And I had arranged to meet Shoaib, as he completed his match-day preparation, and have a bat against him. My crazy idea was that this would nicely enliven an article I was writing for *The Economist* on the biomechanics of fast bowling.

The Indian and Pakistani players were congregated on opposite sides of the Rawalpindi ground. Under the eye of their New Zealander coach, John Wright, the Indians were going through a rigorous fielding drill, racing between bright orange practice cones. Most of the Pakistani players were lounging on the turf beside a pair of tattered nets, snoozing and chatting. There was no sign of Inzy or their team coach, Javed Miandad. Shoaib, training alone, was meanwhile pelting around the boundary.

When he had finished his run, he came over, his barrel chest heaving and drenched with sweat, and apologised for keeping me waiting. Waving away my request for a helmet (which he had promised me in advance) Shoaib then pointed me to the business end of one of the nets. His team-mates, briefly curious, fell silent and watched as he ran in to bowl at me. He bowled pretty fast – fast enough to knock the stumps right out of the ground, which he did twice. But Shoiab was bowling much below his full tilt, and, as I relaxed a bit, I found I could play the ball fairly comfortably. It was a wonderful, Walter Mittyesque experience, in surreal circumstances.

There was no chance one of the Indian bowlers would have indulged my request. Their coachers, perhaps rightly, would never have allowed it. Moreover, cocooned in their celebrity isolation, Indian cricketers are much harder to befriend. Getting in touch with Shoaib, by contrast, had been a doddle. I had got his mobile number from a friend at the Pakistan Cricket Board. And when I had called him, out of the blue, and suggested my idea for a net, he had simply laughed and suggested this time and place. As I was thanking Shoaib for his indulgence, my heart still thumping with fear, he suggested we meet up some time soon for a drink.

I wished he hadn't. Because I would not then have boasted of my new celebrity friendship, at a party a couple of nights later. And my friends, a gang of high-living Punjabis, would not have persuaded me to invite Shoaib around there and then. I duly called him up, and he answered the phone in a voice thick with sleep. Looking at my watch in horror, I suddenly realised it was long after midnight, and he was in the middle of a Test match against India.

'Thanks, man,' said Shoaib, thickly. 'Normally I'd be up for that. But the problem is we're not supposed to go out during a Test ... But, man ...' continued the Express, interrupting my anxious apologies, 'I don't suppose you've got any ladies with you?'

He was great fun, but indicative of the indiscipline that plagues Pakistani cricket. Over the next five years, before his retirement during the 2011 World Cup, Shoaib was fined and banned at least four times – though often subsequently exonerated on appeal. His alleged indiscretions included using steroids, attacking his new-ball partner, Muhammad Asif, with a bat, and criticising the Pakistani board. He missed more cricket than he played, due to bans, injuries and, ahead of the 2009 Twenty20 World Cup, a nasty case of genital warts.

Pakistani cricket was meanwhile beset by more serious blights. One was terrorism. To replace the cancelled 2009 Indian series, the Pakistani board had prevailed upon Sri Lanka to tour Pakistan instead. It promised their team 'presidential-style security'. But as the Sri Lankan team bus was on its way to the Gaddafi Stadium, it was ambushed by jihadists. Six Sri Lankan cricketers were wounded by gunfire and eight Pakistanis, mostly policemen, were killed. Pakistan would henceforward be off-limits to foreign cricketers and it was hard to imagine when they might return. The other main affliction was match-fixing.

Pakistani players were in the thick of the allegations that came to light in 2000: an inquiry by a Pakistani high court judge, Malik Mohammad Qayyum, found two players, Salim Malik and Ata-ur-Rehman, guilty of fixing (though Malik later persuaded a Pakistani court to exonerate him). The judge also recommended that six others be censured for failing to co-operate with his enquiry, including Wasim Akram, a great fast bowler to whom Qayyum later regretted having been too lenient. 'I had some soft corner for him,' he admitted. 'He was a very great bowler and I was his fan, and therefore that thing did weigh with me.' But it hardly mattered: Qayyum's recommendations were largely ignored by Pakistan's cricket board, a body which can make the BCCI seem an orderly custodian of the game. Unsurprisingly, rumours had persisted that Pakistani cricketers were still buyable.

Such rumours lurked in the background of a more outrageous controversy in the Pakistani team. During the 2007 World Cup, held in the West Indies, Pakistan's British coach, Bob Woolmer, was found dead in his Jamaica hotel room. A pathologist's report suggested he had been strangled, and his former charges were questioned by local police. A few of the players were questioned twice. They had been knocked out of the World Cup, by Ireland, just a few hours before Woolmer's death. This was a remarkable upset, leading to open speculation that the coach had been murdered after twigging that the match had been thrown. A subsequent police report suggested Woolmer had died of natural causes. But the coroner kept an open mind, ruling that the cause of his death was unknown.

It seemed Pakistani cricket could hardly fall further. Yet it did. In March 2010 the PCB, to the surprise of many, announced it had imposed life bans on Pakistan's two best players, Mohammad Yousuf and Younis

Khan, banned a third, the former captain Shoaib Malik, for a year, and banned or fined another four of the Pakistani team. This was its response to a disastrous tour of Australia, in which the players had been trounced and often at one another's throats. But the bans were nonetheless absurd, and soon overturned. To no one's surprise, most of the sanctioned players were back playing for Pakistan within a few months.

Mismanaged, unruly and denied their share of IPL riches, Pakistan's cricketers were becoming increasingly demoralised and resentful. What happened next appeared, in retrospect, almost inevitable. Pakistan's decimated side embarked on a tour of England, under the captaincy of Salman Butt. Against a fine England side they were well beaten in the first two Tests, at Trent Bridge and Edgbaston. In the third, at the Oval, the Pakistanis, with their usual flickering brilliance, punched back. They won the Test by three wickets, partly thanks to Mohammad Amir, a wondrously talented 18-year-old fast bowler, who bagged five in the second innings. That set up the series for a dramatic finish, to be played out at Lord's.

Yet the drama that eventually transpired there had little to do with cricket. On the third day of the game, on 28 August, the British Sunday tabloid the *News of the World* ran an exposé of Butt and Pakistan's opening bowlers, Asif and Mohammad Amir, alleging that they had conspired to bowl two no-balls to order earlier in the game.

Such selective fixing, known as 'spot-fixing', which is much easier to engineer and harder to detect than a rigged result, was the new corruption in cricket. It was arranged after one of the newspaper's correspondents, a British Pakistani posing as a member of an Asian betting syndicate, paid Butt's British agent, Mazhar Majeed, £150,000 in marked banknotes in return for a promise to fix matches. To prove his power, Majeed predicted that in the first innings of the Lord's Test the first delivery of the third over and the sixth delivery of the tenth over would be no-balls. These were duly delivered.

The first no-ball, bowled by Amir, was so flagrant and so untypical of the bowler that one television commentator, Michael Holding, all but accused him of corruption on the basis of it. Holding, a former great West Indian fast bowler, struggled to hold back tears as he did so. After first denying the undeniable, all three players were banned from cricket for between five and ten years. They were subsequently tried by a British court, convicted of corruption and sent to prison – in Butt's case, for 30 months. In a separate case, Pakistan's best spinner, Danish Kaneria – only the second Hindu to have played for Pakistan – was arrested by British police on suspicion of spot-fixing while playing for Essex. He was subsequently banned from playing in England and sidelined by Pakistan.

By the time Pakistan's cricketers travelled to India for the 2011 World Cup (which Pakistan was originally supposed to have co-hosted), they were depleted and disgraced, the emissaries of a cricketing pariah. Even their new captain, Shahid Afridi, described them as a 'broken team'. The Pakistani cricket board was also humiliated. In the aftermath of the 'spot-fixing' exposé – which the PCB had at first sought to deny – it had been warned by the ICC to clean up Pakistani cricket or face serious sanctions. Never had cricket seemed more apposite to a nation's fortunes.

Indian cricket was meanwhile sweeping all before it. The BCCI was not about to be admonished by the ICC: it bankrolled it. India's cricketers, with bank balances swollen by IPL loot, were among the world's richest sportsmen. Ranked No. 1 in the world in Test cricket, they were also in fine form. As usual, every Indian expected India to win the World Cup; and that was a reasonable expectation. Yet the Pakistanis, as is their wont, also performed far better than anyone expected.

They beat Sri Lanka, Canada, Zimbabwe and Australia to reach the semi-final, against India in Mohali, which I watched in Nizamuddin bazaar. At one stage they looked on to win that game, too. Batting first, India hit 260, a middling sort of a score, which they owed to six dropped catches. Tendulkar, who made 85, was dropped an astonishing four times. In their reply, the Pakistanis started well: after 23 overs they were 100 for two. But then they lost a flurry of wickets and the scoring-rate dipped. In the end, it was not even close. The Pakistanis were all out in the last over of the innings, 29 runs short.

Afridi, who had been the bowler of the tournament – with 21 wickets at less than 13 runs apiece – was tremendously dignified in defeat. 'First of all I'd like to congratulate the Indian cricket team and the Indian nation for this great victory, and wish them all the best for the final,' he said, standing on the Mohali pitch. The Indians were less delicate. As they proceeded to Mumbai, to play Sri Lanka in the final, their opening batsman Gautam Gambhir vowed to dedicate a possible World Cup victory to the victims of the 2008 Pakistani terrorist attack.

A decade that had promised such hope for Indo-Pakistani relations had ended dismally. Peace was impossible now. Whatever trust had been built up during the Composite Dialogue was gone, and neither country had leaders capable of restoring it. Pakistan had entered a new era of democratic feuding; most Indian politicians were largely indifferent to Pakistan. Manmohan Singh, the prime minister, was one of the few still striving for peace. Promising a new round of cricket diplomacy, he hosted his Pakistani counterpart, Yusuf Raza Gilani, at the game in Mohali. A right-minded man, born in what is today Pakistani Punjab, Singh declared that India and Pakistan 'share the same destiny'. But many Indians would have wondered what on earth he meant by that.

India and Pakistan, in a favourite Indian strategic buzzword, had become 'dehyphenated' in the minds of India's elite. Pakistan was a regional embarrassment, run by feudal lords, medieval mullahs and bullying generals. India was the regional power, admired around the world for its democracy, its growth, its excellent IT companies. Pakistan was a cricketing pariah, India a cricketing superpower. But this wasn't the full story. In one important sense Indian and Pakistani cricket were still strongly linked, and that was by corruption.

Given the nature of his business I was surprised by Salim's directions. 'Come to Dongri police station before three o'clock,' he had said on the telephone. 'Call me when you get there and my boy will come.'

I reached the station, a tumbledown cottage with blue walls and a red-tiled roof, in good time. As I stood waiting, men and boys in lacy Muslim prayer caps flowed by. Across the street a banner was hanging from a wall, announcing, in English, Hindi, Urdu and Arabic, that Eid al-Fitr was coming. Three large piebald goats lay on the pavement beneath it, chewing on a pile of red onion skins, blissfully unaware of the death sentence written over their heads.

Dongri, a Muslim area of south Mumbai, was once best known for its textile mills. Hence 'dungarees', which were made from the blue denim they produced. But the mills are gone now and Dongri is better known as the home turf of the Mumbai mafia. Haji Mastan, Dawood Ibrahim, Chhota Shakeel and other well-known godfathers grew up here, and ran their smuggling, racketeering and narcotics businesses from Dongri's teeming streets. It is the Corleone of India.

After I had been waiting five minutes, a young man wearing a black T-shirt approached and silently beckoned me to follow him. He led me to a doorway a short walk away. Inside was a small concrete room, windowless, painted pink and just big enough to fit four folding chairs and a desk. There were a dozen mobile phones piled on top of it, through which an unshaven, youngish man was sifting. He was barefoot and wore a pair of silk black trousers and a cream shirt decorated with fancy cuffs and epaulettes. As I entered, he briefly looked up, unsmiling, and at once started talking into one of the phones.

This was Salim, as we will call him. He was a mid-tier bookmaker, charged with running a network of small-time illegal bookies in Maharashtra, Gujarat, Rajasthan and Karnataka. Operating out of hotel rooms and by mobile phone, these bookies – 'my boys', Salim called them – took bets on hockey, table tennis or volleyball games, on Indian state or general elections, on American presidential races, even the weather. But mostly they took bets on cricket. And with the World Cup only a few days away, Salim was having a busy time.

He put down the phone and asked what I wanted. He was not solicitous but did not seem very guarded either. Salim, who I had been introduced to by a well-connected Mumbai journalist, knew nothing about me except that I was a British writer who wanted to understand his business. I asked how he expected it to go during the World Cup.

'On a big game, minimum 10,000 bets, minimum, and maximum crores of bets,' he said matter-of-factly. 'Full, full betting, every people betting, family betting, ball-to-ball betting, unlimited betting.' He expected his network to handle several billion rupees worth of bets over the course of the tournament. And if India had a good run – which Salim said they would – it would be a bonanza.

More than half his profits, Salim said, had to be pushed up to his boss – the 'upper one', he called him. This money was mostly sent abroad to middlemen in Europe and the Middle East, via the hawala system, an ancient trust-based means of transferring money across borders that operates widely in the Muslim world. The remainder was for Salim and his boys, and was not inconsiderable. Salim said he expected their share of World Cup loot to amount to several million dollars.

'That's a lot of money,' I said. He nodded. 'Big business, yes, but there are so many things to pay: hotel rents, office rents, lunch, dinner, breakfast. I am handling 150 families. And then there is the police, crime branch, CID, CBI, IB to manage, also the hawala rackets, all need total management.'

Salim's own cut, he claimed, would be 8 to 10 per cent of his network's profits, well over a million dollars for the World Cup.

'So much money…' I said.

Hearing the doubt in my voice, Salim gave me a look of reproof. 'I am rich, sure,' he said. 'But this is risky business. It needs total involvement.'

By law, gambling is heavily restricted in India. As defined by the Public Gambling Act of 1867, India's legal gambling industry extends to some state lotteries, betting on horse racing, and a handful of casinos. Betting on cricket is not allowed. But these strictures have proved as effective at stopping Indians from gambling as the Telegraph Act was at deterring India's drunken cable television operators. In its 2000 match-fixing report, India's Central Bureau of Investigation found that, 'By the middle of the 1990s, with a surfeit of one-day matches being shown on live television … betting had taken the shape of a massive organised racket.'

India's gambling industry has since grown with the economy. One oft-quoted, albeit highly uncertain, estimate suggests it is worth $60 billion a year. The illegal part of the industry, which is estimated to amount to half of the total, is especially big in Gujarat and Mumbai, where it is largely controlled by gangsters.

Salim was given the odds for a big match or popular bet – like a Tendulkar century – from his godfather boss. His job was to pass the odds on to his boys and keep track of their turnover.

'And who is the upper one?' I asked, though I felt sure I knew.

Salim shook his head and fidgeted with his phones: 'Nobody knows and nobody will tell.'

'You don't know who your boss is?'

He shook his head again. Then he turned to speak in rapid-fire Hindi with his accomplice. This was a younger man, wearing an embroidered white salwar kameez. I could make out almost nothing of their talk, except two oft-repeated English words, 'family' and 'risk'.

'OK, I will tell you,' Salim said at length, 'but you must not say I said it.' I agreed not to.

The Mumbai mob rose to prominence during the 1960s and 70s, smuggling gold, electronics and liquor, goods that India's throttling import controls had made scarce. Many of its members were Muslims, drawn from longstanding Saurashtrian smuggling networks and traditional Pushtun moneylenders, based in Dongri. They were also involved in other typical gangster businesses, including illegal drugs, prostitution, bootlegging and extortion. But they soon became best known, around this time, as financiers of Bollywood movies. This was the result of another idiotic regulation. Until 1998, Bollywood was not recognised as a regular industry, which made it almost impossible to get formal funding for film productions. The gangsters filled the gap – by the 1980s they were financing most of the 200-odd films the Hindi film industry churned out each year. It was a useful way to launder money. Hanging out with film stars also tickled the gangsters' fancy. Indeed, some became celebrities in their own right – for example Haji Mastan, a big smuggler of the 1960s and 70s. A former coolie at Mumbai's docks, he became known for driving about the city dressed all in white, in a chauffeur-driven white Mercedes.

In the 1980s Mumbai saw the beginning of a long property boom, so the mafia got into that business too. Real estate is another largely corrupt segment of India's economy. It is one of the main destinations for India's massive untaxed cashflows: an illicit economy estimated to be equivalent to nearly half of India's official GDP.

The gangsters were rarely inconvenienced by the police. They owned many of them, and they had good friends in politics. 'The underworld was always hand-in-glove with the political class,' Julio Ribeiro, a former Mumbai police chief and gangster catcher of the 1980s, told me. 'Basically when the politicians needed money to fight elections, they took it from companies and they took it from the underworld. That's the fount of corruption in this country.'

On Ribeiro's watch the underworld underwent a violent change. A more vicious generation of gangsters emerged, typically Muslim and from Dongri. These killers showed no respect for the turf-agreements adhered to by their forebears, gentlemen dons like Mastan. Dawood, the son of a police constable from Dongri, was one of the new breed. 'In my time Dawood was a small-time muscle man. He was nothing big,' recalled Ribeiro. 'He was the son of one of my head constables who lived in our police lines. He was a good head constable. His contacts were very good: he knew all the criminal elements. But his children ran amok. There were about 11 of them and this fellow was the second.'

The underworld became gripped by a violent power struggle, between the old guard and the new. Mastan was driven off to found a political party, and by the late 1980s Dawood and his gang, D-Company, were the most powerful crew in Mumbai. Accused of many murders, he and his top lieutenants fled into exile around this time.

Yet Dawood's various businesses in Mumbai carried on functioning as normal. This became apparent in the investigations into the multiple bomb blasts in Mumbai, allegedly engineered by Dawood, in 1993. So did the reason why – a corrupt co-operation between the gangsters and powerful politicians and bureaucrats. A high-level commission, presided over by a senior official called N.N. Vohra, was charged with investigating this nexus. 'The investigations into the Bombay bomb blast cases have revealed extensive linkages of the underworld in the various governmental agencies, political circles, business sector and the film world,' it reported, quoting a senior intelligence officer. 'The Mafia is virtually running a parallel government, pushing the state apparatus into irrelevance.'

This was part of a long report. Yet the Congress government of the time permitted only 12 pages to be made public. India's Supreme Court, when challenged on the matter, supported that decision. It ruled that it would be 'severely and detrimentally injurious' to the public interest to publish more of the report. It was widely assumed this was because too many of India's elected rulers had been cited in it.

An investigative weekly, *Outlook*, boldly alleged that the name of Sharad Pawar, Maharashtra's three-time chief minister and future president of the ICC, was among them. On the basis of unpublished material held by the Vohra Commission, the magazine alleged there was a 'definite nexus between underworld don Dawood Ibrahim's associates and former Maharashtra chief minister Sharad Pawar'. Around the same time a leading Gujarat newspaper, *Gujarati Samachar*, ran what it alleged to be a telephone interview with Dawood, in which he confirmed that he had 'good relations with Pawar'. But after Pawar sued *Outlook* and its editor Vinod Mehta for $28 million, the magazine retracted its allegations.

There were calls to cleanse India's rotten political system, and the principal solution seemed obvious. India needed to make the funding of political parties, which the gangsters often supplied, formal and transparent. But as this would have entailed a personal loss to India's corrupt politicians, nothing of the sort has happened. And political corruption has since run out of control in India.

Mumbai's gangsters have been reduced by other means, however. In the aftermath of the 1993 bomb blasts India's security agencies launched a bloody assault on them. Over 600 alleged gangsters have since been shot dead by the police in pre-arranged hits, euphemistically called 'encounter killings'. Nearly 8,000 have been arrested.

The opening of India's economy has been a bigger blow to the underworld, leading to the collapse of their smuggling business. It has also led, more gradually, to the gangsters being pushed out of Bollywood. Over the past decade, a combination of changes to India's foreign investment rules and official recognition of Bollywood has allowed large Indian and Hollywood production companies to invest in Hindi film. Viacom, NBC, Sony and Time Warner alone invested $1.5 billion in India's film and cable TV sector during the decade. Bollywood is now a legitimate business.

This has left gambling as one of the Mumbai mob's last redoubts. The rise of one-day cricket, which provided a huge boost to the industry in the 1990s, was therefore well timed for the mobsters. And in Sharjah, Mumbai's exiled dons had a convenient stage on which to do business, enjoy their celebrity, and remind Indian politicians of their enduring relevance.

'In the 1990s the underworld was hosting whole cricket teams, with impunity, giving the players expensive watches and other gifts. That is how the match-fixing nexus started,' another famous Bombay cop, Rakesh Maria, the head of Maharashtra's Anti-Terrorist Squad, told me. 'The attraction worked both ways. The underworld was struck by the glamour of cricket and the cricketers were suddenly being introduced to gangsters and their Bollywood friends. And then it was easy for them to say, "Why don't you help us to fix games?"'

According to Maria, who had investigated the tawdry matter, some of the cricketers were easily persuaded. 'Greed is something that has no limits,' he said cheerfully. 'When you have a hundred, you want a thousand; when you have a thousand, you want lakhs; when you have lakhs, you want crores. And always in the back of a cricketer's mind he knows he only has four, five years left. Swimming with the tide is much easier than swimming against it.'

Maria was in no doubt that corruption remained rife in Indian cricket, though more subtly than before. 'Spot-fixing is quite an easy thing for a player,' he said. 'It is ... how can I put it? I can tell myself I'm not hurting the team; it's something very small and innocuous. But it's a sin all the same and it's recently become the norm. Dropping a catch, bowling a no-ball, or a wicketkeeper letting a bye go through ... It's very difficult to prove these things.' Maria was smiling sadly.

Match-fixing was above Salim's pay-grade – his mafia boss, he said, was the 'game changer'. But he claimed to believe that most international cricket matches were fixed. '99 per cent are fixed,' he said. 'The full World Cup is fixed. India and Australia are coming in final.'

'But you can't possibly know that! You'd have to control them and every other team in the tournament.'

Salim looked surprised. 'OK,' he said. 'The upper levels do the match-fixing and we have no involvement. Also not all teams are manageable. But we know which team will win. Pakistan is the best team for match-fixing.'

'We hate Pakistanis!' Salim's accomplice chipped in. He looked and sounded very angry.

'Why?'

'Because they say we are not good Muslims. It's like you are Christian and some Christian country-wallah says you are not good.'

'They're probably just jealous,' I said, wanting to placate him.

He nodded. 'We are more successful. Because we do betting, drugs, smuggling. It is the government's fault because they do not give us Muslims opportunity. We do not get government jobs so we must do illegal things.'

'Pakistan is easy, also Australia, South Africa,' Salim continued. 'The England team is too tough. They play for winning the game, not for money. Mostly Asian teams are manageable. South Africans, very easily managed. You know Hansie Cronje? He died in big crash, you know. It was not an accident.'

Salim was certainly exaggerating. But I was still dismayed by his claims. They had the shadow of truth on them. He gave me a consolatory half-smile. 'When you know, nah, this match-fixing, you won't have interest in cricket. In India all persons love cricket, but after knowing the match-fixing, whole craze is going. All over the world it's a business. It's not a game. If the bigger amount is booked on India, nah, then India will not come in final. Because money talks. After full total of betting money seen, then the uppers will decide.'

'How about you?' I asked him. 'Don't you like cricket?'

'At first I was fanatic of cricket. But after coming into this business-line I do not love cricket. Full-on cheaters. Full fraud. How many runs, how many wickets, how many sixers, all are fixed. Cricket is not a game. Sports spirit is not there.'

'Well, if that's right, thanks a lot,' I said.

Salim shrugged. 'You know the song *Sab Ganda Hain Par Dhanda Hain Ye*'? ('It's dirty, but it's our business.') It's like that.'

'But why,' I asked Salim, 'are you working next-door to a police station?'

'That is no problem,' he said. 'They are fixed monthly.'

'So is it actually better to be near a police station?'

'Han,' he nodded. 'It's safe.'

'I am in this business 18 years and also I am an informer,' he said. 'You know that?'

I nodded, for I had heard it.

'Police, Intelligence Bureau, FBI, I am informer for them.'

'What happens if the upper man finds out?'

'Very dangerous,' Salim said and slid his forefinger down the side of his throat.

It was pure Bollywood. So was the song he had referred to – it was the theme song to a well-known gangster movie. I was not minded to believe him.

I looked down to check my tape recorder. But then I looked up and saw Salim's forefinger was still pointing to his lightly bearded throat.

I leaned across the desk. 'Bloody hell!' I said.

The left half of Salim's neck was encircled by a thin white scar, starting at his spine and ending near his Adam's apple. It was criss-crossed with dozens of shorter scars, obviously left by stitches.

'They heard I was informer,' he said.

Salim said he had had his throat slit by a relative of his employer and had been left for dead in the street. But almost as soon as he had recovered, he had returned to work, for the same crime gang, under a different name. 'In this business only the names are known to the bosses,' he said. 'They never meet the people working for them; they never know us. They only know name and number. They never know who is informer and who is working with them.'

'But aren't you afraid they will find you again?'

He shook his head, and then silently to the ceiling. 'Allah,' the gesture meant, 'will decide.'

CHAPTER SIX

Cricket, Caste and the Countryside

By 7am the sun was climbing over Dharavi, a big slum in Mumbai, and a symphony of clanging metal and whirring machinery resounding from its thousands of hut factories. The working day had begun. In cramped and murky spaces, poor slum-dwellers were labouring to produce shoes, clothes, toys and recycled materials, goods worth millions of dollars a year in exports alone. Dharavi, a square mile of low-rise wood, concrete and rusted iron, is one of the biggest slums in Asia. It is also, amid the poverty and filth, astonishingly industrious.

Chetan Jaiswal, a 26-year-old slumdog, had found better employment, working at a stockbrokers in the nearby district of Bandra. We had arranged to meet on a Monday morning, before he left the slum to spend his day 'sitting in front of a computer screen, buying shares for people,' and Chetan was anxious not to be late. He was waiting for me, motorbike helmet in hand, on a busy thoroughfare bordering the slum. Yet Chetan, who was reckoned to be the best cricketer in Dharavi, had time for a five-rupee cup of chai and a chat.

He had had a good weekend. The previous day Chetan had taken four for 14 for his company, Total Securities, playing on Azad Maidan. As we sat down on a roadside seat to drink our tea, he modestly accepted my congratulations. 'I am very lucky,' he said. 'Because of cricket I can live, I can work, I can give money to my family. It means I have my bike, it means I can roam with my friends. Cricket is my life.'

Dharavi, which I had visited often during my time in India, was cricket-mad. The great majority of its million inhabitants, a multitude of poor migrants drawn to Mumbai from all over India, seemed to love the game. Yet there is no record of the slum having produced a single first-class cricketer, and it was easy to see why.

It has no sports facilities. To play games of tennis-ball cricket, Dhjaravi's youngsters had only three nearby yards to choose from, including the Dharavi-Sion Sports Club, which I had visited the previous day. It was optimistically named. Half an hour's walk from the slum, the club was merely half an acre of bare, gritty ground.

This made Chetan's achievements all the more impressive. The son of a poor migrant from Uttar Pradesh, he had learned cricket playing in cramped alleys inside Dharavi. It had been obvious from early on that he had a talent. 'I was always better than the others,' he said with the same imposing self-confidence – the testosterone-whiff of a sportsman – that Arvind Pujara had radiated. So Chetan's father, who worked as a porter in Mumbai's port, sent him as a 15th-birthday present to the nearby Matunga Gymkhana. That gave Chetan his first experience of real cricket, played with a hard leather ball, and he found the adjustment hard. 'I was terrified of the ball,' he confessed. 'I still am.'

Yet he visited the Gymkhana for only a few weeks – it cost 350 rupees a month, which was more than his father could afford. But through hard work Chetan had proceeded to Mumbai University to study physics, where he got another opportunity to play pukka cricket. And despite his fear of the hard ball, he hit centuries in two of his first college games. This sparked the interest of Total Securities.

The company provided Chetan with cricket kit and smuggled him into its side to play on the maidans. And when he completed his studies it offered him a job and wages of 17,000 rupees a month. That was almost twice what Chetan says he would otherwise have earned working in a call-centre. Thereby he had been able to help support his parents and three younger siblings. 'We needed another breadwinner in our family,' he said. 'And by God's grace, through cricket I was able to provide.'

On a national scale, Chetan's sporting achievements were modest. But viewed against the extreme poverty of his opportunities, they were impressive. He was reckoned to be the only semi-professional cricketer in Mumbai's biggest slum. His success was also remarkable in another way.

Chetan and his family are Chamars, members of a Hindu leatherworking community traditionally considered 'untouchable' – that is, defiling to high-caste Hindus. According to an early British ethnographer, George W. Briggs, who studied the community in the early 20th century, 'the Chamar occupies an utterly degraded position in the village life, and he is regarded with loathing and disgust by the higher castes. His quarters abound in all kinds of abominable filth. His foul mode of living is proverbial. Except when it is absolutely necessary, a clean-living Hindu will not visit his part of the village.'

Chamars shared this reviled status with roughly a sixth of India's population – around 200 million people today. In British times, untouchables were referred to as 'depressed classes'. Today they are known by a Marathi translation of that phrase, as Dalits. And they are still depressed. Over six decades after caste discrimination was formally abolished in India, Dalits are among its poorest and most illiterate people. Not coincidentally, since 1947 only one Dalit is known to have played cricket for India.

This is a powerful indication of the elitist turn Indian cricket took after 1947. Yet it also has a peculiar resonance, because of what went before. In the first two decades of the 20th century, Indian cricket had several prominent Dalit stars, most of whom were from a single Chamar family – the remarkable Palwankars.

The eldest Palwankar, Baloo, was born in 1875 in the south Indian town of Dharwad. But the family moved soon afterwards to Poona in Maharashtra, where Baloo's father found work with the army. After some cursory schooling, Baloo and his younger brother Shivram were hired as groundstaff by the local Parsi Gymkhana. There they learned to play cricket, messing about with whatever kit their Parsi employers left lying around. And soon their duties included bowling at the members in the club nets.

In 1892, or thereabouts, Baloo was hired in the same capacity by the local European Gymkhana. This brought him into contact with one of the foremost cricketers of the Raj, Captain John Glennie 'Jungly' Greig (his nickname was earned not by hunting tigers, but by the sound of his full name said quickly). Baloo and Jungly, a Kiplingesque combination, began practising together every morning, the untouchable groundsman wheeling in to deliver his left-arm spinners to the British officer.

This was lucky for Greig, too, because Baloo was a natural. Early appreciations of his bowling note the smooth flow of his action, his ability to turn the ball both ways, and his magnificent control. 'One of the best native bowlers,' the great Parsi bowler Dr M.E. Pavri wrote of

Baloo in 1901. 'Has both breaks and a curl in the air and has a lot of spin on the ball. The most deadly bowler on a sticky wicket.'

Word of the talented Dalit quickly spread around Poona. Soon the city's Hindu Gymkhana was considering Baloo for a grudge match against the local Europeans. Its Brahmin players, members of the Hindu priestly caste, were not keen on the idea of taking the field with a Chamar. But Jungly told the local press they would be mad to leave Baloo out. And sense, if not decency, prevailed. Baloo was picked for the Hindus and helped them to a famous victory. But though his high-caste team-mates would take the field with the untouchable spinner, they would not take tea with him. While they repaired to the pavilion for refreshment, Baloo was directed to a stool on the boundary, where he was served tea in a disposable clay cup by an untouchable servant.

It is a paradoxical image: the poor Dalit bowler in spotless cricket whites, yet shunned by his own team-mates. This illustrates something of the contradictory attitude towards the caste system that prevailed under the British.

They were at once fascinated and appalled by it. Since the early 19th century, British liberals had identified caste discrimination as a great evil and barrier to India's progress. For James Mill, whose 1818 *History of British India* was a powerful influence on generations of colonial officers, it produced nothing but 'indolence, avarice, lack of cleanliness, venality and ignorance'. But unlike other abhorrent Hindu customs, such as child marriage or *sati* (the practice of wives throwing themselves on to their husband's funeral pyre), the British made no serious attempt to end the caste system.

Much as they deplored it, they saw the system as a crucial source of stability, without which 'order would vanish and chaos would supervene'. They therefore enshrined in their laws a highly theoretical and rigid definition of the caste system, which they learned from certain medieval Brahmin texts. These ordered Hindu society into four groups, or *vedas*, as follows: priestly Brahmins; Kshatriyas, a class of warriors and rulers; Vaishyas, the farming and merchant castes; and, beneath these groups the Shudra labouring castes. Untouchables formed a sub-human fifth category, technically outside the caste system altogether.

Caste discrimination was not outlawed until India's independent constitution was adopted in 1949. Yet it was already by then much reduced. Though still widely practised in the countryside, observance of untouchability was hardly evident in India's cities – caste distinctions being hard to enforce where people live crowded together and work outside their traditional occupations. British rule also created unprecedented opportunities for low-caste Hindus. By 1856 a third of the army of Bombay was from the untouchable Mahar community. At the battle of Kohima in 1944, when British and Commonwealth troops turned back the advance of the Japanese, the newly formed Chamar Regiment was in the thick of the action.

By early 1897 Baloo had moved to Bombay, initially to work for the army. And his cricket career soon flourished there. When the Hindus made their victorious debut in the Bombay Triangular in 1906, Baloo was their star turn. He took eight wickets against the Europeans, an achievement celebrated by Bombay's budding liberal intelligentsia, for whom nationalism and eradicating casteism were twin causes. For the *Indian Social Reformer*, Baloo's match-winning turn was 'a landmark in the nation's emancipation from the old disuniting and denationalising ways'. It was well said. The relative ease with which the gifted untouchable found cricketing opportunity in Bombay, at the highest level of the Indian game, shows the extent to which urban India was modernising.

The following year Baloo took 13 wickets against the Europeans, and scored a fifty. The untouchable spin-bowler was now unstoppable. On the inaugural All-India tour of England, in 1911, he almost single-handedly upheld the honour of Indian cricket. Though the Indians won only two of their 14 first-class matches, Baloo's bowling was magnificent. He took 75 first-class wickets at an average of 20.12 runs per wicket. By the standards of a bowler-friendly time, that was not quite as world-beating as it may now appear. At least 20 English county bowlers had better records that summer. But it confirmed Baloo's status as one of India's finest bowlers. His younger brother Shivram, the second of four cricketing Palwankar brothers, was also on the tour. He came second in the Indian batting averages and scored a match-winning century against Somerset.

On his return from England, Baloo was given a welcome reception by the 'Depressed classes of Mumbai'. At this event a congratulatory speech was delivered by a talented Mahar student, one Bhimrao

Ambedkar. Another son of a soldier, Ambedkar was a future scholar, politician and architect of India's constitution. This was his first recorded public appearance.

Baloo was now joined in the Hindus side by one or more of his brothers, Shivram, Ganpat and Vithal. Together they helped deliver four further tournament victories for the Hindus up to 1920. In 1913 the Hindus fielded a side that included all four Palwankar brothers. Contemporary Indian historians, including Ramachandra Guha, who has done wonderful service in rescuing the brothers from obscurity, have tended to focus on the discriminatory slights they sometimes suffered. Yet, at a time when untouchability was still legal and casually practised in much of India, the degree to which they were accepted by Bombay's cricketing elite seems more remarkable.

In 1921 Gandhi launched a national campaign against untouchability. For Gandhi, too, this was a necessary precondition to India achieving *swaraj*, or self-rule. '*Swaraj*,' he declared, 'is a meaningless term if we desire to keep a fifth of India under perpetual subjection, and deliberately deny to them the fruits of national culture.'

The Palwankars were not merely enjoying India's national culture, they were making it. Baloo hung up his bowling boots that same year. But in 1922 the Hindu Gymkhana awarded Vithal Palwankar its captaincy – an honour some felt Baloo had been wrongly denied. Tall and graceful at the crease, Vithal ranked close to C.K. Nayudu as a batsman: they ended their careers with almost the same first-class batting average, a little over 35. But Vithal was a more successful captain. He led the Hindus to three tournament victories in four years. He was also their captain on that memorable day in 1926 when Nayudu destroyed the MCC's bowling on the Bombay Gymkhana ground.

By the time Vithal retired in 1932, the Palwankars had been mainstays of the Hindus side for three decades. Meanwhile the fight against untouchability was one of the hottest issues of the freedom struggle. No wonder the historian Guha has compared the significance of the brothers' achievements to those of black American sports stars such as Jackie Robinson and Muhammad Ali, heroes of the civil rights movement. Yet, despite the remarkable political resonance of their triumphs, the Palwankars are hardly remembered in India today, and then only by a small tribe of cricket aficionados.

That is not because the heat has gone out of caste politics. Quite to the contrary – Indian politics has been transformed over the past two decades by the rise of parties dedicated to serving Dalits and other low-caste Hindus. India's giant state of Uttar Pradesh has been ruled by the biggest of them, the Bahujan Samaj Party, on four occasions, and is now littered with statues of Dalit politicians. But I know of no memorial, anywhere in India, to Baloo the untouchable cricketer.

This is, most obviously, another sign of modern India's obsession with politics. Yet there is another reason why Baloo is not celebrated by Dalit activists – it is that Baloo became a politician himself and ended up on the wrong side of history.

By the late 1930s the campaign against untouchability had broken into two main factions. The more popular was led by Gandhi, who considered untouchability an abomination, but otherwise approved of the caste system. 'I consider the four divisions alone to be fundamental, natural and essential,' he once said. The other faction was led by Ambedkar, who took a more absolutist view of the problem. He saw caste discrimination as inseparable from Hinduism and considered upper-caste Hindus incapable of delivering the equality that Gandhi preached. 'Inequality is the soul of Hinduism,' he declared.

Ambedkar therefore rejected Gandhi's leadership and even Hinduism. In 1936 he declared that he 'would not die a Hindu'. The following year Ambedkar led a low-caste opposition to Congress – the Scheduled Caste Federation – in India's first provincial elections.

He himself stood for a seat in the Bombay assembly. Congress put up his old hero Baloo to stand against him. The former cricketer had remained a prominent champion of his benighted caste. Devoted to Gandhi, Baloo similarly saw the improvement of the untouchables' lot as an ongoing project within Hinduism. He also saw great progress in this regard. In the cities Baloo believed caste discrimination was no longer much of a problem. The election, in the event, was a close-run contest, but Baloo lost this one. Ambedkar won by 13,245 votes to his 11,225.

Ambedkar, of whom there are statues everywhere in UP, went on to greater things. India's constitution is a triumph of liberal values and one of the country's enduring strengths. But in 1956 he died, shortly after converting to Buddhism along with half a million of his Mahar followers, a disappointed man. None of the three political parties Ambedkar established gathered much support beyond his caste. Most Dalits supported Congress, as they would do for the next three decades. Dalits, along with Muslims and Brahmins, were one of the three assured vote-banks that kept Congress in power.

But during the 1980s Dalits abandoned Congress for the Bahujan Samaj Party and other low-caste outfits. The single policy demand of these parties was for an increase in handouts to low-caste Hindus, chiefly by expanding a longstanding system of positive discrimination. On the basis of this, at least half of India's public-sector jobs and places in schools and colleges are now reserved for low-caste Hindus and members of other disadvantaged groups. In Tamil Nadu a staggering 69 per cent of government jobs are thus sewn up. This caste-based patronage, besides having a damaging effect on the institutions affected, has caused huge resentment and enshrined caste identity in Indian politics.

There is little evidence it has improved the lot of Dalits, who remain one of India's poorest groups. Yet in other ways caste is becoming less important in Indian society, as is again most obvious in the cities. Well-educated Dalits, like Chetan the Dharavi cricketer, are no different from any other middle-class Indian. They share the same tastes in film, music and cricket, perform the same religious devotions and probably hold much the same political views. They are unlikely to suffer caste discrimination, especially in the workplace, which is becoming increasingly meritocratic as the private sector expands. When, in 2008, the BSP and other low-caste parties demanded that India's leading IT companies – including Wipro, TCS and Infosys – hire a certain quota of low-caste Hindus, the companies didn't know how to respond. A boss of Infosys told me this was because they had no idea what castes their existing workers belonged to.

In middle-class India, caste is mainly important in the marriage market: as it was for those Brahmin cricketers on Azad Maidan, playing for the honour of their ancestral villages and to keep their small community together. Yet inter-caste marriages are becoming more common. The matchmaking website Jeevansathi.com reports that around 60 per cent of its online matches are across caste lines. The advertisements (or 'matrimonials') that young Indians post on such sites suggest they are increasingly more bothered about a future mate's occupation and level of income than caste. The acronym 'CNB', which stands for 'caste no bar', is displayed increasingly. Chetan reckoned he was typical of this trend. He expected to have a love marriage – even though, by happy circumstance, his girlfriend was also a Chamar. (Dalits, it is worth noting, are no less fastidious about such distinctions than any other Hindu.)

Given this progress, it is striking how few Dalit cricketers have emerged since the Palwankars. Chandra Bhan Prasad, a Dalit newspaper columnist, thinks there is a surge of low-caste cricketers waiting to happen. 'The Dalit middle-class is in its formative stage, busy in settling stage-one priorities like education and housing,' he told me. 'Sport will belong to stage two.' Meanwhile, the absence of Dalit cricketers looks all the more painful set against the cricketing performance of the Hindu priestly caste.

Brahmins account for less than a fifth of India's population. Yet since 1970, according to calculations by Madhusudhan Ramakrishnan of ESPNCricinfo, well over a third of Indian Test players have been drawn from this privileged caste. And that understates its dominance of Indian cricket. A best-ever Indian Brahim side, post-1947, would be almost the best-ever India side. It might look something like this: Sunil Gavaskar, Sachin Tendulkar, Dilip Vengsarkar, Gundappa Viswanath, Rahul Dravid (wicketkeeper), Sourav Ganguly, V.V.S. Laxman, Anil Kumble, Javagal Srinath, Ishant Sharma, B.S. Chandrasekhar. If opened to other castes, Kapil Dev would come in for Sharma; one of the Vijays, Merchant or Hazare, might come in for Vengsarkar. There would also be a heated discussion about the wicketkeeping position. But otherwise India's best team could be entirely composed of Brahmins.

Their prominence is unsurprising. Brahmins, who in ancient times were the only Hindus permitted to read, tend to be India's most educated and privileged Hindus. Nor has their cricketing prowess excited much comment in India. Low-caste politicians are not much interested in cricket. They can also take consolation in Brahmins' dwindling political influence. Up to 1970 around a third of India's chief ministers were Brahmins. By 2012 only two out of 30 were.

Yet a few Indian commentators have been angered by the Brahmin cricket tradition. 'Cricket in India has been a truly casteist game,' wrote Siriyavan Anand in *Outlook*. 'It does not require much disciplinary training to infer that cricket is a game that best suits Brahminical tastes and bodies ... Having too many Brahmins means that you play the game a little too softly, and mostly for yourself.'

Brahminical tastes may be one thing, but Brahminical bodies? If they are of a type, it is not consistent. The difference in height between Vishy and Sharma is more than a foot. Caste and race are not the same thing. In fact, all Indians, whatever their caste, tend to get bigger and lighter-skinned the further north and west they are found.

Yet it is not only critics of Brahmin prominence in cricket who have sought physiological explanations for it. R. Mohan, one of India's most venerable cricket journalists and a Brahmin himself, told me: 'I would think there's a genetic reason for it. Cricket, with its rules and cerebral nature, is a more intelligent game than football or hockey. At the same time it is less physically demanding. So Brahmins, who are not the strongest men, took to it quite readily. They also took to chess. At the same time, I imagine the complexity of cricket put a lot of less intelligent people off.' Mohan is not unusual among upper-caste Indians in holding such views.

I met him in Chennai, a historic stronghold of Brahmin cricket. Almost since its inception, cricket in Chennai and throughout the state of Tamil Nadu has mainly been run, watched and played by members of two Brahmin sub-castes, the Iyengars and Iyers. (The former worship Vishnu and not Shiva; the latter worship both.)

Almost all the state's first-class players were, until recently, Brahmins, mostly recruited from a handful of Brahmin schools. Of the top 12 clubs in Chennai, seven are to this day sponsored by Brahmin-owned companies, including several by India Cements Limited, which also owns the Chennai Super Kings IPL side. The Chepauk Stadium in Chennai is in the heart of a Brahmin-dominated suburb, and its crowds, even today, are reckoned to be up to half Brahmin. This is despite the fact that Brahmins represent only around 3 per cent of Tamil Nadu's population.

Yet this Brahmin grip on Tamil Nadu's cricket is exceptional. The state gave birth to one of India's earliest low-caste political movements, in the 1930s, and it has been run by low-caste politicians for most of the time since. Hence its aggressive low-caste jobs quotas. Mohan told me that his two daughters had both scored 98 per cent in their school-leaving exams, yet had been unable to win a place at a good university in Tamil Nadu. He shook his head sadly: 'It's become a total hotbed of opposition to the upper-castes, which is understandable, of course, because they had a good innings for so long ...'

Even in cricket, the Brahmin grip is weakening. Mohan was formerly cricket correspondent of *The Hindu*, one of India's main English-language newspapers and another Tamilian Brahmin redoubt. The paper is based on Chennai's Mount Road, in a fine stone building with cool corridors, a faint smell of ink and an atmosphere of industry and suppressed excitement. It is a reminder of what wonderful institutions newspapers can be. *The Hindu*'s owners, an extended Iyengar family, have also provided several cricketers to the state side. They include the paper's editor-in-chief, N. Ram, a Marxist intellectual and once a handy wicketkeeper, and K. Balaji, formerly a batsman and now the paper's business manager. (The initial in Tamil names usually refers to the father's name.)

Balaji and his brother K. Venugopal, the deputy editor, warmly welcomed me to *The Hindu*. Yet they suggested my inquiry was at least a decade out of date. Back in the 1970s, when Balaji was playing, the Tamil Nadu side were entirely Brahmin. 'It's not like back then now,' said Balaji. 'Nobody knows or cares about such things.'

All the same, I asked the brothers if they wouldn't mind performing a simple test. I picked up a copy of that day's paper, pointed to the scorecard from the previous night's IPL game, and asked if they would please tot up how many of the Chennai Super Kings team were Brahmins. Of eight Tamilians in the match squad they reckoned that, on the basis of their names, at least six were Brahmin. 'Ah,' said Venugopal. 'That's rather surprising.'

Yet the brothers were also right. Cricket in Tamil Nadu is becoming less centred in Chennai, partly due to the work of the state cricket association, which has helped provide most of its districts with a turf pitch. As a result, more than half the state's current Ranji Trophy side hailed from outside Chennai and, by the brothers' reckoning, more than half were non-Brahmin. The pitch is becoming a little more even.

The only Dalit cricketer known to have played for India since the Palwankars was Dodda Ganesh, a journeyman seamer from Karnataka, who played four Tests in the 1990s. But another, better known, player of that era is often claimed to be a Dalit: Vinod Kambli, Tendulkar's childhood batting-partner. He is in fact from a lowly fisher caste and not a Dalit at all. But that detail has rarely got in the way of what is, after the Palwankars, the second great caste saga of Indian cricket.

The son of a poor mechanic, Kambli grew up in a crowded tenement, or *chawl*, in central Mumbai. He shared a single room with up to a dozen relatives. His father, though poor, was a keen club cricketer. And after seeing that little Vinod had a knack for batting, he started taking him along to games, sitting behind the handlebars of his motorbike, and encouraging him to practise.

When Kambli was 13, his father took him to Ramakant Achrekar, one of Mumbai's fabled coaching gurus. Achrekar declared the boy outrageously talented and arranged for him to be given a place by the Shardashram Vidyamandir High School where he coached. There Kambli met Tendulkar, who was another young batting prodigy, albeit from a middle-class Brahmin family.

Kambli and Tendulkar, the younger of the pair by 18 months, became firm friends. Under the stern eye of Achrekar, they netted together for half the school day and played together for the school team. Achrekar was a tough taskmaster, who sometimes rewarded stupid errors with a whack with a stump. But Sachin and Vinod made few mistakes. Both were brilliant – though Kambli, Achrekar later said, was the more naturally talented.

On Azad Maidan in February 1988, in the semi-final of the Harris Shield, the schoolboy batsmen went berserk. Playing against a slightly lesser cricketing school, St Xavier's (Sunil Gavaskar's alma mater), they put on 664 runs in an unbroken stand. Kambli, by then 16, scored 349 not out and 14-year-old Tendulkar 326 not out. By the time Achrekar – who was not at the ground – learned of this run glut and demanded that Tendulkar, the captain, declare the innings, at least one of the opposition bowlers was in tears. It was the highest recorded partnership in cricket history. And when St Xavier's finally got to bat, Kambli, bowling off-breaks, took six wickets.

Tendulkar began his first-class career with Bombay the following year. He scored a century in his first game, and made his Test debut the year after that. Kambli had to wait a year longer to play for Bombay – which he celebrated by hitting his first ball for six. He made his India debut in a one-day game in 1991, and his Test debut in 1993 against England. He then went on one of the most brilliant opening runs in Test history. Kambli hit four centuries, including two double-hundreds, in his first seven Tests.

Against spin or English military-medium, he was murderous. He loved to dance down the pitch, with his nimble footwork, and hit the ball straight back over the bowler's head. But he didn't like fast, short-pitched bowling, and as soon as opposition bowlers realised this, he started to struggle. Against the West Indies in 1994–95, Kambli was worked over by Courtney Walsh and Kenny Benjamin and had a woeful series. He was dropped soon afterwards, having played 17 Tests and averaged more than 54 per innings. He was only 23. But he would never play another Test match. India was about to unearth several batting gems, in Rahul Dravid, Sourav Ganguly and V.V.S. Laxman, all of whom were more easily managed than Kambli.

He was good-hearted, but a rule-breaker who turned up late for practice and liked a drink or four after the day's play. He still played more than 100 one-day internationals. But Kambli was often dropped, shunted up and down the order, and his one-day record was, for one so talented, undistinguished in the end: an average of 32.5, with only two centuries. The abiding image of his career is not those early centuries or those easy sixes. It is of Kambli at the World Cup semi-final in Eden Gardens, walking off the field in tears after his innings was prematurely interrupted by the rioting crowd. He looks, in retrospect, like a harshly treated cricketer. And in a television interview in 2008, Kambli said he knew where to place the blame. 'I always felt discriminated against by the cricket board because of my caste and colour,' he said.

I wanted to hear more about this, and arranged to meet Kambli at the flat in Mumbai where he lived with his Anglo-Indian wife, Andrea. The couple was out when I arrived. But a maid opened the door and ushered me inside. The flat was tiny and decorated for Christmas, which was just a few days away. Its sitting-room was sparsely furnished, with a huge television, a picture of Vinod and Andrea on their wedding day and a Teletubbies doll. The toy was for the couple's newborn son, Jesus Cristiano Kambli.

After I had been waiting an hour, Kambli burst noisily into the flat, wearing a yellow tracksuit and beaming. Andrea puffed in behind him, pushing Jesus Cristiano in a pram.

As I introduced myself, I gave Kambli my business card. Glancing at it, he attempted a joke. 'Ah, *The Economist*! That's what I call Sachin these days, a big economist!'

'Why's that?'

'He's ... like an economist ...' Kambli said hesitantly, realising that the punchline didn't quite work. 'Economist, you know? I mean he's rich.'

Poor Kambli. He had played for India over 100 times and had a first-class average of nearly 60. His had been a brilliant cricket career. Yet almost the only thing anybody ever asked him about these days was his old school friend. He had naturally assumed this was why I had come to see him too, Tendulkar having scored his fiftieth Test century only two days before. Kambli said he had already received over 150 calls from journalists asking for a comment on this achievement.

He had spoken to as many as he could, though none had offered to pay him and money was a worry.

Kambli had spent most of his cricket earnings and Pepsi advertising fees on the high life or alimony to his first wife. A second career in Bollywood had been a flop. Kambli was a terrible actor. A third attempted career, in politics, was also looking shaky. The previous year Kambli had contested a seat for Maharashtra's state assembly for the Lok Bharati Party, another low-caste outfit. But he had lost. Now he was pinning his hopes on a late return to cricket, in an unlikely bid for an IPL contract. He told me he had been netting every day and was hitting the ball as well as ever. But he was 39, had a gammy leg and hadn't played any serious cricket for a couple of years.

I told Kambli how much I had enjoyed watching him play and he smiled: 'Thank you. That's so nice of you.' He spoke superb English – a legacy, he said, of the convent school he had attended before Shardashram.

I also said his record suggested he had been unlucky and he nodded grimly. Why was that? I asked.

Kambli shrugged. 'I don't know, it's very hard to say ...'

'But you said you were discriminated against ...'

Kambli suddenly looked very uncomfortable. 'I said that because there was an influence. At that time the selectors were influenced by things ...'

'By your caste, you mean?

'My caste, that's what I said.' He was looking very glum.

'Is it what you really think?'

'Out of 100 per cent I think it contributed 1 per cent. Maybe,' he said. 'The other 99 per cent, I don't know.'

That didn't do much for the Bollywood film plot. But I thought it sounded about right. It was the 99 per cent that did for Kambli: the weakness against short-pitched bowling, the reckless flashes to gully and the annoying indiscipline. Perhaps, if he had been from a rich family, if he had had a powerful patron, he would have been given more opportunities. But he had had plenty all the same.

We talked for over an hour, about cricketers and cricket. Kambli was warm and delightful company. But I had a plane to catch, and so stood and made to leave. Kambli, seeing this, then dived into the pram to bring out Jesus Cristiano for me to admire. He hoisted the tiny baby into the air, as if acknowledging the applause of an imaginary crowd, his face shining with delight.

'Look at him! Isn't he beautiful?' he said.

Kambli insisted on accompanying me outside, to help me flag down a taxi and direct the driver. As the taxi nosed into the Mumbai traffic, the cabbie, no longer able to suppress his excitement, swivelled around to me and said: 'Kambli? Vinod Kambli?'

When I confirmed that indeed it had been he, the driver started laughing. 'Kambli! Vinod Kambli!' he said, chuckling fondly, as he savoured the cricketer's name.

Around 6pm in springtime the north Indian sun begins to cool and dip over Shahabpur, a village in Uttar Pradesh. Shadows of mango and poplar trees start to creep across its fields of yellowing wheat. This is when Ravendra Prasad, a 13-year-old Chamar boy, feels the tug of the village cricket pitch.

So long as his father Sarju can spare him from their work, hauling and skinning the carcasses of cattle and buffaloes, Ravendra downs tools and heads for Shahabpur bazaar. Behind it is a rutted wasteland. This is where the village boys gather to play cricket.

One day in March, as the spring harvest was beginning, I accompanied Ravendra there. A few women were threshing corn on the stony outfield, singing harvest songs as, with a rattle and swish, they beat the dry staves on the ground. There would be no time for cricket when the harvest was in full swing. But that was a week away yet, and a crowd of youths and boys were playing hard, in tight-fitting polyester shirts and trousers. They used a splintered bat, a hard rubber ball and piled-up bricks for wickets.

By crowded north Indian standards, Shahabpur is a medium-sized village, a few miles north of the Ganges. The nearest city is Allahabad, 30km away, at the confluence of the holy Ganges and Yamuna rivers, where Ranji's ashes were scattered. The village has around 10,000 inhabitants, who lived in caste-based hamlets, separated by brick walkways and fields of vegetables and wheat. It is in north-Indian villages such as this that the caste system survives in India. Many Shahabpuris do the same work their families have done for centuries, as blacksmiths, potters, washerfolk and so on. They rarely socialise across caste lines, and never inter-marry.

Around a third are Dalits. They are the poorest people in Shahabpur, and Ravendra's family was the poorest of them all. Besides disposing of dead animals, Sarju mended shoes in the village bazaar: hence his nickname, *Mochi*, or cobbler. As a reviled skinner, tanner and leatherworker, he earned a pittance, and no friends. The family's mud-hut was surrounded by a thorn stockade and separated from any neighbour by an expanse of turd-strewn wasteland. Sarju and his wife Sushila, who worked as the village midwife, another unclean occupation in Hinduism, were never invited to the village weddings. When my translator Utpal and I had stayed with them, sleeping alongside the family on string-beds, during an earlier visit to the village, Sarju said we were the first visitors he had ever entertained.

Standing beside me on the cricket pitch, Ravendra pointed out one or two of his classmates among the players. I called one over for a chat, whereupon all the boys, taking this as a signal, abandoned the game and came flocking to join us.

'Are these friends of yours?' I asked Ravendra.

'Not really,' he said boldly. He was a handsome boy and very proud. 'But they let me play with them. There is no discrimination here.

'But,' he continued with a fierce look, 'still their families will not let me enter their homes. They will not give me food and they will not give me a sip of water from their cups.'

'Is this true?' I asked the cricketers.

None replied.

'And when you have houses of your own, will you also deny him entry?'

One or two murmured inarticulately, but none spoke up.

Ravendra spoke for them. 'These things will never change,' he said. And none of his schoolmates contradicted him.

I had returned to Shahabpur that day because of a bigger game of cricket. India were playing Australia in Ahmedabad, in the World Cup quarter-final, and I wanted to see what interest the game held in the village.

It was not obvious it would hold any. Indian cricket started in the cities and it has more or less remained there. Between 1932 and 1979 there were ten village-born players among Indian Test cricketers, according to Richard Cashman's researches – but all learned their cricket after migrating to the city. Unlike England, India had developed no rich tradition of village cricket. Yet this was changing, like so much else in India, mainly due to the spread of television.

The first black-and-white TV sets started appearing in Shahabpur in the late 1980s, driven by a craze for a serialised version of the *Ramayana* broadcast on Doordarshan. Around the same time, local men began migrating to work in India's thriving western cities, which brought a modest infusion of wealth to the village. This had since become the backbone of the village economy. By the time I visited Shahabpur, roughly a third of the workforce was absent at any given time, working on building sites and in slum factories in Mumbai, Pune and elsewhere. They returned periodically, to their wives and children, with a few thousand rupees, new clothes and city ways. Both changes, television and migration, had helped bring cricket to the village.

This history was described to me by a member of Shahabpur's former ruling family, Amresh Singh Pratap. In British times, his grandfather had ruled a vast local estate, consisting of 70 villages. The family now owned only 100 acres of orchards in Shahabpur and an elegant fortified bungalow, which had been built by its 19th-century British owner. 'Cricket started here sometime in the early 1990s,' he told me, sitting in the garden of this splendid property. 'You'd see village lads playing in tattered clothes, on a field or a dried-up pond, with a country-made

bat and ball. You saw this in the 1990s, very rarely in the 1980s, never in
the 1970s. Back then they were playing only kabaddi, in the lanes and
in the fields, like they do cricket today. Kabaddi, rugby without a ball,
that was the evening game for boys back then.'

When home from his boarding-school, in the 1980s, Amresh often
played cricket with the village boys. This was his main point of contact
with them. Yet he preferred the chase to cricket. His greatest sporting
regret, Amresh told me, was having failed to 'bag a stripes' – tiger-
shooting now being banned in India.

On the morning of the India–Australia game, I had arrived at
Allahabad railway station aboard the night-train from Delhi. Armod
Pandey, one of the many journalists who have helped me on my travels
across India, was waiting on the platform. He had a motorbike helmet
on his head, and another in his hand.

Sharing Armod's motorbike, we rode through the streets of Allahabad,
once one of the most elegant cities in India. An important headquarters
of the Raj, it has many fine colonial buildings – All Saints' Cathedral,
the high court, the university buildings. They looked magnificent and
woebegone in the grey light, as we whizzed past, enjoying the cold
morning air. In the empty streets, cows were picking through the piles
of rubbish that were everywhere. After Delhi, Allahabad looked dirty
and poor.

There was also, unlike in Delhi, very little to show that the World
Cup was on. There were not many billboards of any kind in Allahabad
and I spotted only one, put up by a telecoms company, that referred
to cricket. 'Keep cricket clean' it read, above a picture of some aging
cricket stars. Allahabad was not all that into cricket. Mohammad Kaif,
that unlikely celebrity, is probably its most famous cricketing son.

Leaving the city, we crossed a road-bridge over the Ganges, flowing
milk chocolate brown far below. Shortly after, we left the tarmac road
and turned onto a hard mud trail, which led through fields of ripening
wheat to Shahabpur.

Arriving in the village, we went directly to the house of Anwar Ali.
One of the richer villagers, Anwar worked as a clerk in Allahabad and
he had helped me a great deal during my previous stay in the village. He
was waiting for us outside his small brick house, and greeted me with
a diffident hug. A delicious breakfast of fried eggs and oily parathas

was also waiting. After eating together in silence, we went outside to sit beside Anwar's small wheatfield, to drink tea in the warming sun and catch up.

Anwar wasn't interested in cricket. 'Cricket? Ah, nahin, boss,' he said, amused at the mere idea that he might be. He was 50, had never played the game and rarely watched it. He had electricity at his house, unlike Sarju. Yet Anwar had no television set because his wife considered the medium unIslamic.

Anwar preferred the sports of his youth, especially wrestling, which had been the main tamasha in Shahabpur before cricket arrived. Until the late 1990s, the village had held an annual fair, with a livestock sale, travelling circus and a grand wrestling tournament. It was held on the wasteland where Sarju's mud hut now sat. Beside this shack was a small shrine dedicated to a local wrestling champion, one Pahalwan Baba. The man himself had been long-forgotten. Yet every day his shrine was draped with a clean red loincloth, signifying his purity and devotion to the god of wrestlers, the Hindu monkey-deity Hanuman.

That ancient sporting culture was rapidly fading. Yet it was still evident in parts of north India, as Anwar had previously shown me. He had taken me to a wrestling tournament in the nearby village of Nawab Ganj, held to commemorate Gandhi's birthday.

The wrestling took place on a small sandy mound, the *akhara*, in a field filled with thousands of men and boys, squatting, standing or perched in the branches of the surrounding trees. As soon as we arrived, I was grabbed by the crowd, and pushed by hundreds of eager hands towards the *akhara*. Almost before I realised what was happening, I had been hoisted up its sandy slope, and displayed to the crowd.

'Come and see the journalist who has come from England to see our wrestling!' the master of ceremonies shouted through the dozens of tinny speakers that festooned the village trees. 'He has come to see our wrestling!' he shouted, as I was garlanded with marigolds and raucously cheered. 'What an honour! What an auspicious day!' It was nice to be appreciated.

Yet such gatherings were becoming rarer every year around Shahabpur, as Kabaddi and wrestling became scarce. The village youths preferred cricket – including the small crowd of teenage boys who had gathered outside Anwar's house, to watch me digesting my breakfast.

Unlike Anwar, all said they were mad about cricket and played the game whenever possible. All had a favourite player – either Tendulkar or Virender Sehwag. Most watched cricket at home on TV. Though, as there was no cable television connection to the village, none of the boys had seen the IPL. One or two had scarcely heard of the new Twenty20 tournament.

Nor had any heard of their most famous cricketing neighbour, Kamran Khan. An 18-year-old fast bowler, who came from the nearby village of Nadwa Sarai, Kamran had briefly made a name for himself in the IPL. The son of a poor woodcutter, he had been taken to Mumbai by a freelance cricket scout, where he was spotted by the Rajasthan Royals. He had then played for the Royals during the second IPL season, in 2009. He was small, slight and inexperienced with a leather ball. But he could bowl fast, with a slingy action, and he was successful at first. His captain at the Royals, Shane Warne, nicknamed him The Tornado.

Here was a wonderful rag-to-riches advertisement for India's wildly popular new cricket tournament. Under the headline 'A ticket to stardom for Indian youngsters', the *Times of India* reported: 'Kamran had played just tennis-ball cricket earlier and was so poor that he had slept on railway platforms on occasions. Besides, his parents had to die as the family couldn't afford proper medical treatment. All that changed once he had the ball in his hands, and Kamran, inspired by skipper Shane Warne, produced some magical spells.'

But his luck didn't last. Kamran's form dipped and he was not retained by the Royals. He was hired in 2011 by the new Pune Warriors side, but his uncoached bowling action was ruled illegal soon afterwards. He was subsequently banned from bowling and paid off by the Warriors. The Tornado was last spotted back in Nadwa Sarai, working in his brother's field, wearing a Pune Warriors shirt.

As the sun climbed high, Armod, Anwar and I set off on a stroll through Shahabpur. All but the poorest hamlets, I noticed for the first time, had a few television sets. Only the lowliest Dalit mud huts, which had no access to electricity, had none.

In the Chamar hamlet of Godown – named after the still-visible ruins of a British indigo warehouse – Ram Kishore, a retired government worker, said he had bought a black-and-white set to watch the *Ramayana* in the late 1980s. He estimated that five of the hamlet's 45 households now possessed one. Like many of the villagers, he also said he was looking forward to the World Cup game later that day.

At the approach of two o'clock, when the quarter-final was due to begin, we were still ambling around Shahabpur, through its wheat fields and hamlets. I was hugely excited about the game: the quarter-finals were when the World Cup got serious. And the Australians, led by their aging captain Ricky Ponting, promised to give India a tough match. But when the clock struck two and the Australians went in to bat in Ahmedabad, there was no rising buzz of television sets over Shahabpur. There was a power cut. In fact, Anwar admitted sheepishly, the village never had electricity in the afternoons. So there never had been any prospect of watching the game there after all.

We walked back through Godown, where Kishore was listening to the game on a radio. Actually this, he said, was how he had to follow cricket these days, even when there was electricity. His old black-and-white television had recently been burnt out in a power surge.

That was almost the only radio commentary I heard in Shahabpur. Almost none of the villagers were following the game. The only public place to watch it was a mobile phone shop in the bazaar. Its owner had set a Chinese mobile handset with a tiny television screen on the counter. A small crowd of boys were crushed around it, watching tiny flickering images of the Australian innings. Ravendra was among them.

We repaired to drink tea in the bazaar, while I followed the cricket score on my Blackberry. In their innings, the Australians managed 260 for six – a good but, as it would turn out, beatable score. Dusk was falling fast now, turning the wheatfields grey.

We said our farewells, climbed onto Armod's motorbike, and bumped through dark fields back towards the Ganges. Hitting the tarmac road, the scene abruptly changed. Here, there was electricity. So, in every roadside village, shops and chai-stalls flickered with silver television light and a rasping cacophony of cricket commentary, audible above the engine's roar.

Throngs of men and boys were gathered outside the shops, spilling onto the road, craning their heads towards the flickering cricket images inside. In that remote slice of north India, we must have passed a cricket crowd of thousands. Everyone, all the way to Allahabad, seemed to be watching the game.

CHAPTER SEVEN

Cricket à la Modi

'What about Monsieur?' said the waiter, in the direction of my lunch guest. But there was no response. Lalit Modi was bent over his BlackBerry. The waiter paused, then lifted his head from his notepad. A look of surprise crossed his face, then one of mild disdain. This could be an interesting contest, the high-handedness of a super-rich Indian versus French hauteur.

The waiter gave a cough, which was almost a groan. 'Is Monsieur ready to order?'

'Eh?' said Modi, without looking up. 'Ah, get me a fondue.'

'A ... what?' said the waiter, appearing baffled. This was a fine Mayfair restaurant, the most expensive I could afford. It was not a ski-chalet.

'Fondue. You don't have a fondue? OK, what have you got that's vegetarian?' said Modi, momentarily looking up from his phone.

'Monsieur is ... a *vegetarian*?' asked the waiter, as if the word was unfamiliar. 'Then how about a tomato confit with some goat's cheese?' he said briskly, wishing to end a disagreeable encounter.

'Fine,' Modi snapped. 'And get me some potatoes with that.'

'Potatoes for Monsieur?'

'Yeah, I like potatoes. I'll have some potatoes on the side,' said Modi, dismissing the waiter with a small wave. The Frenchman paused, looking shocked, then bowed briskly and stepped away.

Even by rich Indian standards, Modi could be very rude. In fact this was one of the reasons he was here in chilly London, wearing a blue fleece jacket indoors and looking tired, anxious and far older than when I had seen him last on Indian television a few months before. He was 47, slightly built. The stark autumn light, flooding through a nearby window, showed up grey streaks in his hair. Around Modi's mouth I could see the lines caused by his relentless smoking.

Modi finally put down his BlackBerry and looked up. 'So then …?' he said.

He was not speaking to journalists at this time. He had agreed to meet me because we had a slight personal connection and our conversations would be, selectively, off-the-record. Yet he looked nervous, and it was no wonder.

'Is it true they've taken your passport?' I asked.

Modi shrugged. 'I'm waiting to hear.'

'People are saying you're going to seek asylum in Iceland …'

'No,' he said glumly, 'though we have good friends there …'

'So you expect to be here for a while?'

He shrugged again. 'I hope not.'

Modi hated the cold. And he hated his anonymity in grand, hard-to-impress London even more. He wanted to be home in Mumbai, in the heat and the action, doing deals and wielding influence. He wanted to be running the world's flashest, richest, most insanely popular new sports tournament, the Indian Premier League. For Modi was the IPL's creator and, until recently, its impresario – its 'chairman and commissioner', according to the job title he had awarded himself.

For the first three years of the tournament, Modi had been ubiquitous in it. Strolling across the pitch before the games, barking out orders with a look of manic command, BlackBerry in hand, Modi was ever-present and watched by a television audience of millions. Then the cricket started, and still Modi flickered on to Indian television screens, enthroned in a VVIP box or seated on the boundary alongside the league's celebrity team-owners, laughing, cheering and singing team songs. He had a television crew follow him around to ensure this coverage of himself. 'Modicam' his retinue called it.

Six months before we met in London, ahead of the third IPL season, Modi had appeared on the cover of India's best-selling weekly magazine, *India Today*, in what was by then a familiar image. Dressed in his customary Armani suit, he was grinning and leaning dandily on a cricket bat, with a cheerleader hoisting her pompoms either side of him and a screaming crowd behind. 'Billion dollar baby' read the headline.

Four billion, more like – for that was what the IPL, after just three six-week seasons, was estimated to be generating in annual revenues. It was the apogee of India's cricket boom. It was a powerful symbol, too, of India's wider take-off. The IPL was a 'global representation of India and what the modern-day India stands for,' Modi had said. But that had turned out to be truer than he would have wished.

The IPL was rich, glamorous and inventive, a tearaway T20 craze among India's exuberant and swelling middle class. But strip away the glitter and the noise, and its first renditions had been a poor sporting contest. And the trauma the IPL had caused to cricket was immense. With the force of India's turbo-charged cricket economy behind it, the IPL could pay the world's best cricketers enormous wages. International cricket, a uniquely collaborative sporting culture, worked out over decades, had been instantly devalued as a result. Many wondered what this might mean for Test cricket, the game's most distinctive, sophisticated and least profitable format. Would it even survive the competition? India's cricket bosses hardly seemed to care: they were too busy counting their money. The IPL had become an emblem of India's cricketing hegemony at its most destructive. It also appeared, like India, to be rotten with corruption.

Hence Modi's flight to London, in exile and disgrace. He stood accused by the cricket board of gross financial misdeeds. The government of India was also out to get him. So were the Mumbai mafia. How could such a powerful man fall so suddenly, many asked? And then they looked at his life story and wondered how he could have been given such enormous power over cricket in the first place.

Modi was born rich, the son of one of north India's great Marwari business families. His grandfather, Gujarmal Modi, was a sugar baron and confidant of Jawaharlal Nehru; the company mill-town he founded in 1933, Modinagar, a short drive east of Delhi, still bears the family name. His father, Krishnan Kumar Modi, helped oversee a vast expansion in the family business. Thereby he had formed one of India's biggest conglomerates, with interests in tobacco, chemicals, fashion, food, education and retail.

Lalit inherited his forefathers' commercial instincts. He had a great flair for business. In conversation, he was never happier than racing through the structures of some complicated deal, spitting out revenue, profit and cost projections, challenging his listener to follow his arithmetical gymnastics. I rarely could. But Modi's formal education was less to boast of. After attending some of India's most expensive schools, he went to Duke University in North Carolina, where he got into his first major scrape. It was over a drug deal that went wrong. Modi and three other students were allegedly mugged while trying to buy cocaine. Seeking vengeance, they turned on another student whom they blamed for the robbery. Modi was subsequently arrested and pleaded guilty to charges of possessing cocaine, false imprisonment and assault. He was put on probation for five years but, after pleading ill health, permitted to return to India.

Everyone commits youthful follies. But Modi's seemed indicative of some deeper character traits. He was reckless, self-destructive even. And when challenged he could be aggressive. 'So long as people agree with Lalit, he's fine,' one of his oldest friends told me. 'But if you tell Lalit he can't do something, he'll just go for you, and he won't stop.'

Back in Delhi, Modi was set to work in the family business. But he soon got bored of the tobacco business. He wanted his own success. So, after causing another scandal (by marrying a friend of his mother's, a divorcée nine years his senior), he moved to Mumbai and started a media company, Modi Entertainment Network. This was in 1993, just as India's television revolution was beginning and the opportunities for a well-capitalised, well-connected entrepreneur were immense. Modi formed a string of lucrative joint ventures with foreign media companies including Disney, Fashion TV and ESPN, whose content MEN agreed to distribute in India. Yet Modi, at once controlling and unpredictable, could be a difficult partner. Several of these promising ventures soured, leading to legal battles and eventual divorce. Almost anything Modi touched seemed to become controversial.

Modi's interest in cricket dates from around this time. He had previously shown little enthusiasm for the game. When I asked him if he actually liked it he looked momentarily embarrassed. 'Sure, I like all sports, always participated in sports,' he said vaguely. But Modi was interested in money, and during his ill-fated student days he had been impressed by the revenues American sports churned out. He became convinced that Indian cricket was a seam of undiscovered gold, waiting to be mined.

In 1995, shortly after launching his media career, Modi pitched his idea for a new 50-over tournament to the BCCI: he even registered its name – Indian Cricket League Ltd (ICL). Amrit Mathur, who would become CEO of the Delhi Daredevils IPL side, was part of a four-man team hired by Modi to plan the contest. 'We had it all worked out, city-based teams and with lots of entertainment,' he told me. 'It was going to be pretty much like the IPL has turned out.' But the BCCI said, nothing doing.

Foiled by the board, Modi resolved to join it. He got himself elected to the cricket association of the small Himalayan state of Himachal Pradesh, but his involvement there was short-lived. He then resurfaced in Rajasthan in 2005 on a firmer wicket. The state's Hindu nationalist chief minister, Vasundhara Raje Scindia, a member of the royal house of Gwalior, was an old friend of the Modis. She was also controversial. At a time of galloping growth in Rajasthan – fuelled by a property boom in and around its lovely pink capital of Jaipur – Scindia's government was alleged to be more than usually corrupt. This looked bad for Modi, because he was said to be advising his old friend. He was often seen in Jaipur, staying in a suite at the luxury Rambagh Palace hotel; investors began speaking of Modi as a route to the chief minister. The opposition Congress dubbed him Rajasthan's 'super chief minister', a grand vizier to the state's maharani leader. Ahead of Rajasthan's next election, in 2008, the Congress party sought to capitalise on these allegations with a campaign poster that asked: 'Who is Lalit Modi?'

He has been convicted of no wrongdoing in Rajasthan. Yet Modi clearly did well under Scindia in one respect. With her help he managed to get hold of the Rajasthan Cricket Association from a family, the Rungtas, that had ruled it for 38 years. He launched his campaign surreptitiously, joining the association under an abbreviated version of his name: as one 'Lalit Kumar'. 'I didn't give my full name because in those days my name would crop up and all of a sudden – pssch! – people would want to cut off my entry,' he later confessed. Scindia then introduced an ordinance, the Rajasthan Sports Act, which disenfranchised most of the association's members, hand-picked by the Rungtas, in favour of Rajasthan's 32 district cricket representatives. In February 2005 they were then persuaded to elect Modi, a man with little history in Rajasthan or cricket administration, president of the RCA by a single vote. Modi was now on the inside of Indian cricket. India's cricket bosses quickly recognised his potential. Most had got into cricket before the television-fuelled boom; Modi had come in, bristling with enterprise, because of it. He was unabashedly commercial, the most enterprising administrator Indian cricket had seen. At a Test match in Mohali he was presented to the media by I.S. Bindra, Dalmiya's great rival, as the coming man of the BCCI. 'Cricket in India is a $2 billion a year market,' Modi declared. 'We are sitting on a gold mine. Our players should be played on a par with international footballers and NBA stars, in millions of dollars and not in measly rupees.'

No one in the BCCI paused to question Modi's probity, his divisive character or his scandalous history. Instead they gave him the keys to drive Indian cricket to yet greater profits. After Sharad Pawar took over the BCCI in 2005 he made Modi head of its marketing committee, with responsibility for negotiating commercial contracts. Modi proceeded to raise $150 million from a pair of sponsorship deals, with Nike and the Sahara Group, and $630 million from selling five-year broadcast rights to Indian cricket to Nimbus. That was a deal that would have historic consequences.

It helped convince Zee TV's Subhash Chandra – Indian television's historic monopoly-buster – to launch his rebel Indian Cricket League.

In August 2007 Kapil Dev unveiled Zee's first 50 signings for the ICL. They were better than the Indian board had been expecting. Zee had recruited several high-class veterans, including the West Indian Brian Lara, the Pakistanis Inzamam-ul-Haq and Muhammad Yousuf, and the South African Lance Klusener, each signed for around $400,000 a year. The calibre of the ICL's Indian contingent was much lower, the BCCI having threatened to ban any player who joined Chandra's revolt. 'Our stand is very clear. Players who take part in the ICL will never be eligible to play for the country again. It is up to the players to decide what they want to do', said the board's secretary, Niranjan Shah. Nonetheless, the ICL had bagged a few jaded big-name players, Dinesh Mongia, Deep Dasgupta and J.P. Yadav, and a lot of promising young cricketers, including most of the Hyderabad state side.

The BCCI feared that if Chandra's rebel tournament became established that exodus would grow. Only a handful of Indian cricketers could play for India, after all, and Zee was offering salaries far in excess of what India's state associations paid. Chandra also had powerful friends. Laloo Yadav, India's railways minister, promised him use of his ministry's many grounds. Jokingly, he also urged the BCCI and Zee to settle their argument with a cricket match between their best players. Digvijay Singh, a Congress leader with the ear of the Gandhi family, wrote to Pawar imploring him on Chandra's behalf to 'prevail upon the hardliners in the board and make them understand the sentiments of millions of cricket lovers in India'. India's anti-monopoly watchdog, the Monopolies and Restrictive Trade Practices Commission, meanwhile let it be known that it would investigate any attempt to ban cricketers playing for the ICL. It was a fine old Indian scrap.

Pawar sought to manage the conflict. 'There is no confrontation between the BCCI and ICL,' he announced, perplexingly to most observers. Yet he had already set in motion a plan to fix Chandra. Modi had demanded Pawar's permission to resurrect his own scheme for an officially sanctioned domestic tournament. Owned and run by the BCCI, it would be bigger, glitzier and richer than anything Chandra could pull off, and it would feature all India's star players. Pawar gave Modi the go-ahead, plus a promise of $25 million seed-money for the venture.

Many others on the board were sceptical, or so Modi later claimed. 'Mr Pawar and Mr Bindra, they were the ones who backed me,' he told me. 'Everyone else was saying it's not possible. They didn't understand what I was proposing. They said, "This tournament of yours, it's a bloody useless idea."

'But I had already made so much money by then. I had locked-in contracts for four or five billion dollars. So they basically said, OK, let him do it, he's done so much for us, let him do it and let him fall flat on his face. And that's basically how it started.'

Over tea at Wimbledon in July, Modi outlined his ambition to Andrew Wildblood, a heavy-hitter in the sports management giant IMG. Though IMG was locked in a longstanding payment dispute with the BCCI at the time, dating from an India–Pakistan one-day series it had helped organise in Toronto in 1998, Wildblood was gripped. A new domestic Indian cricket tournament, harnessing the tearaway cricket enthusiasm of India's tens of millions of new consumers, could be enormously profitable. Indian television executives, after all, had been demanding one for years. And now the board, in fear for its threatened monopoly, was right behind the idea. Wildblood agreed to go away and flesh out a plan for the new league. Modi meanwhile embarked on a tour of the cricket world, to warn the world's best players away from Chandra. 'We basically started pulling out all the guns. I went all around the world, country to country, board to board, persuading them not to have anything to do with the ICL,' he recalled. 'Fuck, players were being wooed left, right and centre at this time. Brian Lara's a prime example. I made four trips to London to meet Brian, saw him, saw his agent, told him to hang on. But Brian just felt we would never launch and [the ICL] had already launched, so he was just going to go ahead and play with them.'

By early September IMG had produced a draft design for the IPL, cobbled together from British and American sports. Like Chandra's upstart ICL, it would use Twenty20 cricket, the short, fast, knockabout format introduced in England in 2003. As in English football – to which its name paid homage – the league would be city-based. Its eight teams would be privately owned under a franchise arrangement with the BCCI. Unlike in America's Major League Soccer and National Football League, the board would own the league, not the team-owners. But these investors would be guaranteed a large share of the league's central revenues: initially including 80 per cent of television and 60 per cent of sponsorship revenues.

The IPL was unveiled in Delhi in September at a ceremony attended by India's top cricketers, including the holy trinity of Rahul Dravid, Sourav Ganguly and Sachin Tendulkar. The inaugural six-week tournament, Modi announced, would begin in April 2008, with prize money of $3 million – three times what Chandra was promising. Unlike the ICL, it would also have the blessing of foreign cricket boards. To encourage them, Modi also announced the launch of a new international T20 tournament, the Champions League, in which the best two IPL teams would compete against the Twenty20 champions of Australia, England and South Africa. Representatives of all three countries' cricket boards attended the launch, as did the South African president of the ICC, Ray Mali. A few foreign players were also present, including Australian Glenn McGrath and New Zealander Stephen Fleming, both of whom had recently pulled out of negotiations to sign for the ICL.

Cricket had seen nothing like this. The IPL promised to align the interests of the Indian board and private investors behind a tournament that had nothing whatsoever to do with international competition. If it took off, the players would earn more from playing six weeks of T20 in India than from a year of Test and one-day cricket for their countries. The threat to international cricket was obvious. The IPL threatened to tear a six-week hole in the international calendar – and what was to stop it spreading? Modi did nothing to reassure those who worried about this.

'Cricket is a very old and traditional game,' he declared. 'We have something new and are trying to put it into reality. We have taken some bold steps. We're going forward and trying to change the world order in that scenario.'

Yet Modi was not quite as confident as he seemed. He now urgently needed to sell IPL television rights and teams for sums that would justify the expectations he had raised. And neither sale was straightforward. Hitherto, Indian cricket fans had only been interested in India's national team, and there were plenty of experts who doubted whether their interest could be aroused by a tournament in which national pride was not at stake. Nor was it absolutely certain that they would even go for Twenty20. Just as the board had been slow to embrace one-day cricket in the 1980s, so it had turned its nose up at the game's new shortest form. But this doubt, at least, was soon allayed.

Just six days after the IPL's launch, Yuvraj Singh walked out to bat against England in the inaugural T20 World Cup in South Africa. India were in utter control, on 155 for three, which made this a perfect situation for Yuvraj. Though an ordinary Test batsman, with a brittle temperament, he was a rare hitter of the ball, as he was about to demonstrate. He proceeded to hit the fastest international fifty, off only 12 balls. It included six sixes off a single over, bowled by Stuart Broad. Five days later India beat Pakistan by five runs to win the T20 World Cup: and India promptly went wild for T20.

Modi's sales pitch was now a lot easier. In January 2008 he sold ten-year television rights to the IPL for a little over a billion dollars, to a consortium of Multi Screen Media, the Indian division of Sony, and a sports marketing agency called World Sport Group. The figure was based on Modi's estimate that each IPL game would be worth a million dollars in advertising revenues – a number he had more or less plucked from the air. Later that month, at an auction in Mumbai, the eight IPL franchises were sold to a who's who of Indian tycoons for a total of $723.5 million, payable over a decade in annual instalments.

The cricket world was astounded. To put these sums into perspective, the England and Wales Cricket Board, the world's second richest, had total revenues in 2007 of £93 million. And the Indian cricket board had just landed the best part of $2 billion, in less than a fortnight, for a tournament that didn't yet exist. The commentator Harsha Bhogle was following an Indian tour to Australia at the time. 'The Aussies were completely amazed,' he told me. 'I don't think they'd realised how much money there is in India.'

Yet again Indian cricket seemed to encapsulate India's national fortunes. The economy was putting on a blistering growth spurt, having expanded by over 9 per cent in each of the previous three years. This was up to Chinese standards, and India's bullish finance minister, Palaniappan Chidambaram, predicted that 'double-digit growth' was around the corner. Sober observers thought that unlikely: India, with its rotten infrastructure and paralysing politics, was not China. Moreover, for anyone minded to look, there were signs that the current growth rate was unsustainable. Bubbles were expanding in India's property market, inflation was soaring, India's roads, ports and airports were clogged with traffic – all signs of an economy overheating. But few middle-class Indians – including respected economists who should have known better – were minded to doubt the economic miracle they saw unfolding around them. The high growth rate was a source of tremendous national confidence and loudly celebrated. India, for so long poor and embarrassed, was at last emerging as a global power – and the IPL seemed to many Indians like a powerful symbol of that.

Modi and his retinue encouraged such thinking, by talking endlessly of the money to be made in the tournament. 'Why is the IPL so associated with money? It's because we have always kept talking about money,' the IPL's CEO, Sundar Raman, told me. 'Does this happen in the English Premier League? Do people talk endlessly about what such and such club is worth or player is paid? No. They talk about team loyalty and fan following and traditional rivalries. And the IPL will eventually move towards all of that.'

The identity of the new team-owners encouraged more money talk. They included some of India's richest businessmen, the most conspicuous beneficiaries of the boom times. Until the mid-1990s India was reckoned to have only two billionaires, together controlling around 1 per cent of GDP. By 2008 it had over 40 and they controlled more than a fifth of the country's output.

In a venal age, many of these tycoons had become popular celebrities, embraced by India's bullish middle class. This gave Modi another selling-point for his nascent tournament. India's richest man, Mukesh Ambani, bought the Mumbai franchise for $111.9 million through his Reliance Industries conglomerate. Vijay Mallya, an airline and brewing magnate, paid $111.6 million for a team in his home town of Bangalore. The Hyderabad team went to a big media group, Deccan Chronicle Ltd, and the Chennai one to India Cements, a company controlled by the BCCI treasurer, N. Srinivasan. GMR Group, a construction firm, bought a franchise in Delhi.

Shahrukh Khan – aka King Khan – one of Bollywood's leading lights for two decades, acquired the Kolkata team for $75 million, in partnership with the husband of one of his co-stars, Juhi Chawla. Another Bollywood starlet, Preity Zinta, bought a side in Mohali in a consortium that also included her boyfriend Ness Wadia, a member of one of India's oldest Parsi business families. The only foreign investors were a consortium led by a British sports-media entrepreneur, called Manoj Badale, who had briefly owned the Leicestershire county side; it picked up a franchise for Modi's old stamping ground, Jaipur, for $67 million. The consortium also included Lachlan Murdoch, son of Rupert, and Suresh Chellaram, Modi's Nigeria-based brother-in-law.

These were powerful people and Modi naturally took the credit for bringing them in. 'All of them, every one of them, from Mukesh Ambani to Vijay Mallya to GMR group, to the Deccan, to Shahrukh, I approached,' he told me. 'Preity, Ness, everyone was personally approached by me, and sat with me. I mean they had no idea what the hell this was, no one else went to them. It was all done directly by me, one on one. Everyone was a friend of mine. No one else was going to come.'

Yet the investors were getting a good deal. In the early years of the tournament, they would collect around $10 million a year from television revenues alone, sufficient to cover the annual repayment costs of a $100 million franchise. With additional revenue from tickets, ground sponsorship and merchandising, Modi estimated the franchise owners should not lose more than a couple of million dollars a year, including their franchise fees. 'I gave everyone an assurance,' Modi recalled. 'I said, "Guys, you're signing ten-year contracts. This could either be a dud or it could be big. If it's a dud I guarantee we'll walk away from it ourselves after a year or two. So that's the maximum downside."'

This was high-rolling stuff. Wadia told me how Modi had first approached him and Zinta to invest in the IPL at a society wedding, on a beach in Thailand. 'Lalit said this is going to be big and he told Preity, "Look, it will help your career, it'll raise your profile."' We were sitting together in Wadia's lofty Mumbai office, overlooking 50 acres of mothballed cotton-mills which his family owned. Once the heartbeat of a great industrial city, this was now one of the world's most valuable tracts of real estate, and Wadia had been charged with turning it into office blocks and luxury apartments.

The great-grandson of Pakistan's founding father, Muhammad Ali Jinnah, he was another spoiled super-rich kid. But he had more charm and a lot less ambition than Modi. He was friendly, in an absent-minded way, and gave an impression of not being terribly bright. He liked to suggest he had been drawn to the IPL as a means to express his own frustrated sporting ambitions. 'You know, I would have liked to be a professional sportsman but my father would not have allowed it,' he once told me sadly. But when I reminded him of this, sitting in his office, he seemed embarrassed. 'Umm, I wasn't so much a cricket person,' he said, in his public-school accented English. 'But I would say I was a sport person. At one time I used to play squash, badminton and tennis all in the same evening!'

Like Wadia, around half the IPL's investors, including Reliance, GMR and India Cements, had no obvious commercial tie-up with cricket. But they were impressed by Modi's pitch and, being family-based firms largely unencumbered by the views of shareholders, their bosses were more or less free to invest as they pleased. Another sort of IPL investor saw in cricket an opportunity to flog other products. In the case of the Bollywood stars, this meant themselves. In the case of Mallya, it meant his airline and booze. Indeed, the fact that advertising alcoholic drinks is technically illegal in India made this especially desirable. Mallya named his team Royal Challengers Bangalore after his best-selling Royal Challenge whisky; just as he had named his Kingfisher Airlines, launched in 2003, after his best-selling Kingfisher beer. Kingfisher also became the official sponsor of the IPL's umpires and of five other IPL teams. 'Mallya got the concept immediately,' Modi said approvingly.

Another auction, in February, produced more big-money headlines. The team-owners bid annual wages of $42 million to hire 78 Indian and foreign cricketers on three-year contracts. A few traditionalists reviled this exercise as a 'slave auction' – most Indian cricket fans loved it.

The costliest pick, India's T20 captain Mahendra Singh Dhoni, was bought by the newly named Chennai Super Kings for $1.5 million. The most expensive foreigner, the walloping Australian all-rounder Andrew Symonds, went to the Hyderabad-based Deccan Chargers for $1.35 million – much to his astonishment: 'If I could tell you why, that would probably be quite a good news story, but there is no sort of logical sense to what each player's worth,' Symonds told the *Sydney Morning Herald*. Six players went for over a million dollars, including three so-called 'icon players', Tendulkar, Dravid and Ganguly, whose sides, Mumbai, Bangalore and Kolkata, had promised to pay them 15 per cent more than their nearest team-mate. This made them among the world's best-paid sportsmen, earning as much per week as top English footballers.

In fact there was an obvious logic to the bidding: team-owners paid through the teeth for Indian internationals. Ishant Sharma, a young fast bowler, went to Kolkata Knight Riders for $950,000; Shane Warne, the great Australian leg-spinner, to Rajasthan Royals for a mere $450,000. Robin Uthappa, a journeyman India one-day player, was bought by Mumbai Indians for $800,000; the Australian Adam Gilchrist, one of the most destructive batsmen in the history of cricket, went to Deccan Chargers for $100,000 less. This was partly because Indian stars could draw a crowd. But it was also because the franchises would have to field at least seven Indians in their XIs, putting a premium on Indian talent.

It was madness and utterly compelling, just as Modi had hoped. He presented the auction in faux ideological terms, as a display of the impartial force of the market. 'I believe in free markets deciding everything,' he once said. 'Let people decide. In certain cases you might lose, in others you might win.' Middle-class Indians loved that idea. Yet this was a market defined and regulated by Modi, who had enforced a $5 million salary cap per franchise. That was far more generous than it needed to be – most of the players having signed pre-auction agreements with the BCCI to play for much smaller sums than they were eventually bought for. Sharma's reserve price was a mere $150,000. Yet Modi had, in effect, made sure to inflate those sums. This ensured his new creation eye-catching headlines, the grateful support of the world's players: and also upset the economic balance of world cricket.

Symonds, of all people, had acknowledged the risk in this, even before the player auction. 'The way things are heading, loyalty is really going to become a major issue, particularly when you can make more money in six or eight weeks than what you can in a whole season,' he said. 'Loyalty versus money always makes for an interesting debate. Who wouldn't be tempted to take a job offering more money for less work?' To cricketers used to playing all day, day after day, the IPL looked like a spectacularly good deal.

Some in the BCCI made placatory noises about their commitment to defending the primacy of Test and international cricket. But it was hard to see in their actions any long-term plan for cricket beyond perpetuating their own heft and privileges. The IPL was the vision of no one with a serious interest in cricket's future good. It was primarily a response to Chandra's attempted putsch, created as a defensive measure to shore up the BCCI's jaded monopoly. However redolent of the new, zesty India the tournament would come to seem, it was in this way an indication of how little India was changing at the top.

On a misty evening in April 2008 I turned up at the Feroz Shah Kotla to see what all the fuss was about. The previous evening the first IPL match had been held in Bangalore. Pitting Mallya's Royal Challengers against the Kolkata Knight Riders, it had surpassed even Modi's wildest hopes for the new T20 tournament. The lasers and fireworks were spectacular, the dance music deafening. There were models on stilts and a delirious full house. Sharad Pawar was jeered. The Washington Redskins cheerleaders, prancing around in little yellow shorts, almost caused a stampede. Then there was the cricket.

Opening the innings for KKR, the New Zealander Brendon McCullum hit 158 off 73 balls, including 13 sixes – a feat of hitting that was previously almost unimaginable. The stadium was in ferment, with Shahrukh Khan dancing gleefully for the cameras as his side notched up a total of 222 for three. It was a rubbish game of cricket, with Bangalore all out for 82. But, for millions of Indian viewers, this was the cricket of their dreams. It was purest tamasha.

As the sixes flew from McCullum's bat, Modi gazed around the Chinnaswamy in wonder. 'It was only when Brendon hit what he hit that I knew it would work,' he told me. 'I was sceptical till then, I had my doubts, I was always afraid deep down. At the end of the day, if the consumer didn't buy it, there was nothing more we could do. But it was incredible. It was slam-dunk cricket, the ball was being hit out over the ropes, you had people screaming and shouting and jumping and women and children and Calcutta city glued to the TV. The next day I went to Brendan and said: "Thank you very much for making my tournament a success."'

By the time I turned up to the Kotla the crowd was a gyrating, buttock-rolling mess. The game, between Delhi Daredevils and Rajasthan Royals, had already begun. As I worked my way towards my seat, through a scrimmage of whirling limbs, I caught glimpses of the green luminescence of the pitch and cricketers in blue shirts. But I had no idea which team was which or who was doing what.

Reaching my seat, I grabbed the arm of a man jumping up and down next to it, waving a card printed with the figure 6 above his head.

'Who's batting?' I screamed in his ear.

He shook his head, grinning joyfully, to indicate he had no idea either. 'Sorry!' he shouted, and took off again.

There were still some who doubted Modi's claim that a sports revolution had begun. They included senior figures in IMG, which was being paid lavishly to produce the tournament. The doubters questioned, in particular, how long Indians could remain interested in a contest in which the outcome hardly seemed to matter.

A handful of IPL teams quickly attracted local followings, especially in the traditional cricket centres of Mumbai, Chennai and Kolkata. But the loyalties of most IPL viewers were fungible. They were bestowed, game to game or at best season to season, according to the biggest India star on view. Or according to the biggest hitter of sixes – or 'DLF maximums', as they were known in the IPL, after the construction company that had paid $50 million to be the tournament's title sponsor.

IMG also feared the IPL would stretch the patience of female viewers. Most Indian households had only one television set and 'the Indian housewife', an archetype much fretted over by TV executives, was believed to wield ultimate power over the remote control. This fear was heightened by the unprecedented cricket bombardment that the IPL represented. Its first season featured 59 matches in 45 days. Wasn't that too much tamasha even for Indians?

Apparently not. With average attendances of 58,000, the IPL drew the second biggest crowds of any tournament after America's National Football League. And its television ratings were stunning. The IPL's inaugural season drew a cumulative TV audience of over 100 million people watching at home, based on the conservative estimate of India's main eyeballs counter, TAM. Many others watched, uncounted, in restaurants and bars. Amazingly, around 35 per cent of these spectators were women. The tournament's final, played between the Rajasthan Royals and Chennai Super Kings in Mumbai, was watched by at least 36 million.

Almost as wonderfully for advertisers, the tournament's viewership was otherwise fairly consistent. It suffered none of the precipitous drops seen in international tournaments when India was not involved. The IPL's cumulative television audience was almost 20 per cent higher than that of the 2007 T20 World Cup as a result. Indians, it seemed, would watch any game so long as there were Indian celebrity cricketers on view. 'In the IPL there are always Indians playing, so it's always your team playing,' Multi Screen Media's CEO, Manjit Singh, told me excitedly.

Better still, the IPL was most popular with India's youngest consumers, those aged 18 to 35. Their fickle attention was the Holy Grail for advertisers in a consumer goods market predicted to quadruple over the next decade and a half. 'Fifty-over cricket got a huge crowd, no doubt. If Tendulkar's batting, if India's winning, everyone watches it,' G. Srinivasan, the league's head of marketing, told me. 'But cricket was not cool before Twenty20. That's why young people love the IPL.'

What was the appeal? Three reasons were most obvious, including, to be fair, the cricket. But it was not the main reason for the IPL's success. Even by the slapstick standards of T20, the first IPL season was a poor sporting contest. It provided plenty to shout about, with roughly a quarter of the runs scored as sixes, mostly by foreign players. They occupied nine of the top ten spots in the tournament's batting averages and eight of the top ten in the bowling averages. Yet because the franchises were only allowed to field four foreigners at any time, the standard of IPL play was very patchy.

Set alongside the Australian, South African and Pakistani stars who provided most of the best performances, India's best players looked like overrated celebrities, and the lesser ones looked like over-promoted club players. Dhoni came 12th in the averages, which made him the highest-placed Indian to have played more than five matches. Tendulkar came 30th. Deluged with easy money, some pampered Indian cricketers seemed hardly to care about their performances.

'All the focus is on money, fame, celebrity, when it needs to be on the team,' Jeremy Snape, a former England one-day spinner working as a sports psychologist with the Rajasthan Royals, told me during a later IPL season. 'I tell the players that constantly. But at the end of the day, when the guy goes back to his hotel room, he opens the paper and he's on a double-page spread with a Bollywood star, he's just done 15 commercials and he's paid X millions ... It can be distracting.'

But these shortcomings were not admitted by the IPL's organisers or the television commentators, who were in fact employees of the board. Their job was not to criticise the cricket, but to sing the tournament's praises. And they did so slavishly, led by two former India captains, Sunil Gavaskar and Ravi Shastri, who also sat on the IPL's governing council. Shastri hailed Modi as 'Moses' – for bringing cricket to its promised land. Yet, for unimpressed Indian cricket fans – and there were some – the tournament also offered a genuine cricketing compensation. This was in the success of its least-fancied team, Rajasthan Royals.

Under thrifty management, the Royals had spent less on players than any other side. After the player auction Modi had actually fined the franchise for failing to spend enough. They were the only team not to have hired a big Indian star. But they had instead hired several good foreigners and, in Shane Warne, an inspired captain. He gave his younger team-mates blokish nicknames – the 'Goan Cannon', 'Rock Star' – and told them they were great. Accustomed to India's more whip-cracking style of leadership, they adored him for this. 'For me there is God and then there is Shane Warne,' said Yusuf Pathan, one of the team's stars.

'There will be no one else like him. He changed our attitude towards the game in such a short time. All of us who played under him were ordinary domestic players. He made us into world-beaters.'

The Royals won seven of their last eight games to reach the final, against Chennai. They won that game off the last ball, with their Australian captain at the crease. Whatever cricketing credibility the IPL had, it owed largely to Warne. Even Modi was in awe of him. 'What Warnie did in the locker room …' he told me wonderingly, 'I mean, how Warnie kicked their butts … amazing. He's fantastic, a great, great guy. Warnie is the one person you need to talk to.'

Another aspect of the IPL's appeal, as Sundar Raman had acknowledged, was money. At some IPL grounds, the incoming batsmen's salary was flashed up on the scoreboard as well as his batting average. And the tournament's gusher of ad revenues, its fat wages, its soaring 'brand value', seemed to make as many headlines as the cricket. 'Indian Premier League valued at over $2-bn; KKR richest team' (*Indian Express*, 10 May 2009); 'IPL brand value doubles to $4.13 billion' (*Times of India*, 22 March 2010). This is how some Indians enjoyed the IPL. It was a new form of Indian cricket nationalism, a substitution of commercial for sporting success.

The volume of advertising that was driving this success was unseemly. The IPL was sodden with it. There were ad breaks between innings, between overs and in any half-beat pause in the play. By the second season Modi had introduced a seven-and-a-half minute 'strategic timeout' – a euphemism for an extended ad break – into each innings. Many viewers found this annoying. Many switched channels during the breaks. Yet it was possible that some actually enjoyed this advertising assault.

It identified Modi's baby with the hungry new consumerism of these high-growth times. This was another great change coincidental with the IPL. In 2004 India had about 20 shopping malls; by 2012 it had more than 300, selling Nike trainers and Timex watches, snazzy foreign brands that wealthy Indians had long been denied access to. This development was graphically evident in a new city on the outskirts of Delhi, Gurgaon, which was built by – and sometimes referred to as – DLF, the IPL's title sponsor. A cluster of steel and concrete high-rises, Gurgaon mushroomed in the 1990s to provide the plush office and living space that India's crowded capital lacked. And when foreign companies swarmed into India after its economy was opened, Gurgaon is where many set up offices. Their neon-lit logos cluttered the city's skyline, vying for the highest perch, in front of the smokiest mirrored glass, to advertise American Express, Coca Cola, Nokia, Motorola, Microsoft and other famous firms. Nowhere in India is so reminiscent of China's tearaway growth.

When I first visited Gurgaon, I noticed my driver, Chandra, shooting astonished sidelong glances at its skyscrapers and malls. I asked how it had looked when he had previously visited the city. 'Sir, forest ...' he said. Chandra could not have afforded to shop in DLF's malls; but he still liked the IPL. This was one of the big contradictions within the tournament – and of Indian television more generally. Only a tiny portion of wealthy Indians could afford the snazzy mobile handsets, cars and motorbikes advertised on it. Many have expressed a fear that this will generate resentment and social unrest. It may. Yet, so long as India can maintain its recent high growth, creating a promise, at least, of greater opportunity for all, those fears are probably exaggerated. Laxmi, the goddess of wealth, is one of Hinduism's most popular deities: poorer Indians also aspire to her blessings. 'I'm sure at some level these ads generate frustration for many people. A sort of, you know, "Here's that damn car again and I still can't buy it" feeling,' Uday Shankar, the boss of Star TV and a keen observer of Indian society, told me. 'But I am also sure the experience generates hope.'

It was appropriate that the man most associated with India's new culture of shopping was one of the IPL's most prominent investors. This was Mallya, India's self-styled 'King of Good Times'. A middle-aged roué, famous for his collections of luxury homes, classic cars, yachts and Bollywood starlets, he was an emblem of Indian excess. Every Kingfisher Airways flight began with a video message from Mallya in which he assured passengers, in his fruity bass voice, that the cabin crew had been 'picked by me personally' and instructed to treat every customer 'as if you are a guest in my own home'. It was a line that said a lot about Mallya. He was ambitious, impressive, yet faintly scurrilous and, like many wealthy Indians, had little facility for irony. If any gesture spelled the death of Gandhian frugality, it was when Mallya snapped up the Mahatma's sandals and spectacles at a 2009 auction in New York for $1.8 million.

When I met him at a later IPL players' auction, in Bangalore, Mallya was giving the movers and shakers of Indian cricket a headache. 'Up with Mallya until bloody 3am,' a well-known cricket agent mumbled to me one morning, looking pale and unwell as he slunk back to his hotel room. 'It's not the drink that's the problem. It's that he insists we drink *his* bloody drinks.'

Since inheriting United Breweries as a young man, Mallya had turned a modest south Indian business into the world's second biggest purveyor of alcohol. But this success was despite the noxious hangovers induced by some of its best-selling beer and liqueurs. Kingfisher beer was rumoured to be laced with glycerine to help preserve it during the Indian heat. That was not true. But drink three or four and it could feel like it.

'Now,' Mallya said warmly, as we sat down together in his hotel bar, 'What'll you have?' A rotund 55-year-old, he was wearing a silk designer tracksuit, white patent leather cowboy boots and diamond studs glinted in his ears. I suggested a glass of wine, which was the only drink I could think of that UB didn't sell.

'Excellent idea!' he exclaimed, 'We'll have a bottle of my new Kingfisher red!'

According to Mallya, the key to the cricket business was India's youthful demography. 'We'll have over 100 million consumers added to our middle class in the next couple of years and these are not people who want to live like their parents or grandparents did,' he said.

'This is a whole new generation of Indians, better educated than their parents, earning more, spending more. We've transitioned more from a saving economy to a spending economy. Whether it's clothes, cars, apartments, everything – people want a better quality of life and they are moving away from traditional Indian customs to Western customs. India is changing rapidly. Indians are doing things they didn't do five, seven years ago.

'They have more spending power, they are much more willing to spend and they're watching television to find out how. You know when I was growing up there was only one bloody television channel, Doordarshan? Now there are 150 TV channels, 200 TV channels, all of which are making an impression on people. The youngsters are more impressionable than the older generation. So what is happening is the youngsters are spending and living well. And the parents are saying, well, hang on, I've been working hard, putting my money in the bank for 30 years, and now I might as well spend a bit of it myself and have a better life too!

'In this context the IPL is a brilliant idea and has in my view a fantastic future, because it's cricket, which is like a religion in India, because the format is so exciting it attracts the youngest viewers, and thirdly because, for these reasons, the highest advertising revenues in India are developed through cricket. We've never had something in India so exciting, glamorous and international as this league. So, as the franchises share in the revenue generated by the league, and because these revenues can go only one way, north, and rapidly north, the prospect of ever-increasing income to the teams is high. And for me the double whammy is that it gives me a fantastic platform for my brands.

'The business concept,' said Mallya, raising his glass, 'is sound.'

'And how does your personal image help in marketing it?' I asked.

Mallya surveyed me briefly. 'I don't look for personal glory,' he said. 'It is the media who have branded me "King of Good Times" and given me this great persona. It started off with my being damned by everybody saying, "Here's this young playboy who's inherited his father's business and he's going to drive it into the ground because all he's interested in is horses and fast cars and God knows what ..."

'It used to make me very angry. But now I have no qualms. At the age of 28 I had all the hobbies and interests of a 28-year-old. I could not be expected as a 28-year-old to have the same hobbies and interests of a 50-year-old.'

'But you still have the same hobbies now ...'

'So what!' said Mallya sniffily. 'That's called sustainability. I'm not a changing chappie. I may be 55, but I'm still young at heart and young in the mind. If I spend money, have yachts and planes and cars and everything else, for crying out loud, I spend my own money. I don't live on anyone else. I have said to hell with all that's written about me. It's free publicity and I might as well be the bloody brand ambassador myself. I have never been shy of living my life in an open and transparent way.'

The third aspect of the IPL's appeal, after tamasha cricket and tamasha prosperity, was arguably most important: Bollywood. Bringing Bollywood, or at least Bollywood stars, into cricket was Modi's big idea. 'Bollywood was always the key,' he told me. 'You had all India's men interested in cricket and the women and children follow films, so if you can get them all together, it was always going to be huge.' I had seen a vision of this six months before the IPL began, at a one-day game between India and Pakistan in Jaipur.

My wife and I had been invited to the game by an enigmatic friend, Suhel Seth, an advertising guru and socialite. If 200 people run India, as is often said, only half-jokingly, many are to be seen at the frequent parties Suhel threw in his south Delhi townhouse (a stone's throw from the home of Lalit's tycoon father, K.K. Modi). Modi junior met us at the stadium gates to dispense our match passes. We were late and the then-boss of Rajasthan cricket was irate, urging Suhel to get a move on because the game was about to begin.

It was the last of a five-match one-day series, which India – 3-1 up so far – had already won. Both teams were therefore resting their stars. But from the state of the ground, it might have been a World Cup final. This was my first experience of watching cricket in one of India's smaller cities, where cricket fervour is undiluted by the distractions of metropolitan life. The atmosphere in Jaipur's small Sawai Mansingh Stadium was unlike anything I had experienced.

As Salman Butt and Imran Nazir walked out to begin the Pakistani innings, the noise in the stadium was stupendous. Perhaps that was why I failed to notice a large white sofa positioned on the boundary at deep midwicket. But I could not fail to spot its intended occupant, Shahrukh Khan, or 'SRK' to his fans. The film star wandered into the stadium a few overs into the Pakistani innings and began a slow perambulation of the boundary. The Jaipur crowd duly lost its mind. It became a sobbing mass of 30,000 SRK maniacs, most of whom wore a moustache.

Shahrukh, a 42-year-old star, had ruled Bollywood for two decades. Born into a middle-class Delhi family, he got his break acting in television dramas in the late 1980s. Having graduated to the film industry, he had since acted in over 70 Hindi movies, generally as himself, a slightly gawky, likeable and charismatic clown. He was paid around $3 million a picture for this shtick.

Being self-made, his success was unusual in Bollywood, which is dominated by a handful of film dynasties. Shahrukh was also reckoned to be the film industry's canniest businessman: these days he made his films through his own Red Chillies Entertainment company, through which he would also invest in the IPL. He was the first Indian film mogul to appreciate the money-making potential of conjoining Hindi cinema and cricket.

Hence his appearance at the Sawai Mansingh, just a few days after the release of his latest movie. A song-and-dance confection called *Om Shanti Om*, it was chiefly memorable for a routine in which SRK danced in a pair of tight silver trousers with dozens of Bollywood babes, while lip-synching: 'All hot girls put your hands up and say "Om Shanti O-om!"' His extremely pretty co-star, Deepika Padukone, was also at the game, unrecognised as the huge star she would shortly become. She was sitting shyly behind my wife and me in the plush VIP box to which we had been led.

It provided a superb view of the game, which was entertaining in itself. Mohammad Yousuf and Shoaib Malik had come together at 77 for three and were playing beautifully. They made a pleasing contrast, the elegant and wristy Yousuf and Shoaib more of a stiff-armed biffer. But when SRK suddenly surged into our box, surrounded by bodyguards and flunkies, the game was suddenly forgotten.

The film star made a bee-line for Rajasthan's governor, a former Indian foreign secretary called S.K. Singh, who I happened to be chatting to at the time. With a look of reverence on his shiny, wrinkle-free face, Shahrukh launched himself at the governor's feet. Having thus demonstrated his humility, he rose, beaming to all around him, as the VIP crowd of politicians, judges, army officers and their wives simpered in star-struck wonder. My wife, whose affections are not easily bought, was simpering too.

As Shahrukh was introduced to her, his eyes locked briefly on to hers, then darted away, then returned for a last fleeting inspection of her face. 'Sooo pleased to meet you,' he said in his friendly baritone as Mian flushed pink. I was impressed.

Back at his pitch-side sofa, Shahrukh gave a television interview – for the benefit of over a hundred million people watching the game at home – with live India–Pakistan cricket as the backdrop. This was priceless publicity for *Om Shanti Om*, which was of course name-checked in the interview. The stunt had been arranged by Modi. But some of his colleagues at the BCCI were unimpressed. One later accused Shahrukh of disrespecting cricket. Playing hurt, the film star vowed never to attend another game in response. The redoubtable Niranjan Shah then waded in, to say he had no objection to 'Shahrukh or any other film personality' coming to watch India play 'as long as they are not promoting their films'. *Om Shanti Om* was meanwhile on the way to becoming Bollywood's biggest ever box-office hit.

Bollywood stars flocked to the IPL like drunks to a free bar. And it was no wonder. After the first season, polling by the BCCI suggested as many viewers were tuning in to ogle film stars as to watch cricket. A survey by the *Economic Times* showed that of the top ten individuals most recalled by IPL viewers, only five were cricketers. The IPL was razzle-dazzle entertainment spiced by sport, not the other way around. 'It's fast-paced entertainment, it's fun, it's glamorous, it's got stars,' Multi Screen Media's affable boss, Manjit Singh, told me. 'And yet it also has the elements of a sport.'

'Cricketainment', as Modi called his melding of sport and glamour, handed an obvious advantage to franchises owned by film stars. Shahrukh's KKR was from the start one of the most popular and profitable IPL sides, despite struggling to win two games in a row. Kings XI Punjab, the Mohali franchise, similarly benefited from Zinta, who had been one of India's biggest stars for a decade. Entering her mid-thirties, she was now on the way out as an actress. Too old to play the cutesy tomboys that were her stock-in-trade, Zinta was finding it hard to get good roles. Throwing herself into the IPL was therefore an excellent way for her to remain on-screen, and stave of the threat of midde-aged anonymity.

Most other franchises also tried to buy in some 'glamour quotient', as Indian marketers refer to Bollywood stardust. Delhi Daredevils paid a Bollywood action hero, Akshay Kumar, over $2 million to act as its brand ambassador. The Daredevils' boss, Amrit Mathur, also told me he could sell 15 per cent more tickets for a home game against KKR merely by floating a rumour that Shahrukh would attend.

Some Indian fans found this celebrity onslaught wearing. But it was more belittling for Bollywood. Until a decade or two ago, cinema was more important to Indian imaginations than cricket. From the 1940s to the 1980s Hindi films were the country's main source of entertainment and a popular art form that at its best bristled with intensity and national purpose. In the films of the 1950s and 1960s, now remembered as the greatest Bollywood age, directors like Raj Kapoor and Bimal Roy produced all-India epics, often celebrating the lives of the plucky poor, especially new arrivals to the fast-growing cities.

In the 1970s Bollywood reflected a darker mood, as naive optimism gave way to anger at the corruption and brutality that seemed inherent in Indian society. The star of this time was Amitabh Bachchan, a son of Allahabad, who dominated his cinematic era as no other film star ever has. Playing tough guy heroes, typically forced into crime by cruelty and injustice, Bachchan was the greatest hero Indian popular culture had ever produced. His films were national legends, endlessly playing in the thousands of single-screen cinemas that dotted India's cities and small towns. They made Bachchan one of the most powerful men in India. When he was injured on a film set in 1982, Indira Gandhi flew to Bombay to be by his bedside. He recovered, stood for parliament for Congress and won the election with almost 70 per cent of the vote. There was no danger of the 'Big B' suffering Tiger Pataudi's electoral indignity.

But Bollywood's subsequent history is less inspiring. The best contemporary Hindi films are at least superbly produced. In recent years the spread of new multiplex cinemas, which draw an affluent middle-class audience, have also led to the release of interesting niche movies, higher-brow and less musical than the popular norm. Yet the days of Bollywood providing India with national stories, reflecting the hopes and anxieties of millions, are long gone. The most successful films tend to be convoluted love stories, involving implausibly rich and sanitised characters, who wear Western designer clothes and speak Hinglish ('*Array bhai! Shit! Chalo, let's go!*'). Often filmed outside India – in London or the Maldives – they project a rich, Californian-flavoured and, in fact, non-existent India. The singing and dancing are often wonderful. But the plots are often incoherent and the characters two-dimensional.

That is not just my view. On a week-long tour through Andheri and Juhu, the north Mumbai suburbs where Bollywood lives and works, I heard it expressed by many top directors, producers and actors. When I asked one of India's most famous actor-directors whether Bollywood had made any good films in the past two decades, apart from his own, he looked pained. 'Difficult,' he said. 'It's difficult to think of even one. But please don't write that I said it.'

One reason for this slide is television, which has warped the market for Hindi films in several ways. In particular, it has created huge competition for Indian eyeballs, leading to the closure of many single-screen cinemas, and shortening the average cinema run of any film. A big hit used to play at the cinema for several months – or, in the case of *Sholay*, Bachchan's biggest hit, for many years. But only a serious blockbuster now runs for even a month.

The growth of Indian cricket has exacerbated this pressure. During the IPL or a big one-day tournament, Indians simply stop going to the cinema, which has squeezed the calendar for possible film release dates. Cricket, not Bollywood, is now India's biggest form of entertainment. 'Whenever movies and cricket compete in our country, cricket wins,' Rajesh Sawhney, boss of Reliance Entertainment, one of India's biggest film production companies, told me. 'The IPL has altered the whole media landscape of our country. For two months of every year you now have a dark period in the multiplexes of India.'

The upshot is that, to have much chance of success, Bollywood films must light up the box office within a week or two of their release. This has encouraged film producers to rely on a small stable of established stars, like SRK, a constellation that has hardly changed in two decades. With so much focus on the main star, the producers appear meanwhile to have given rather little thought to their scripts.

A related reason for Bollywood's bad, or at least out-of-touch, movies is the people who make them. Unlike television – a meritocracy by Indian standards – the Hindi film industry is more or less a closed shop, dominated by a few dynasties whose creative talents have not obviously increased over time. Like cricket, Hindi film has always been controlled by an elite group. But whereas in cricket this is becoming less true as its talent pool spreads, in Bollywood the barriers to entry have risen. One of the biggest film families, the Prithviraj Kapoor dynasty, was started by a star of silent Indian cinema in the 1930s and is now into its fourth generation. Prithviraj's great-granddaughter Kareena Kapoor is India's biggest female star and her cousin Ranbir one of the biggest stars of all. Such Bollywood royals are as super-rich and pampered as the characters they often play. No wonder their films seem largely unconnected to the lives of almost any Indian.

I had a glimpse of Bollywood's elite culture on a film set in wintry Srinagar. The film, called *Rock Star*, was being directed by Imtiaz Ali, a young self-made director from Jamshedpur, the Tata steel town. With this background, unusual in Bollywood, Imtiaz was considered to have a rare common touch: his two previous films, *Love Aaj Kal* and *Jab We Met*, had both been smash hits. This was why I had sought him out, and he was wonderfully thoughful and kind. Rather to my surprise, many Indian film people are. But I couldn't see any evidence of a common touch in *Rock Star*, which was clearly pitched at a Westernised, middle-class audience. It was a complicated tale of a young Punjabi rock star and his doomed love affair with a beautiful Kashmiri, a story that flitted through India, Italy and the Czech Republic. The film set was one of the most pleasantly sophisticated, Anglophone and polite workplaces I had ever experienced. With a budget of $11.5 million, Imtiaz had assembled the cream of Bollywood technicians and producers. All were friendly and interested to discuss Hindi film. But none, apart from Imtiaz himself, seemed to hold it in particularly high regard.

When I asked the film's well-known cinematographer, Anil Mehta, to name the last popular Bollywood film he had enjoyed, he pulled a face. 'That's a difficult one,' he said. He had tried to like a recent blockbuster, *Dabangg*. 'We all did. But really I didn't. Being of the elite, Western-educated, I naturally prefer Western films.'

When the cameras were rolling, the actors spoke their lines in Hindi. But as soon as Imtiaz shouted 'Cut!' most of the actors and crew spoke in English. It was also the home language of Bollywood's foremost dynasty, according to Ranbir Kapoor, who was playing the lead in *Rock Star*. 'Hindi is dying,' he told me earnestly, over a cup of the Darjeeling tea that Imtiaz prescribed for all his shoots. 'The language you hear in the films of the 1950s, its beauty, that's gone. Today's actors can't even speak proper Hindi.'

Ranbir said he was an exception: 'I've always been very good at Hindi. I made sure I had a Hindi diction coach when I was young because I wanted to be a Hindi film actor.' That was a reasonable ambition for Ranbir, given his lineage. 'I grew up in musical settings, story settings, with musicians and directors passing through,' he said. Most of them spoke in English too. 'So who did you practise your Hindi with?' I asked Ranbir. 'The maid,' he said.

Until a couple of months previously Ranbir's co-star, Nargis Fakhri, had spoken no Hindi at all. She was a Bollywood debutante, a gorgeous American model with long brown hair and big brown eyes. She was mesmerisingly lovely.

During a lunch break, I spotted Nargis, dressed in the elaborate costume of a Kashmiri bride. She was having mutton curry spooned into her mouth by an assistant so as not to smudge the henna patterns painted on her hands. Rather diffidently, I asked how she had come to be here. 'It was an accident, I really don't know, I'm the wrong person to ask,' Nargis blurted out between mouthfuls of curry. 'Look, I'm 100 per cent American. I'm from Queens, New York. How did I get here? I mean, who are all these people talking funny?'

Until a few months beforehand, Nargis said, she had known almost nothing about India. Then, while modelling in Copenhagen, she had received an email asking her to go to Prague to meet Imtiaz. He had spotted her picture in Vijay Mallya's Kingfisher swimwear calendar, one of India's raunchiest licit publications. He had assumed she was Pakistani and would know Urdu. Indeed, Nargis's father was Pakistani. But she had barely known him and had grown up in America with her Czech mother. She didn't know any Urdu. Her only experience of the subcontinent had been a brief visit to Mumbai, and she hadn't been impressed by it. 'I mean, have you been to Bombay?' she asked me. 'Dude, it's gross. I was, like, standing looking out my hotel window thinking, "You know what? This is gross."'

But Mumbai is where Nargis ended up, taking crash courses in Hindi and acting. 'I had five hours of Hindi in the morning, then five hours with Imtiaz in the afternoon, doing crazy things, staring at the wall, that kind of stuff. It was awful and I cried every day,' she said, while the assistant hovered with the loaded spoon.

'Then we started shooting and I cried again. I thought, "What am I doing in this crazy, fucked-up job?" I mean, it's exhausting mentally and physically, and it's lonely. I only have my mum and my sister, and I mean they're not going to come over here. It's 16 hours away.'

'Cheer up,' I said. 'You're going to be rich and famous. Isn't that great?'

'Oh, I don't know. Not really,' said Nargis. 'I don't care what I do really.' Then Imtiaz politely suggested it was time to start filming again, and, with a heartbreaking smile, she returned to being a Bollywood star.

⁂

The ICL, Subhash Chandra's rebel creation, was meanwhile limping along. It was launched on a misty evening in November 2007 at a small municipal cricket ground outside Chandigarh. Kareena Kapoor – cousin of Ranbir, girlfriend of Tiger Pataudi's son – did a dance routine. Then there was some crash-bash T20, in front of a chilly looking crowd, for which Tony Greig, a paid-up ICL cheerleader, provided exuberant commentary. The Chandigarh Lions beat the Delhi Jets that night.

I watched the ICL on television now and again. But I can't remember much more about it than that: north Indian mist, small crowds, Greig shouting, and the garish pink shirts of the Chennai Superstars, which strangely reminded me of Rwandan prison uniforms. Himanshu Mody, Zee's business chief and the rebel league's architect, winced to recall them. 'Awful,' he agreed, sitting in Zee's Mumbai headquarters. 'They were painful to look at.'

Over the next few months, Zee managed to secure a few more venues for the ICL: in Gurgaon, Chennai and Ahmedabad. But the stadiums were small, most of the ICL's players were old or third-rate and the cricket was even worse than in the IPL. The ICL's television ratings were much worse, roughly a quarter of the IPL's. The tournament that had inspired the IPL now looked like a pathetically poor imitation of it.

Financially, the ICL was disastrous. By November 2008, when a series of ICL 'internationals' – pitting teams designated as Pakistan, India, Bangladesh and the 'World' against each other – opened in Ahmedabad, Zee was $40 million down on its investment. It still hoped to recover that money. Indeed, a recently concluded ICL T20 tournament, won by the Lahore Badshahs, had gone well. But that hope was ended, on 26 November, by the amphibious assault on Mumbai by Pakistani terrorists. As the bullets flew, Inzamam-ul-Haq, captain of the ICL's Pakistani contingent, demanded that Zee send him and his team home. There would be no more ICL matches after that. The rest of the league's players were also laid off, some with their wages unpaid. The league was a failure, which left its creator, Himanshu Mody, rueing his involvement in it. 'I always liked Test cricket, to be honest,' he told me. 'I also don't mind one-day cricket. But T20, I don't know, it's more like entertainment than cricket. It's just a tamasha.'

But the IPL appeared to be unstoppable. In March 2009 the BCCI cancelled the IPL's television contract, claiming Multi Screen Media had broken its terms, including by carrying too much advertising. After a complicated renegotiation, it then resold the rights to the same broadcaster for almost twice the money, $1.6 billion over nine years. The values of the franchises were rising at a similar clip. Around the same time Raj Kundra, the British husband of Shilpa Shetty, a former Bollywood actress, bought an 11.7 per cent stake in Rajasthan Royals for $15.4 million. That implied the team's value had doubled in a year.

Yet the tournament was also causing increasing concern. Foreign cricket boards had long since reconciled themselves to India's ability to control the international calendar. But they were now confronted with a possibility that India could, in effect, control their contracted cricketers. Symonds, who had warned of this danger, now seemed to illustrate it. A hard-drinking larrikin, he had often been in trouble with the Australian board, and his IPL windfall coincided with a worsening of his indiscipline. Within a few months of the first IPL season ending, he was censured for skipping an Australia team meeting to go fishing, getting into a pub brawl and getting drunk. His troubles may have had nothing to do with the IPL. But for those who worried about the effects of showering cricketers with money, they were discouraging. By 2009 Symonds' international career was finished and a new career as a freelance T20 specialist beckoned.

Shrewdly, the foreign boards sought to avoid forbidding their players from getting their share of IPL gravy. But this was not always possible. The English board was finding it especially difficult to accommodate the IPL in its schedule, because it clashed with the beginning of the English county season. Instead, disastrously, it set out to compete with it.

In June 2008 a helicopter landed on the turf at Lord's and disgorged a moustachioed Texan financier, Allen Stanford, and crates of $100 bills. This marked the launch of one of the most bizarre entanglements in any sport. It was a deal between Stanford, England and the West Indies, to hold five Twenty20 matches between England and the West Indies a year, each of which would be played for a winner-takes-all jackpot of $20 million. But within a year Stanford had been arrested and charged with running a $7-billion Ponzi scheme. He was convicted and sentenced to 110 years in prison. For anyone tempted to consider that the BCCI had a monopoly on greed and recklessness among cricket administrators, this tie-up was a forceful counter-blast.

The IPL had a more serious rival at home – India's democracy. In March 2008, the government called a general election that was set to clash with the forthcoming IPL season. With the police unable to cover both events, India's irascible home minister (and former finance minister), Palaniappan Chidambaram, demanded that the tournament be postponed. Modi refused. Denouncing the government, he declared that he would instead stage it, at only a fortnight's notice, in South Africa.

This was an act of chutzpah that caused great offence, fatefully for Modi, to India's rulers. Yet at the time it seemed an act of brilliance. Despite the disruption, IPL2 was another great success. South African crowds packed the stadiums; Indian fans seemed unabashed by the IPL's banishment. An estimated 122 million – nearly 25 per cent more than the previous year – watched the tournament at home on television. 'You have to hand it to Lalit Modi all right,' commented the perspicacious Australian cricket writer Gideon Haigh. 'One wonders how soon people will get sick of doing that.'

The IPL returned the following year to a bullish country. After a brief blip occasioned by the meltdown in global finance, by 2010 India's economy was again growing fast, at almost 9 per cent a year. And India's entertainment industry, driven by exuberant advertising, was growing much faster. 'If you talk about an industry poised for huge growth, it's this one,' Multi Screen Media's Manjit Singh would later tell me. 'The demographics are right, incomes are going up, ad revenues are going up, cable subscriptions are going up.' History suggests that when a country's average annual disposable income per capita reaches $800, television advertising revenues swiftly double. India's was around $650. 'We've got the demographics and the incomes that say "entertainment!"' said Singh. 'It makes for what we could call a compelling money case,' he chortled, while miming throwing wads of money at me across his desk.

Ahead of the third IPL season, Modi announced that two new franchises would be auctioned off and added to the league. He also had other new innovations to visit on the Indian game. He sold exclusive online rights to the IPL to Google. 'We are now taking our event truly global for the first time,' he raved. 'Google gives us access to 500 million pairs of eyes every single moment of the day.' Another deal, with Colors, a Hindi entertainment channel owned by the global media giant Viacom, pushed cricketainment to new levels.

It would involve Colors producing four IPL spin-offs, including a singing competition, 'IPL Rockstar – Music Ka Tadka', in which aspiring singers would perform at stadiums before the games, and coverage of after-match parties, known as IPL Nights, which would be attended by cricketers, models and high-paying guests. A third spin-off was an Oscars-style IPL awards show, a lucrative format already well used in Bollywood. But the cricketainment jewel, which was scheduled to follow IPL3, was a version of the American reality stunt show, *Fear Factor*, starring 13 Indian and foreign cricketers.

According to Colors' then-boss, Rajesh Kamat, 'the crème de la crème of Indian cricketers' were signed up for the show, to jump off cliffs and retrieve food from barrels of snakes under the eyes of its Bollywood host and former Miss World, Priyanka Chopra. Announcing the Colors deal, Modi declared, 'Our partnership with Colors takes the IPL cricketainment quotient into an all-new orbit. I have always maintained that the IPL is a cricketing carnival like no other and with this unique partnership that we have entered on behalf of our franchisees, we are delivering on our promise to extend the IPL franchise beyond cricket, beyond the IPL season and quite frankly beyond imagination.'

For Kamat, the deal looked like TV paydirt. 'Thirteen cricketers, on Colors, doing stunts? Wow!' he told me. 'It would have hit the ball out the park. Absolutely. The image of the channel would have gone through the roof. Thirteen cricketers gets you talked about for three or four months. And that buzz value puts a sheen on the whole channel. That's important. Because we have soaps that drive our bread and butter. Cricket's not only about ratings, you know. It's about image.'

From outside Kamat's office window there came a faint throbbing of Bollywood dance beats. In a car park far below, a crowd of Colors employees were playing an inter-departmental cricket match with a plastic bat and tennis ball. Half the players were young women wearing tight jeans, mini-skirts and strappy shoes. Whenever a wicket fell, music thundered from a pair of giant speakers installed in the car park. None of the players looked a day over 20: the Licence Raj had ended before they were even born.

As I walked down the stairs on my way out of the building, I passed yet another pretty young woman, fashionably dressed, who was pressed against a window watching the game. I asked who was playing, and she shot me a brief glance. 'They're playing cricket,' she said briskly, turning back to the window.

Approaching its third season, in April 2010, the success of Modi's baby was phenomenal. But there were warning signs. After only two six-week seasons, the league was reckoned to be worth $4.13 billion. Yet it was run by a secretive volunteer organisation, the BCCI, which did not appear to consider itself bound by the most basic rules of corporate governance. The IPL's governing body, on which Tiger Pataudi and other grandees sat, was barely functioning. And the tournament was beset with possible conflicts of interest. N. Srinivasan was the BCCI secretary, president of Tamil Nadu's cricket association and also owner, through his family company, of Chennai Super Kings. Mallya, the Bangalore franchise owner, also ran the BCCI's marketing committee. His stepdaughter worked for the IPL. The in-laws of Sharad Pawar's daughter and political successor, Supriya Sule, it emerged, owned a stake in Multi Screen Media, owner of the IPL's broadcast rights. Modi's brother-in-law and stepson-in-law owned stakes in the Rajasthan and Punjab franchises.

Modi himself was a bigger worry. Ensconced in a luxury suite at the Four Seasons hotel in Mumbai, he had assumed the mantle of IPL god-creator. 'If you really want to see power,' wrote Bobili Vijay Kumar, sports editor of the *Times of India*, 'you need to walk into his IPL headquarters in Mumbai; of course, that is easier said than done. Right at the entrance of the plush five-star hotel, there are close to ten NSG-style commandos, all armed to their teeth. You walk through the gate at your own risk. There is an IPL help-desk next to the reception. When you say you have an appointment with Modi, a call is quickly made; only on confirmation, the hotel staffer reveals the floor number. Another one steps forward and punches in the card that gives you access to the floor. When you step out of the lift, the corridor is eerily silent. In the far corner you can see another bunch of armed guards; nobody is allowed here without valid IDs.'

Unhindered by the BCCI, Modi made almost every important decision in the IPL, involving billions or merely thousands of dollars.

Colors' boss, Kamat, gave me an illustration of this. 'Everyone had said no to *Fear Factor*,' he told me. 'But then I got to see Lalit. I sat with him, started telling him the idea, and he just said, "OK, wait." Then he made five phone calls, including with Shane Warne, and started speaking values, then and there. He was able to take decisions. That was his clout.'

In his way, Modi was brilliant. He was feverishly industrious. 'I've never seen anyone work as hard,' Pataudi told me, wonderingly. He was obsessed with excellence, refusing to accept India's usual shoddy standards. 'Whatever anyone says about him, Lalit made sure the organisation of the IPL was world class,' one of the team managers told me, and then illustrated this with a story of how, after returning from another visit to Wimbledon, Modi had upgraded the lanyards used for IPL passes with a better sort he had seen there. Yet it seems amazing in retrospect – no, it seemed amazing at the time – that India's cricket board had given so much power to this Icarus of corporate India.

Brilliant as Modi was at making deals, he was equally good at making enemies. He paid no attention to the first rule of Indian public life: Indians can forgive almost any indiscretion by their leaders in return for a show of grovelling humility, however implausible it might be. But Modi was no groveller. 'You want tickets for the game?' he told a government minister, 'Fine, go buy them.' Though gracious to those he approved of, he could be astonishingly rude. He had little respect for anyone's authority but his own. He seemed genuinely to believe that the IPL was the biggest thing in India, and that he alone ruled it. Manically driven by his desire for power, excellence and self-validation, he offended almost everyone he had dealings with, from the government to the lowliest hack reporter. The IPL could not have happened without him, at least not as it did. But Modi was far from indispensable. And even those who had profited most from him were tiring of the IPL's chairman and commissioner.

The Rajasthan Cricket Association had got rid of him in early 2009, shortly after his mentor Scindia was voted out of office. The BCCI, under new leadership, was also losing patience with Modi. Pawar, now installed at the ICC, had been succeeded as president by a dour Maharashtrian lawyer called Shashank Manohar. And he and his ally Srinivasan were becoming uneasy about how the league was run. After IPL2 they had demanded, over Modi's head, a renegotiation of terms with IMG, which had been paid nearly $10 million for its work in 2008. This looked bad for Modi, who had negotiated IMG's terms, and he made matters worse by rallying the franchise owners against changing them. Manohar and Srinivasan were furious.

They were also concerned by the almost daily controversies that attended the league: endless rows with journalists over access to stadiums, with Hindu nationalists over the cheerleaders' scanty dress, and so on. No one at the BCCI was shy of an argument. But Modi seemed to go out of his way to create them. 'Controversy was always something I wanted in the IPL,' he told me. 'You look at England and football – players having girlfriends all over the place, having affairs. People are interested, some people find it aspirational. Some may disapprove of it, but it still gets their attention, they're still reading about it.' That was all very well, but the endless controversy was becoming compromising. Ahead of the third IPL season India's tax authorities declared they were reviewing the BCCI's charitable status. They had the temerity to suggest that the cricket board was, in fact, a commercial operation.

By the time IPL3 began in March 2010, Modi was running out of friends. He was also engulfed in a new scandal, which grew bigger by the day. It started at an auction of the two new franchises, in Mumbai, just a few days before the season began. As the deadline for bidding passed, the sale appeared to have been completed: only two bids had been lodged. Yet Manohar suddenly cancelled the auction. He would later suggest it had been rigged. Modi denied it. Yet some queried the unusually stringent conditions he had imposed on the bidding process: including a stipulation that any bidder must have collateral of a billion dollars. That had put paid to a lot of other potential bidders – leaving only two in the running: a consortium led by Videocon, a Pune-based electronic company, in which Pawar was alleged to have an interest, and a Gujarati conglomerate, the Adani Group, which was linked to Pawar's sidekick, Praful Patel. (Both politicians denied having had any involvement in the bids.)

A fresh auction was held two weeks later in Chennai, without the stringent conditions, and this time Videocon and Adani lost out. The biggest bids were made by the Sahara Group, another giant conglomerate, with financial services and other interests, which bid $370 million for a franchise in Pune; and a consortium called Rendezvous, made up of several Maharashtrian and Gujarati business families, which bid $333 million to own a franchise in the Keralan city of Kochi. These two bids almost matched the total cost of the existing eight IPL teams only two years before.

Facing the cameras, Modi declared himself proud that the IPL was 'on the upswing'. Yet the results of the auction were unexpected, and privately Modi was rumoured to be in a panic. As he opened the winning bids, one of those present, who was no friend to Modi, claimed to have heard him turn to Manohar and mutter: '*Margaye, boss!*' 'I'm dead!'

The third IPL season was by this time rattling along. Ratings were strong and the quality of the cricket had improved. But behind the scenes the tournament was in turmoil. The investors in Rendezvous accused Modi of dragging his heels on finalising their franchise agreement, while trying to force them to withdraw their winning bid. Satyajit Gaekwad, a former Congress MP related to one of them, later alleged that Modi had offered them $50 million to 'just quit the game and get out'. Even by Indian standards of corruption, that sounded a bit improbable. Modi strenuously denied the allegation and threatened to bring legal proceedings over it. Yet it added to an impression that something was going seriously awry.

Rendezvous clung on nonetheless, seeking the protection of senior figures in the Congress party, including their mentor, Shashi Tharoor, an urbane Keralan politician, junior foreign minister and novelist. He was an unusual Indian politician. A former UN diplomat, who had been elected to parliament the previous year, Tharoor was an intellectual and genuine cricket lover. He had been instrumental in steering the Rendezvous investors to Kerala, a state mainly associated with football. And he now steeled them to resist the pressure they claimed Modi was subjecting them to. Manohar, impatient with the stand-off, ordered Modi to sign off on the franchise agreement. But an hour after he had done so, Modi hit back in a series of inflammatory messages on Twitter.

'Who are the shareholders of Rendezvous? And why have they given this hundreds of million dollars bonanza?' he asked, and then answered the question himself by tweeting a list of the franchise's shareholders. Among them was a Kashmiri woman, Sundanda Pushkar, who stood to own 4.7 per cent of the franchise, which she had been given as 'free equity', or rights convertible into shares. She was also known on the Delhi cocktail circuit as Tharoor's girlfriend.

Pressed by a Twitter follower for further details of this, Modi tweeted, 'a big? I was told by him [meaning Tharoor] not to get into who owns Rendezvous. Specially Sundanda Pushkar. Why? The same has been minuted in my records.'

There are tacit rules to India's complicated corporate sector, and Modi had just breached one. He had declared war on a government minister. Three days later tax inspectors descended on the IPL's offices in Mumbai and Modi's suite at the Four Seasons. In parliament the BJP opposition was meanwhile howling for Tharoor's head. So were many in his own party. Effete and self-delighting, Tharoor had upset many in Congress with his frequent mockery for the mucky business of Indian politics. And now he appeared as venal as the next elected Indian. He protested himself innocent and his girlfriend, Pushkar, renounced her equity in the Kochi franchise. But Tharoor was not widely believed and, on the order of Sonia Gandhi, was forced to resign from the government.

Having lost its minister, Congress sought revenge. The day after Tharoor's resignation, the *Times of India* splashed on the details of a confidential tax report into Modi, which had been leaked to its reporter by a senior figure in Congress. 'Mr Lalit Modi,' the report began, 'has had a trail of failed ventures and defaults till four years back but has a lifestyle now that includes a private jet, a luxury yacht and a fleet of Mercedes S Class and BMW cars all acquired in the last three years.' The report also claimed that Modi held stakes in three IPL teams: Rajasthan Royals, Kings XI Punjab and Kolkata Knight Riders. It further alleged that he was 'deeply embroiled in both generations of black money, money laundering, betting in cricket (match-fixing of certain IPL matches).'

'IPL has turned out to be a huge scam,' declared a senior BJP politician, Yaswant Sinha, as more inspectors descended on the league. The offices of Multi Screen Media, World Sports Group, and three IPL franchises were all searched. So were those of India Cements, Srinivasan's company, and, again, the offices of the IPL and BCCI.

The officers of the BCCI were deeply alarmed. They feared the board had been dishonoured. They also feared its monopoly over the affairs of Indian cricket was at risk. On the last night of the IPL season, 25 April 2010, Srinivasan's Super Kings beat Mumbai Indians to win the third IPL. Minutes after the game ended, Modi was suspended for 'alleged acts of individual misdemeanours'.

The following day, Manohar spelt out the charges against him. In thinly veiled language, the board accused Modi of involvement in a possible effort to rig the aborted franchise auction, of allowing irregularities in the ownership arrangements of the IPL franchises part-owned by his relatives, and also referred to allegations that a kickback, of anything up to $80 million, had been paid by Multi Screen Media during the renegotiation of TV rights. What is more, Manohar sniffed, the board objected to Modi's 'behavioural pattern'.

At least some of this sounded like bluster. That Modi's relatives held stakes in the Rajasthan and Punjab franchises was well known, and their ownership pattern looked unremarkable. It would also emerge that the board had had more oversight of Modi's operations than Manohar let on: Srinivasan, not Modi, had been signing the IPL's cheques. In a subsequent attack on Srinivasan, Modi would claim to have fixed the IPL's second player auction so as to ensure the England all-rounder Andrew Flintoff went to his team, as indeed he did, for $1.55 million. (Srinivasan denied the allegation, which he said lacked 'substance or truth'.) But with the board against him, Modi was toast.

In fact, the allegations against him kept multiplying. In an email dripping with venom, the boss of the England cricket board, Giles Clarke, wrote to the BCCI to accuse Modi of plotting 'to destroy world cricket's structure and especially that in England, and create a new league.' He referred to a lunch held in Delhi between Modi and the bosses of three of the biggest English counties, Lancashire, Yorkshire and Warwickshire, at which Modi was alleged to have discussed plans to expand the IPL to England.

This would create further clashes with the international calendar. Yet Stewart Regan, the Yorkshire chief executive, wrote, 'Modi believes that most star players would take the money rather than spend months playing county/state or indeed Test cricket. Indeed, if he wanted he could even launch IPL Tests & ODIs.' That really would be changing the world order. Modi subsequently sued Clarke; the matter was settled, confidentially, out of court.

Still Modi tried to cling on. His lawyers produced a 160-page defence, backed by 15,000 pages of supporting documentation. He challenged his suspension in the high court, then in the Supreme Court. Few honorary positions can have been fought over more fiercely, or expensively. But

Modi, whatever the merits of the charges against him, had offended or alarmed too many people. Pursued by the establishment, he had run out of friends. 'If somebody has committed some mistake,' said his former Pawar, sadly, 'he will have to face the music.'

In September 2010 the board finally managed to sack Modi. It then sought to purge his influence from the IPL. The generous retainers paid to the governing council members were scrapped. So were the Rajasthan and Punjab franchises, leading to another protracted legal battle, from which the teams would emerge victorious. The board also withdrew the longstanding corruption charges against its former supremo, Jagmohan Dalmiya, thereby rehabilitating him as a member. The prospect of Modi and Dalmiya, two formidable and aggrieved Marwaris, joining forces in exile had simply been too awful to contemplate.

I met Modi in London a couple of weeks after his sacking, for two long lunches. He had already been in exile for some time, living with his wife and three children in a vast Mayfair flat, serviced by half a dozen servants that he flew out from India on rotation. He claimed to be in London for his safety, a well-known Mumbai gangster having put out a contract on his life. That didn't look good for Modi either; he said it was because he had refused to fix IPL matches.

Meanwhile, he was being investigated by the Indian government for possible tax evasion and foreign exchange transgressions. His Indian passport was about to be revoked. He was understandably glum. Diwali, the Hindu festival of lights, was approaching and Modi said this would make him miss Mumbai all the more. 'I've never spent a single Diwali outside India,' he said bitterly. 'It's a 24/7 witch-hunt. This has never happened to anyone in the history of India, not even to a hardened terrorist who wants to blow up the country.'

Modi's brittleness, his lurking volatility, was always evident. He was unrelaxing company. But he was polite, even amiable, and straightforward in a way. It had not been easy to persuade him to meet me and, at a delicate time, I had half-assumed he would go back on that promise. But he did not – and Modi was also known for this. When he said he would do something, he usually kept his word.

Wary though I was of him, it was hard not to be impressed by the IPL's creator. Not many could have done what he had done. Even his vanity seemed somehow heroic. 'At the end of the day charges have been thrown up. And you know, as far as I'm concerned I want to take this to its logical conclusion,' Modi said. 'It's very important to me to clear my name. The truth will prevail.

'It's not that the truth can't prevail … if they had anything that could pin me down, anywhere, they'd have put it in the public domain by now.

'I mean, every agency is investigating and they haven't got anything. The trail's run dry. Obviously the trail's run dry … because there isn't anything. And at the end of the day there's going to be a public backlash.'

But there was no sign of that. Modi had changed cricket. At one time he had seemed almost to rule it. But now he was gone, at least for a while, and he would not be missed.

CHAPTER EIGHT

With the Daredevils

A couple of days before the start of the fourth Indian Premier League season, I drove through the gates of the Roshanara Cricket Club, a tree-girdled refuge from the noise and exhaust fumes of north Delhi. It was one of India's great cricket venues: the Roshanara was the scene of the meeting in 1927 between Arthur Gilligan and the Maharaja of Patiala, which hastened India's arrival as a Test-playing nation.

Five years later, shortly before the Indian side embarked on its inaugural Test tour, the ground hosted a dramatic contest between the club and a Viceroy's XI. It demonstrated where cricketing power lay in India at the time. The teams fielded eight Indian princes between them, including two England Test players, Duleepsinhji, who scored an elegant 173, and the Nawab of Pataudi (senior) who took six wickets in the second innings. But the most remarkable performance was from the Maharaja of Porbandar, soon to be unveiled as India's captain. On his first-class debut, he scored 22, his career-best score.

The Roshanara is now frequented by a sort of north Delhi nouveau riche, so less exalted. Its small colonial-era clubhouse has been clumsily extended, at the cost of its former elegance. Inside it is cluttered with ugly furniture and rubbishy prints of 19th-century London. As I walked through, making for the cricket pitch that the clubhouse backed on to, it was deserted save for a couple of skinny waiters lazily flicking cloths at drink-stained tabletops.

Yet outside, on the Roshanara's historic ground, there was cricket being played. In the furnace heat of an April morning, the Delhi Daredevils, gym-honed men in coloured T-shirts and fluorescent vests, were playing a last practice match ahead of the new IPL season.

The South African Morne Morkel was running in to bowl. With his long torso upright and his legs a-whirr, he looked like a cartoon character going at full pelt. Yet he was an imposing sight. Moving through his simple, brutal action, Morkel hurled the ball – much, much faster than television can ever suggest – at the Australian James Hopes, who dabbed it into the off side and ambled through for a run. The practice proceeded at this leisurely half-pace, a bloodless display of high-class cricket skills. Clapping and encouraging one another, the fielders then jogged into new fielding positions, and Irfan Pathan took the ball.

This would be a big tournament for Irfan. At the age of 26, India's most promising all-rounder since Kapil Dev was suffering a mid-career crisis. Beset by injuries and poor form, he had not played a Test match for three years or any cricket for a year. It was a long time since he had been celebrated for his curving in-swingers and carefree hitting. Irfan was more likely to be written about these days for his bad back or his Hindu girlfriend. Yet despite his troubles, he had just been handed a three-year contract by the Daredevils worth $1.9 million a year.

To see him bowl, that looked like a gamble. Irfan was running in hard but he was not bowling at all fast and his control was woeful. He was spraying the ball all over the place. His fellow Daredevils, mostly young Indians on a fraction of his wages, clapped and shouted encouragement after each wild delivery. But Irfan looked embarrassingly bad.

This would be a big year for the IPL too. Following its shift to South Africa in 2009 and the turbulence of 2010, its investors were anxious to see stability and profits. That was a realistic prospect; Multi Screen Media was already predicting a 20 per cent increase in IPL advertising revenues. Yet there were also some fresh doubts about the tournament.

The 2011 World Cup had ended only a few days before and many wondered whether Indian cricket fans, exhausted by the patriotic fervour occasioned by India's victory, could be bothered to watch Kolkata Knight Riders against Chennai Super Kings. The absence of the IPL's Svengali, Lalit Modi, was another worry. He was still in London, fighting his many lawsuits and demanding the return of his passport, and it was unclear how the tournament would manage without him.

The Rajasthan and Punjab teams had won a reprieve from the courts. But the cricket board was still trying to erase Modi's fingerprints from the IPL. It had declared that there would be no more cricketainment.

The IPL Nights parties and contract with Colors had been cancelled. There were even rumours that skimpily dressed cheerleaders would be banned. From now on, the BCCI declared loftily, the tournament would be all about cricket. That was a big worry for its investors – because cricket had never been the point of the IPL.

The turmoil had highlighted how vulnerable the franchise-holders were to the vagaries of the board. They had much less power than their counterparts in American basketball or English football. But it was also clear that they were not willing to be pushed around. The IPL team-owners were not weak and cash-strapped like the foreign cricket boards the BCCI was accustomed to bullying. They were some of the richest and most formidable people in India.

'The BCCI is the most powerful cricket body. It dictates what happens in world cricket,' I had been told by P.B. Vanchi, the boss of GMR Sports, which owned the Daredevils. 'But what the BCCI has to realise is that the franchises are run by people who are very relevant in this country. We are major businesses, nation-builders, you can say. We have more than influence. We understand how to respect others and how to get respect from others.'

That sounded like a challenge. And certainly no one could doubt the influence of Vanchi's big boss, G.M. Rao, GMR's founder. Until the early 1980s, he had been a small-time jute-miller in the south Indian state of Andhra Pradesh. Yet as India's economic growth began to accelerate, Rao saw that demand for infrastructure – power stations, roads and airports – would follow. Such things were controlled by the government and Rao had proved exceptionally adept at winning contracts to build them. He was charming, astute and generous. He knew what made politicians tick. With these skills, Rao had developed one of India's biggest firms, with assets valued at $5 billion.

Set against GMR's main business, the Daredevils were a mere bauble. Rao had been persuaded to buy the team by a cricket-loving son. Yet owning an IPL team in Delhi also fitted well with his wider business strategy. He had bought the Delhi franchise for a relatively cut-price $84 million. According to Vanchi, this was because other bidders had been put off by Delhi's nasty, politicised environment. 'They were afraid of dealing with the politicians, they were afraid of dealing with the Delhi police,' he said. But access to Delhi's powerful politicians was something

GMR actually wanted. It was in the process of building a $3 billion international airport in the city, a task that demanded dozens of permits and good relations with unions, police and other civil authorities – and therefore strong political support.

'Let me tell you,' said Vanchi, when we had met in Bangalore, at the pre-season player auction. 'In Delhi I have the opportunity to invite powerful people as our guests. One of the days we get the Sonia Gandhi family into the stadium. Every day we invite six or seven cabinet ministers and their families to the match, and they all love it! Everybody in the Delhi knows the Daredevils are GMR. Through that they know that GMR owns the airport and also owns the Delhi Daredevils. Access to cricket is a big value in India.'

The cricket team was also starting to look like a decent business in its own right. After three IPL seasons, GMR claimed to be around $15 million out of pocket on its investment, including the annual repayments of its franchise fee. That was less than half the losses of some other team-owners.

'The young boys of Delhi carry the maximum money in their pocket – their ability to spend money, I tell you, it's amazing,' said Vanchi, unburdening himself after a long day buying cricketers. 'I have a bigger demand for a 25,000 ticket than a fucking 5,000 rupee ticket. So I raise the price and then they want to know, "Is there anything more expensive than that?" That's the Delhi market. My most expensive tickets get sold three months in advance.'

This was the upside of operating in India's flash, prosperous capital. But there was a downside, which Vanchi, a native of slower-moving, civilised Chennai, was finding hard to get used to. 'Delhi people will be nice to you one day, and the next they will kick you in the back,' he said bitterly. 'Delhi has no heart. Delhi has no head. Delhi only has physique. You know, people think that as you go south, India gets narrower, but it's totally the opposite in a way. As you move south, India is far more entrepreneurial, far more broadminded. Today I can't buy the loyalty of people in Delhi, I just cannot. What they want to know is, "What is there for me?"'

He was tired and sounded overwrought. 'I've never loved Delhi,' said the boss of the Delhi Daredevils. 'The people in Delhi are never warm. They have a tendency to display their wealth and they're cut-throats. They're like, "money, money, money". Everything is money.'

'And how are you finding building a fan-base?' I asked.

'Building a fan-base in Delhi is very difficult because there is no factor like loyalty in Delhi,' he said glumly. 'There are only interests.'

After Irfan finished his spell, I walked slowly around the Roshanara boundary, pacing myself against the heat, to where the Daredevils' CEO Amrit Mathur, was sitting. At around 35°C, it was very hot, but in the invigorating way of early summer. It was still bearable by Delhi standards. The sky retained a hint of blue. It was not yet washed-out summertime grey.

I paused to watch Irfan jog to the boundary for some water. He looked superbly fit, with muscles bulging through his sopping blue shirt. Tossing back the empty plastic bottle to a servant, he said '*dhanyavad*', a Hindi word for 'thank you' that Delhi wallahs use sparingly. Then he jogged bravely back out to the wicket.

Amrit was sitting under an umbrella, watching the play. He waved cheerily as I approached and urged me to get into the shade. A dapper middle-aged man, wearing a pair of sporty blue sunglasses, Amrit was considered one of the good guys in Indian cricket. A former senior civil servant in the India railways, he had run its cricket operations for over a decade, while also being known as an unusually competent officer of the BCCI. That was why Modi had hired him, back in 1995, to draft a blueprint for his putative Indian Cricket League.

Amrit had also attended the momentous 2003 tour of Pakistan, as the Indian team's media manager. When I had called him up and asked if I could follow him and the Daredevils through the forthcoming season, he had said it would be his pleasure.

There were two important issues I wanted to resolve during the season. I wanted to decide, on the basis of a careful look at the IPL, whether it was actually any good. Its standards of play had clearly improved, especially the batting, which – as in T20 generally – was becoming ever more inventive. The IPL's standard of fielding, a big weakness in the opening seasons, had also got better, which perhaps suggested the tournament had raised the basic skills in Indian cricket. But did this make the IPL a proper sporting contest?

Until around about the inaugural T20 World Cup, in 2007, few international players had taken the shortest format very seriously. 'Hit and giggle' is what some called it. But now, chiefly because of the IPL, it was the game's most lucrative format. A top Australian player such as Shane Watson, who was in demand for all formats, should soon expect to have to play T20 for four months each year: including two months in the IPL, six weeks in Australia's Big Bash League, two weeks in the Champions League, plus a couple of weeks of international T20 games.

This deluge of T20 had not come at much cost to Test or one-day cricket yet. To maximise profits, the game's administrators had simply squeezed T20 games into an already packed cricket calendar. But if T20 expanded further, both Test and one-day schedules would have to be cut back. And this looked almost inevitable. The BCCI had already demonstrated its willingness to expand the IPL in search of ever-greater profits.

Thus the addition of the new Pune and Kochi teams this IPL season, which meant there would be 72 games, up from 60. And the board was also coming under increasing pressure from the franchise-owners to increase the duration of the tournament. That was not so much because they wanted to play more cricket. It was because they wanted more access to their star players, to help them sell sponsorship and advertising packages. Hence the second issue I wanted to resolve. Whatever the IPL was worth, I wanted to know whether, despite its recent upheavals and the faddishness of the Indian cricket fan, the tournament was here to stay. There was probably no bigger question in cricket.

Amrit also had doubts about the league, though not about whether it was any good. No one making his bread from the IPL could afford such thoughts. He was concerned about the viability of the IPL's business model, especially given most of the teams' failures to build reliable fan-bases. The Daredevils, despite having done fairly well on the field in previous seasons, had not recruited many loyal fans, as Vanchi had intimated. Cricket's roots are not deep in Delhi, nor is there much sense of civic pride in the city. In 2007 the Daredevils had launched a fan club with the aim of recruiting 100,000 members within a year. But after three years it had only 25,000 members, and had been closed down.

This mattered because, as the franchises' share of television and other central revenues decreased, the teams would be increasingly reliant on merchandising and local advertising to make money. Lacking a loyal support-base would make this much harder. In the absence of many committed fans, the Daredevils were meanwhile relying on their main celebrity cricketer, Virender Sehwag, to draw a crowd. A local Delhi wallah, he had played for the team since the league's inception, and Amrit said it was impossible to stress how valuable this had been: 'People come to the ground because Sehwag is playing, not to support the team.'

GMR had therefore made sure to retain him for this season, despite there having been a compulsory clear-out of the IPL squads at the end of the previous one. This was intended to give the two new franchises an equal opportunity to hire good players. To retain a player, the franchises had had to pay him a generous increment; the Daredevils were paying Sehwag around $2.2 million a season. Mumbai Indians had similarly retained Tendulkar, on a rumoured salary of $4 million. Dhoni had been kept on at Chennai Super Kings, for around $3 million. Most other players had been thrown back into the player auction in Bangalore, much to the annoyance of the eight original franchises. 'Let's just say it doesn't help to build team loyalty when you lose your team,' Amrit said delicately.

He hoped he had got a good new squad. It was hard to be sure. T20 was still comparatively new and it was not yet clear what a winning formula looked like. In India, spinners and really fast bowlers (like Morkel) had been most effective. Yet there remained a suspicion that T20 was so unpredictable that picking a successful team was something of a lottery. Nonetheless, there were reasons to fear for new Daredevils. The franchise had hired no really top batsman to support Sehwag and the hard-hitting Australian David Warner, who it had also retained. It also had no top-class spinner and looked to have paid too much for some second-grade Indians, Irfan included. Amrit acknowledged that he had been expensive. 'But we wanted a top Indian all-rounder, which left us little choice,' he said. 'There's a major shortage of them.'

As one of India's most photogenic stars, Irfan brought more to the squad than cricket skills. This was good news for the team's sponsors. 'It's not that the sponsor tells us who to go out and buy,' said Amrit. 'But, of course, we understand who has got commercial appeal ...' Sehwag and Irfan featured on almost all the Daredevils' billboards that were then going up around Delhi. There was no sign of Morkel, who had been hired to take wickets not to sell shirts.

While we chatted, the practice was ending. The new-look Daredevils congregated on the wicket to shake hands and exchange high-fives. As in every franchise, the international players, Indian and foreign, had only met up with the squad in the past week, which made forging a team spirit hard. Some of the franchises were therefore trying to accelerate the bonding process. The Rajasthan Royals, under the direction of their in-house psychologist Jeremy Snape, were playing at being Rajput warriors, with real elephants for props. Nita Ambani, wife of the Mumbai Indians' proprietor, had a habit of delivering windy pep talks to her team, focusing on her family's business success. The Indian press wrote a lot about Nita's talismanic effect on her cricketers, and she was said to believe what it wrote.

But there was little evidence of team spirit in the IPL. Teams that went on losing streaks often collapsed, as Punjab had done the previous year, and KKR always did. The Royals, who had played consistently above the sum of their talents, were the exception: probably more because of their captain, Shane Warne, than the elephants.

I watched the new Daredevils troop in for lunch. They left the wicket in a tight huddle, but by the time they reached the boundary line they had hived off into three distinct groups: first came the Indian team players, Sehwag, Irfan and Ajit Agarkar; then the foreigners, Morkel, Hopes, Travis Birt and Aaron Finch; then a gaggle of lesser Indian players, traipsing diffidently in behind them.

Four days later I turned up at the Feroz Shah Kotla to watch the Daredevils' curtain-raiser against Mumbai Indians. It was an evening game, and the streets outside the stadium were hot, dark and snarled up with hooting traffic. The dark outline of the Kotla loomed above, shining a beacon of silver neon light into a starless sky.

Having not yet received my press pass, I had begged a ticket for the game from a contact at IMG. It gave me access to a VIP box on the third tier of the stadium, which had been reserved for the Delhi District Cricket Association. Its glass wall provided a fine view of the stadium, which was decked in the Daredevils' blue and red colours, and heaving with 30,000 tamasha-seekers.

A thunder of dance music and cheering vibrated through the glass as Tendulkar led the Mumbai Indians on to the field. GMR's marketers had attempted to bill the Indians as the Daredevils' great foe – because if the Daredevils were to become a proper sports club they would need a grudge rival, and the Mumbai team were an obvious candidate. But for most spectators the game was primarily an opportunity to see Sachin.

The VIP box was seriously overcrowded with friends and relatives of the DDCA. It was going to make the game hard to watch. A crowd of overweight children lined the window, almost blocking out the view. No one else seemed to mind much, however. Perhaps they were already thinking of supper, as a delicious scent of garlic and masalas wafted around the room. Next to me sat a high court judge's bodyguard, with a pistol sticking out of his waistband. 'Sachin-bhai!' he murmured, as the Mumbai Indians captain directed his fielders. He sounded unsure, as I was, whether we were inside the stadium or not.

Craning to see over the children's heads, I watched the game begin. Two World Cup winners were straight into the action: Harbhajan Singh was bowling to Sehwag, who hit his fourth ball for a 'DLF maximum'. The crowd roared, giant speakers thundered out a snatch of the Daredevils' anthem *Khelo front foot pe!* ('Play on the front foot!') The word 'Monstrous!' flashed up on the Kotla's giant television screen. Then the Delhi crowd resumed chanting Sachin's name.

Their hero responded by running out Sehwag with a smart throw from fine leg, where a giant red and white advertisement for Karbonn mobile phones had been painted on to the pitch. The crowd roared, either in exultation or in disappointment. And it continued roaring as Mumbai's best bowler, the Sri Lankan slinger Lasith Malinga, cut through the Daredevils. He took five wickets in three overs, including four clean-bowled with his trademark yorkers. The Daredevils were all out for 95, a wretched score. Yet it was impossible to know whether the churning, hollering crowd was happy or sad.

This was not merely a case of 'bad strokes cheered just as lustily as good strokes,' as Neville Cardus wrote sniffily of the Lancashire leagues. From the muffled detachment of the VIP freeloaders' box, the crowd seemed to be cheering anything that moved. It screamed when runs were scored, when wickets fell or the Daredevils' cheerleaders – Eastern Europeans in hot pants – waggled their pompoms. It yelled when Tendulkar's face flashed up on a giant TV screen. It cheered the Mumbai Indians' owners, Mukesh and Nita Ambani, when they flashed up, looking rather shy. They were perched on an enormous pitch-side sofa and obviously trying hard not to look at the cameras. Arun Jaitley, the Delhi cricket association's BJP boss and his Congressman sidekick, Rajeev Shukla, had managed to squeeze themselves on to the sofa alongside them. They probably thought the crowd was cheering them.

The Mumbai Indians knocked off the Daredevils' runs for the loss of only two wickets: the result of the game was never in doubt. Tendulkar, batting through the innings, made 46 not out, including a six that raised the biggest cheer of the night. Irfan, in his first game for a year, had a miserable evening. He was run out for a duck and bowled only 2.5 overs, including the last ball of the match, which Tendulkar hit for four. It really was a rotten game.

I had quite enjoyed it, though. It was wonderful to see Malinga, with his eccentric brilliance. And the sight of the heaving Kotla was thrilling. But as a contest the game was a non-event, as T20 games often are. The outcome was decided inside the first seven overs, when the Daredevils lost four wickets. There is usually no coming back from such a start in T20, so everything that followed was predictable. This would be a dismal feature of the season: too few of the nail-biting finishes on which the format depends for most of its drama.

The problem with T20 is not, as some purists gripe, that it is not cricket. It is absolutely cricket. It is played on the same pitch, with the same implements, and features many of the same batting strokes, bowling deliveries and fielding positions as any other form of the game. The best cricketers, like Tendulkar or Sehwag, usually excel at it. As the closest thing to street-cricket – the hit-it-or-get-out games that millions of Indian children play – T20, you might even argue, is somehow *real* cricket. But this does not make it very good.

T20 cricketers are certainly skilful. 'Some of the things the younger batsmen are trying out, it just amazes me,' Adam Gilchrist, captain of Kings XI Punjab, told me. But the thrill of big-hitting palls in the absence of an interesting contest. 'T20 is like a porn movie,' W.V. Raman, a former India batsman, put it to me, 'I mean, it's OK for a bit, but how long can you watch the bonking?'

A bigger problem, even in a tight run-chase, is the lack of much serious competition between bat and ball, which is the fundamental drama of cricket. It is almost always primarily a batsman's game, and in India especially, but T20 grossly exaggerates that bias. The shortness of the game, the miserly allotment of only four overs per bowler, small boundaries and flat pitches: the conditions in which T20 is played are designed to maximise hitting. T20 bowlers are cannon fodder – even Malinga is. For all his wicket-taking prowess in the IPL, the Sri Lankan still concedes seven runs per T20 over.

Thus slapped about, T20 bowlers cannot build pressure, which kills their craft. In T20 a bowler has no time to soften a batsman up with bouncers or a carefully chosen arrangement of deliveries. Against a snorting, risk-oblivious T20 batsman, most of these balls could get hit for six. In T20 any hittable ball is therefore a bad ball, including the traditional length-and-line deliveries that are the basis of bowling skills.

Another big problem with T20, wherever it is played, is how little it ever really matters. High-risk batting is, in a way, not risky at all, because it comes with an appreciation that, at any moment, the batsman is liable to get out. So he cannot really be blamed when he does. Compared to other cricket formats, it seems to me, batsmen in T20 tend not to look very upset as they trudge back to the pavilion. Their only serious crime would be not to attack: so long as a batsman is out swiping, he has more or less done his job. This makes T20, for all its speed and noise, fatefully bathetic. Ashis Nandy, India's obtuse cricket theorist, had it right: compared to traditional forms of cricket, T20 is a debasement.

I asked Gilchrist how it compared to Test cricket. A thoughtful man, he paused to reflect on the question, imparting a sense that he wanted to get this one absolutely right. 'There's just nothing so exhilarating, so exciting, so physically and mentally challenging as Test match cricket,' he said, sitting in his cherry-and-silver Kings XI kit, on the other side of a restaurant table.

'Look ...' he said, and paused again, slightly awkwardly. 'I don't want to get too carried away here ...'

'Go on.'

'Well look, Test match cricket is a five-day game. Think about that, five days of sport! To be able to look across at your team-mate at the end of that, to know you've planned for it, fought it out, gone through so much together, knife-edge twists and turns in the game, being physically exhausted on day three, so mentally exhausted on day four that you struggle to get up in the morning, and then hopefully, you know, you come out on top. It's just very, very hard to describe how great that is.'

'And how's T20?'

'Ah, it's a good game,' Gilchrist said.

I was often surprised, reading over the notes I took during half a dozen Delhi Daredevils games, by how exciting I found them at the time. I hadn't quite remembered that, because the thrill of T20 is in the moment. And as soon as it becomes clear who will win – sometimes very early on in the game – the moment is past.

Filing out of the Kotla, after the Daredevils had received their first hiding of the season, the crowd seemed happy and calm. No one seemed angry, rowdy or, by hard-living Delhi standards, terribly drunk. But nor was anyone within earshot discussing the game. It was already gone and forgotten.

The Daredevils' second match, in Jaipur against the Rajasthan Royals, went almost as badly as the first had. Sehwag got out early, and the rest of the batting collapsed. The Daredevils' final score, 151, looked just about competitive; but the Royals passed it with ease. Rahul Dravid, who had been snapped up cheaply by the Royals after being ditched by Bangalore, top-scored with 38, including an on-driven six off Irfan of unforgettable elegance. Irfan got smashed, going for 32 runs in three overs.

I showed up the next day at Jaipur's Sawai Mansingh Stadium, home of the Royals. It was being prepared for their next game, against Kolkata Knight Riders, and was in a state of chaos. The Royals' British CEO, Sean Morris, a former Hampshire cricketer, was looking hot and angry, battling workmen, policemen and officers of the Rajasthan Cricket Association. The main row concerned a temporary VIP stand he was having built for the Royals owners, including the film star Shilpa Shetty. Naturally, the officials also wanted bum-space on it. 'Just wait till tomorrow,' Morris growled as he strode past. 'It's going to be the biggest bloody fight you've ever seen.'

I walked out on to the lush green outfield, enjoying the feel of its spiky turf underfoot. The match wicket, into which the stumps had already been sunk, had a glistening brown patina of polished mud. A policeman was guarding it, slouched behind the stumps like a drowsy umpire.

In the covers, some workmen were touching up an advertisement for Karbonn mobile phones, slapping red paint on to the grass. Their bare legs were stained bright red from the knee down: from a distance they appeared to be morphing out of the ad. I wandered over to talk to them, which proved difficult. They were Bengali sign-painters, it turned out, who migrated to Jaipur for the duration of each IPL season. They spoke no English, little Hindi and, over 1,000 miles from home in humid Kolkata, were almost as foreign to Rajasthan as I was. They complained about its dry desert heat; yet seemed happy enough. They were earning 500 rupees a day for painting the cricket pitch, more than double what they earned in Kolkata.

I had come to the stadium looking for another migrant, the Royals' captain Shane Warne. Tendulkar notwithstanding, he was the most influential cricketer in the IPL. After taking 1,000 wickets for Australia, Warne was now aged 41 and otherwise retired, living the life of a globetrotting celebrity. A fixture on British and Australian chat shows, he also did a bit of cricket commentary, played competitive poker and had a reputation for chasing glamorous women – all successfully. Anything competitive Warne put his mind too, he usually came off best.

Even now, with a stiff, middle-aged shoulder and hardly any practice, he was one of the best bowlers in the tournament. Though he had lost some of his variations and guile, he retained his near-perfect control and his greatest attacking weapon, his tremendously forceful character. Against the best international batsmen, let alone callow Indians half his age, Warne was still an intimidating presence on a cricket field. He had been too good for the Daredevils. Spot-on from his first delivery, Warne had taken two for 17 and the man of the match award. There was no more intriguing cricketer or advocate for the IPL.

We arranged to meet that evening at the team hotel, the Rambagh Palace, another former Modi haunt. As I sat waiting for him on a torch-lit veranda, listening to a Rajasthani band and the genteel chatter of European holidaymakers, I worried that I might not recognise Warne. His face had recently undergone some considerable change. Once rather pudgy, his features were now sealed in a permanent wrinkle-free spasm. He claimed not to have had Botox treatment, but no one quite believed him. Under floodlights, Warne's new face took on an unearthly sheen, the light sliding off his cheeks and making his California-perfect white teeth sparkle. It was the face of a middle-aged film star, not a cricketer, and the makeover was not appreciated by all of Warne's fans. 'The outrageous falsity of his new eyeball area raises the question of what it means to be handsome,' pondered the Australian writer Clive James. 'Surely, at any age, it must mean to look like a human being.'

But Warne turned up punctually for our interview, as no self-respecting film star would. He was wearing a blue tracksuit and carried a BlackBerry in one hand and a packet of Benson & Hedges cigarettes in the other. He introduced himself politely, almost as if people had been having trouble recognising him. But he was unmistakeably Warne, the weirdness of his new face much less acute on the softly lit veranda.

He was friendly but slightly awkward at first, a practised but not actorly celebrity. He knew I wanted his considered opinions, not just some anecdotes about his career, and maybe he was uneasy about that. Warne was a very serious man. But off the pitch, he sometimes tried hard to dispel that impression. The banter he dished out on Twitter to his celebrity pals and thousands of slavish followers was beyond inane. Yet when Warne got talking about cricket, with his enormous forcefulness and certainty, his thoughts and recollections flowed.

I congratulated him on his bowling against the Daredevils and asked how much practice he'd been putting in. 'Not too much,' he said. In fact, not really any, it turned out. Warne hadn't played a game since the previous IPL season, and his pre-season practice had consisted of bowling at a wall in Los Angeles, where he had gone to visit his girlfriend, the British model Elizabeth Hurley. 'I had a couple of sessions by myself, up a laneway, just bowling up against a wall, catching the ball, that sort of thing,' he said, lighting a cigarette. He took a long drag, exhaled and then gave a rueful smile. 'I lost a ball in someone's garden. It spun a bit, hit a bin and went over a gate. I thought I'd better not climb in and get it.' So that was how the IPL's greatest bowler trained for the tournament.

I put it to Warne that T20 wasn't up to much, but he was not having any of that. 'Not at all,' he said forcefully. 'I think it's a good game. I think it shows off real skill, it shows off fielding talent, and I think only good players will do well at it. There are a few exceptions. But most of those who do well in T20 are good cricketers.'

I said that made it sound like it wasn't cricket. But Warne wasn't having that, either.

'Captaining Twenty20 is probably the most satisfying out of any form of the game. That's because you've got no time. You're always on the clock and you can't say, "Hang on a minute, just let me figure this out." You've always got to be a couple of overs ahead of the game. Every ball's alive.' Gilchrist, I noted, had said the same.

Warne saw plenty of innovation in T20 too. 'Each year there's something new going on. In the last couple of years it's been slow balls and bouncers. Now we're going to see set plays coming into it more, like firing in the last ball of the over as a wide yorker or a bouncer maybe, to give the batsman one. That's going to frustrate the batsman who's not getting strike.'

'People have a go at Twenty20 not because it's not good,' he said. 'The problem is only that the administrators get greedy, so there's too much of it. There's also too much help for the batter, but that's a problem in all cricket, not just Twenty20. It's becoming hard work for the bowlers. You need more grass on the wicket to make it a bit more sporting. All everyone wants to see is runs: fours and sixes. I want to see contest, a real contest between bat and ball.'

'But isn't that the whole point of T20, fours and sixes?'

He shook his head. 'Having a fast bowler coming in whizzing the ball past people's ears, that's good to watch. I think the crowd likes that too. I think they like spinners bowling and someone running down the wicket to hit him for six too. And you know, cricket is all about mental. How you think, your attitude to the game, how much you want to improve, how you think about a situation. It's a bit like life really. And I think Twenty20 and the IPL has taught me a bit of, you know what? Some days I'll do well, some days I'll not do so well …'

A party of elderly Australian tourists suddenly emerged from the darkness beyond the veranda, wearing knee-length shorts and red Rajasthani turbans. 'It isn't Warnie? My God, it isn't Warnie! Warnie?' one shouted, jabbing his finger at the cricketer.

'Aussie! Aussie! Aussie! Let's hear you! Go, Aussie! Aussie, go!' he shouted, jigging up and down, with one hand on his loosely tied turban to prevent it falling off his head.

Warne gave a kind smile. 'Listen guys, we've got an interview going on here. How about I come over for a photo when we're through?'

'How often does that happen?' I asked, as the elderly tourists retreated, cackling with excitement.

'All the time,' he grimaced, reaching for his cigarettes.

I asked Warne how he thought India had changed since he had started visiting the country, 15 years before.

'People are a lot more confident now,' he said. 'They won't be pushed around. They won't get spoken down to. Where before too many Westerners maybe came here and just demanded things. In cricket or whatever, people came from all over the world and thought they were superior. They came to India and sometimes they forgot their manners.'

He was right. And it was perhaps truer of Australian and English cricketers than most visitors. Until a decade ago, few had a good word to say about India. But now you couldn't keep them away.

'These days if you speak to Indians like that ...' said Warne, tailing off. 'Look, it's financial. For cricket, full-stop, this is where the money comes from.'

'How have you found captaining Indian players?' I asked.

'Calm, you gotta be really calm here,' he said. 'Occasionally you've got to shout, if they're making the same mistakes game after game. But most of the time it's about putting your arm around them and making them feel important.'

It sounded facile but Warne was revered by his players, and not only because of how he praised them. He treated them fairly, which was not usual in India. He told a story about how, after the Royals' owners had tried to foist a well-connected player on the team, he had threatened to quit. 'I said, "Fine, it's your team, but if you do that I'm going home. I've made my decision and made the squad, and if you want to put someone in for political reasons, that's fine. But put me on the next plane back to Australia. I'm not getting involved in the politics of India and I won't have that at the Royals. Everyone's treated the same."'

Warne was said to be earning around $2 million a year from the Royals. No wonder he was so enthusiastic about the IPL. But when I asked him to compare it to Test cricket, he – like Gilchrist – suggested this was not a useful comparison. 'For me it's always about Test cricket,' said Warne. 'I don't think there are too many people who will say, "Look at him: he's a great Twenty20 player, what an unbelievable player." They'll say, "He's just a Twenty20 player."' So it was a good game then, but not that good.

After the interview ended, Warne picked up his remaining cigarettes and went over to where the Australian tourists were sitting. It had been an hour since they had interrupted us, but he had remembered his promise of a group photo. It must have made their holiday.

As I made my way towards the exit, I stopped to speak to a group of Royals players, Dravid, the Australian Shaun Tait and the New Zealander Ross Taylor, who were eating dinner together on a nearby table. It was a lovely Rajasthani evening, the fading heat of day ruffled by a desert breeze. When I finally left the hotel I saw Warne, sitting alone on the lawn, bent over his BlackBerry. Maybe he was talking to Hurley, or to his three children in Melbourne, or to his half a million followers on Twitter.

Midway through the season, the Daredevils had played seven games and lost five. The pre-season fears about the squad were looking to be justified. It was too reliant on Sehwag. He had helped win a game against Punjab with a blistering half-century, but was now struggling with an injury. And when he failed, so did the team.

The Daredevils' lack of a decent spinner was another big shortcoming, especially in away games, for which the opposition naturally arranged turning pitches. Irfan was having a terrible time. And the Daredevils' cut-price Australians, Hopes and Birt, were not putting in the match-winning performances expected of foreign cricketers. Worst of all, as defeat followed defeat, it was being said the Daredevils no longer minded losing. They had started to expect it.

This disappointment didn't seem to affect the atmosphere at the Kotla, which was packed for almost every game. That was the upside of the Delhi crowd's lack of loyalty: it didn't much mind when Delhi was losing. There was always something else to cheer. Against Kings XI Punjab, Warner, the explosive but unreliable Australian hitter, thrashed a brutal 77. Against Bangalore, the loudest cheers were for a half-century by Virat Kohli, a World-Cup winning batsman playing for the Royal Challengers; and also for a lingering embrace on the giant TV screen between Vijay Mallya's 23-year-old son Siddharth and his Bollywood girlfriend, Deepika Padukone. The crowd wasn't too fussed about Kohli's team-mate Chintu Pujara, who struggled to make seven, then hit a long-hop to midwicket. With his orthodox technique, lovingly honed on the railway ground with his father Arvind, Pujara was not much good at T20.

Against KKR, the biggest cheers by far were for Shahrukh Khan. I sat behind the boundary-side sofa where he was sitting: the crowd bombarded it throughout the game with screaming and pleading for a wave, a smile, a look. Every half-hour or so, the film star obliged, turning to flash a grin over the top of a well-plumped cushion. And the crowd went wild. Meanwhile his team were putting the Daredevils to the sword.

More often, I watched from the press box, among an unhappier crowd. There was no great enthusiasm for the IPL there. 'The only thing you have to remember is that it's complete rubbish,' a senior correspondent of *The Hindu* told me glumly. Indian newspaper journalists can be rather an insecure lot. Less well paid than TV reporters, whom they tend to despise, they protect their dignity jealously. And these cricket reporters, all deeply serious about the game, did not feel it was well served by the IPL.

All the same, few would criticise the tournament in print. That would have been considered almost unpatriotic, so closely had the league, as a great Indian creation, become associated with national success. Some newspapers were also deeply invested in the IPL, which made it hard for their journalists to cover it objectively. The *Times of India* owned internet rights to the tournament and the Deccan Chronicle owned a team. Indian sports editors were also unsure *how* to cover the IPL. Most reported it as they would a 50-over game, with pre-match reports predicting the important face-offs: Malinga versus Sehwag, Warne against Tendulkar, and so on. But that gave T20 too much respect, when Sehwag was just as likely to get out swiping at a journeymen Ranji player as to be out-thought by Malinga. Traditional match reports also seemed unsuited to the format, because no one ever really cared about yesterday's game.

In his pokey office in Connaught Place, Delhi's central business district, Amrit was starting to feel the strain. 'When the team's losing, the sponsors start losing interest, fans stop interacting with you on Facebook, the owners get upset, everyone's unhappy,' he said miserably. 'No one wants to support a losing team. You wouldn't believe some of the abusive messages we're getting on Twitter and Facebook.'

I hoped he wasn't worried for his job. Amrit had been very kind and helpful, and it wasn't his fault the Daredevils squad had been badly chosen. His troubles also extended off the pitch. The franchise relied on the Delhi cricket association for use of the Kotla and other facilities, and its officers were running Amrit ragged. Under IPL rules, the local associations were entitled to 20 per cent of the match tickets in return for allowing the franchises use of their facilities. In practice, Delhi's cricket bosses considered the figure of 20 per cent a matter for constant renegotiation. And this being Delhi, the franchise was additionally being pestered by the police, judges and the municipal government, all of whom wanted their share of match-tickets, as befitted their lofty status.

As a result, Amrit was rarely able to put more than 60 per cent of the Kotla's tickets on sale. The rest were given out as freebies. Whatever the advantages to GMR of doing business in India's capital, this was a steep tax on it. The facilities begrudgingly provided by the Delhi cricket association were also invariably filthy and broken. 'Their groundstaff are no good, their kit is not clean, their people just don't care,' Amrit moaned.

Bigger concerns about the tournament were starting to emerge. Television viewership was down 25 per cent. Audiences for Hindi soaps, which had suffered during the earlier IPL seasons, were meanwhile holding up. This was the first sign that the IPL was not fated to grow inexorably, and Amrit did nothing to hide his fears.

'I'm extremely worried about the IPL,' he said. 'It's a consumer product, and like any consumer product it needs changing and freshening up all the time. We've taken the consumers for granted. You know, we've got to be very careful about this. We don't want to end up with no one watching in the stadium, as if it's Lancashire against Sussex.'

This was already the case in Kochi. The Kochi Tuskers Kerala franchise, a controversial addition to the IPL, was in deep trouble. Its investors, a consortium of wealthy Gujarati and Maharashtrian families, had been steered to Kerala by their political protector, Shashi Tharoor. They had planned to market their team in the Arabian Gulf, among its prosperous Keralan expatriate community. But the BCCI wouldn't allow any matches to be played outside India; and with only a million or so people, Kochi was too small to support an IPL team. Besides, most of the locals preferred football.

Sensing they were in trouble, the Kochi consortium had beseeched the BCCI to let them move to Ahmedabad in Gujarat even before the season had begun. But the board had refused, and now the Tuskers' home games were playing to a half-empty stadium. Saddled with an annual cost of $33.33 million a year just to repay their franchise fee, the investors were anticipating huge losses.

Most had until recently known nothing about either Kerala or cricket: they had made their money in diamond trading, construction and manufacturing. This had been obvious when I met some of the Kochi investors at the player auction in Bangalore. 'Ah, Murali is Murali!' enthused one, Dhaval Shah, a Mumbai real estate tycoon, shortly after he had agreed to buy the great Sri Lankan bowler for $1.1 million. 'He's an off-spinner, right?'

I asked Shah whether he thought the consortium had paid too much for the franchise. A third of a billion dollars, their winning bid, seemed a little steep for something with no physical assets. But, of course, Shah said he was not remotely worried. 'Because the IPL has a bit of everything for us,' he said, 'business, cricket, fun.' I admired his insouciance.

The Kochi franchise looked doomed. Some, especially in the Kotla press box, predicted the IPL was too. Even Amrit, in his gloomier moments, seemed half-tempted by that idea. But I was pretty sure it was wrong. Even with its reduced viewership, the IPL was easily India's most popular television show. By one estimate, the Mumbai–Delhi game at the Kotla had been watched by 40 million people.

Most, I am sure, did not find the game especially 'monstrous!', but they still watched it. In fact, as the IPL entered its fourth year, I sensed many Indians were taking a more measured view of the tournament. They weren't quite so mad-keen on the IPL. But for a quiet evening at home in front of the television, it was easily entertaining enough. Strip away the hype, and the IPL was a cricket tournament that a lot of Indians considered to be quite enjoyable. Few thought it was great. It was lowest common denominator cricket. But given how many Indians like cricket, this was sufficient to make the tournament an enormous, cricket-changing success.

Yogesh Visht was perhaps a typical lukewarm IPL fan. He worked for Genpact, a big outsourcing company based in Gurgaon. I was introduced to him after asking Genpact's boss, Pramod Bhasin, to introduce me to a random sample of youngish cricket fans in his employ. Pramod, one of India's most genial and respected businessmen, said he would be delighted. He was a keen cricketer himself, a miserly left-arm spinner for Genpact's cricket team, which had just won the Royal Stag Corporate Cricket Cup (named after another of Vijay Mallya's whiskies).

Yogesh, a human resources manager, was known to his colleagues as a diehard cricket fan. A 32-year-old Brahmin, he lived with his wife, parents, four brothers, their wives and a pack of children in a large house on the edge of Gurgaon. We arranged to meet there one Sunday afternoon, to watch the Daredevils play Kochi on television.

He showed me to a smart front room with a television set and furniture still wrapped in shop plastic. The room was obviously rarely used. Yogesh and his brothers mostly watched TV in their bedrooms with their wives. Fortunately, Yogesh's wife quite liked the IPL, which he said he watched most evenings after he got home from work. That was usually around 9pm, just in time to catch the second innings of the evening game.

Yogesh took great pride in his work at Genpact. His family was prosperous; it owned three nearby houses and a couple of shops in what had been its ancestral village, before Gurgaon subsumed it. But Yogesh was the first member of the family to have been to university and to work for a Western-style company.

'Working at Genpact I've come to understand the importance of communications and standard of living,' he said. 'We definitely want to move out from this particular community.' I liked Yogesh's house a lot. It was a pleasant blend of rural and modern, comfortably modern, but with cows and buffalo nosing at the doorstep. But he seemed embarrassed by this. He wanted to move to a modern flat in the middle of Gurgaon, with better access to good schools. His parents, understandably, were resisting the idea.

Determinedly upwardly mobile, Yogesh talked about his interest in cricket as if it was another aspect of his career. His favourite player was Tendulkar, he said, 'because of his focused approach, his effort. He's been doing absolutely fine for India for 20 years. That kind of application, that energy and ability to concentrate, it can teach you a lot for your professional life also. It shows that if you put a lot of concentration on your targets, you can achieve anything.'

'And what about his batting?'

Yogesh looked briefly nonplussed. I couldn't help thinking that maybe he wasn't quite such a big cricket fan after all. It turned out that he mainly liked watching India play. 'IPL is not like watching your country playing,' he said. 'When it is your country, you have more excitement. Even Test cricket is all right, so long as Sachin or Sehwag is batting. IPL is also enjoyable, but at a different level.'

In fact, Yogesh admitted, he increasingly found himself watching Hindi soaps when he came home from work, not the IPL. He said he was starting to find the league a bit boring. And I suddenly realised that, while we had been chatting, Yogesh hadn't even switched the television on to watch the match. There was a power-cut, it turned out, and Yogesh was reluctant to turn on the back-up generator for the IPL.

The IPL wasn't the only business showing signs of a slowdown. After a tearaway year in 2010, India's growth rate was slowing. The moderation was gradual at first, and there was little reason to fear India's great economic surge was coming to an end. Yet it was surprising, and its main cause, a drop in private investment, was worrying. India's private companies were the most dynamic part of the economy, the real cheerleaders of the new India. So what was taming their animal spirits?

The coalition government, led by Congress, was part of the problem. To woo poor voters, it had been splurging on welfare payments, fuel subsidies and other blandishments. To pay for this, it had borrowed heavily from state-owned banks, crowding out private borrowing. Yet another reason for slowing investment was more dramatic, and Indian business was also to blame for it. This was the paralysing effect of a series of large corruption scandals.

The first of these was the meltdown in the IPL the previous year. But it was soon overshadowed by much bigger alleged scams. In late 2010 a government auditor accused the telecoms minister, Andimuthu Raja, of handing mobile phone licences to eight companies at 'throwaway' prices. It was estimated this had entailed a loss to the Indian treasury of $40 billion. The affair dominated Indian newspapers for weeks, sustained by a tantalising sub-scandal. The income tax department, it emerged, had been tapping the phone of a well-known Delhi lobbyist, Nira Radia, and some of its transcripts found their way into the newspapers. They suggested she had been trying to influence the government's telecoms policy. Some of India's most senior journalists were accused of assisting her. And Radia's clients included some of India's most exalted businessmen, including Ratan Tata, boss of that great Parsi company the Tata Group. Now the 'mother of all scams', as it was dubbed, seemed to have everything, a colossal theft carried out by a coterie of crooked politicians and businessmen, aided by pliant journalists. Radia and her journalist friends were not charged with any offence; Raja was forced to resign and imprisoned on corruption charges.

Like the IPL scandal, this scandal seemed deeply significant. Indian mobile telecoms were, alongside the outsourcing industry, the country's biggest industrial success story. Every month 16 million new users were signing up to the networks. That the industry appeared to be as corrupt as any other Indian sector was therefore a blow to the very notion of the dynamic new India.

Smallers scandals followed. It emerged that politicians and army officers had been grabbing apartments in Mumbai built for war widows – forcing the Congress chief minister of Maharashtra to resign. A luxury new town near Mumbai, it was then alleged, was being partly built on land acquired from the government at a knockdown price. This season of scams, as the newspapers called it, invited some uncomfortable national introspection. Indians had invested great pride in their buccaneering private companies – or 'Indian Inc.', as the newspapers called them. They looked to them to improve on the lamentable performance of India's corrupt government. That is why they were seen in such a patriotic light, as national champions, delivering the growth that would raise India from the Third World. But the telecoms and many lesser scandals, also in mining, construction and even the revered IT industry, made it seem as if Indian business and government were not in contrast to each other, but in bed together.

Was India becoming an oligarchy, a democracy stage-managed by a corrupt super-elite? India's growth spurt, it was becoming clear, had shaken up Indian business far less than many had been expected. About three-quarters of India's GDP was controlled either by the state or by family-run firms that predated the economic reforms of 1991 (including among them about half the IPL's team-owners).

Hounded by the media, the government was gripped by uncertainty. Senior officials, the traditional agents of high-level corruption, began asking their political masters for every order in writing. India's administration was paralysed by the controversy. The daily business of granting licences and clearances, to allow businesses to make investments, was not getting done. No longer greased by corruption, the wheels of the Indian state were grinding to a halt.

Anti-corruption protests flared in many Indian cities. The most important, led by an aging Gandhian called Anna Hazare, took place in early April 2011, at an 18th-century observatory in central Delhi called Jantar Mantar. As the new-look Daredevils were meeting up at the Roshanara ground, Hazare, lying on a small dais at the observatory, launched a 'fast unto death'. It was intended to force the government to adopt a new anti-corruption law.

The scene at Jantar Mantar was so archetypally Indian it felt like a film set. Gathered around the simple charpoy where Hazare lay weakly, a crowd of long-haired yogis, Gandhians in khadi, villagers in traditional dress and thousands of middle-class well-wishers had gathered to sing songs and chant slogans in support of his protest. Hazare held some eccentric views, including that officials convicted of corruption should be hanged. But in this febrile time, he had become a sainted figure in India. A thicket of television cameras pointed at his prostrate form, to provide 24-hour, India-wide coverage of his sacrifice. Behind the cameras, hawkers had set up food stalls from which, rather indelicately, a delicious smell of chana masala – a spicy hash of chick-peas and fried potatoes – wafted towards the dais.

Nothing suggests the theatricality of Indian public life so much as the fast unto death. Gandhi carried out at least half a dozen. And scores are still held, in both India and Pakistan, every year. Occasionally, they turn out grimly. An Indian poet, protesting against army atrocities in her insurgency-wracked state of Manipur, has been fasting for over a decade. She has been force-fed through a tube, by court order, throughout that time. But her case is unusual. Most political fasts are a well-understood performance. Not only does the hunger-striker not die, he or she may barely lose weight. In the pleasant confines of the Lahore high court, I once interviewed some Pakistani lawyers whose solemn undertaking to 'fast until death' amounted to skipping lunch.

But Hazare's fast, televised across India, was generating a lot of political heat. By the time I showed up, three days in, it was easily the country's biggest news story. Sympathy fasts and candle-lit vigils were being held in many cities. Bollywood stars and Kapil Dev had declared their support for Hazare.

The Congress-led government implored him to eat but, lying wan and hungry on his string-bed, he denounced it. Hazare objected especially to the fact that Sharad Pawar was sitting on a high-level anti-corruption committee. Pawar promptly resigned from it, but Hazare was unimpressed. 'If one Pawar goes, another will come,' he said.

In a roped-off area beside the dais, there were more hunger-strikers. They included a 24-year-old IT engineer from Chennai, who had flown up to join the protest the night before. He was called Ballaji, was very fat and looked extremely uncomfortable. 'It's my first fast unto death so I want to make sure I do it properly,' he told me, adding that he had not even touched a drop of water all day.

'But aren't you allowed to drink water?' I asked him. 'Everyone else is, even Anna Hazare. Isn't that right?' I asked the other fasters.

They nodded vigorously.

'Thank God!' said Balaji, accepting a cup of water.

I asked him why he was protesting. 'Everyone's corrupt, all of us, and it has to end,' he said. 'When I drive my car badly and get stopped, I pay a bribe. If I want a birth certificate or a copy of my school certificate, I pay a bribe. Whenever I have any sort of dealing with the government, I pay a bribe.' His father was a police inspector in Chennai and very proud of his stand, he added.

'How long do you think you can you keep it up?'

'I don't know because this is my first time,' he said enthusiastically. 'But I've taken 20 days off work.'

Like cricket matches and Bollywood dramas, political protests have their special rhythms, and this one was speeding up. A troupe of drama students, men and women wearing black kurtas and jeans, marched faux aggressively through the crowd, shouting sardonic reworkings of Bollywood lyrics. 'The country's so corrupt, socha hai?' ('... have you thought of that?') Small sub-protests were erupting in front of the television camera, with protesters shouting for world peace or free medical care. In the thick of this democratic tumult, unmoving and lost in thought, I spotted Ashis Nandy, the sociologist and cricket theorist.

He greeted me warmly and, unasked, gave voice to his reflections. 'It's deeply interesting. Spontaneous. There's a mythic subconscious here that has lasted for thousands of years, a tradition of fasting and peaceful protest against cruel acts of authority. Even if the people don't know it, the myth lives within them.'

I asked the professor if he had enjoyed the recently concluded World Cup and his pensive expression unfolded into one of pure joy. 'Yes indeed. I watched it in Australia of all places. It was a very nice event. There was a lot of nationalistic fervour, but a lot of generosity too. Genuine feelings. I enjoyed a lot.'

'But of course, you won't be watching the IPL?'

'Oh, I wouldn't say that. Of course, I'm not really interested. But I might, you know, switch it on.'

On the dais, a young man wearing a white salwar kurta began strumming a guitar and crooning the words to a patriotic Bollywood song. *'Bharat humko jaan se pyara hai,'* he softly sang as the crowd murmured with emotion. 'India is dearer to us than life itself.'

Viewed from the pavilion, a line of snowy Himalaya peaks soars above the Himachal Pradesh cricket ground, from deep mid-on to a fairly wide third man. It is in Dharamshala, home of the Dalai Lama and his Tibetan government-in-exile, and there is no lovelier place in India, or perhaps anywhere, to watch cricket. I was sitting alongside Anita Mathur, wife of Amrit, awaiting one of the last games of the Daredevils' dismal season and watching the sunlight glinting on the spectral Himalayas, speechless with wonder.

The ground was the second home of Kings XI Punjab. And it was now rapidly filling with a boisterous crowd of 20,000 Punjabis, who had driven up from the plains. Most had no view of the mountains because of the stands behind them. Instead they were making do by ogling the cheerleaders, young white women wearing spangly white vests and leggings, who were warming up on their boundary-side podiums.

'They have no idea what they're doing,' said Anita, watching the girls and the reception they were getting. It turned out she knew a thing or two about cheerleading, having been a cheerleader herself, while attending an American school in Liberia. 'They're hopeless,' she said. 'Like all the IPL cheerleaders. But the main thing that worries me is those girls really have no idea what's going through the minds of those men.'

The IPL's cheerleaders were not from the higher echelons of their profession. Mallya's experiment with the Washington Redskins' troupe had been expensive and short-lived. Most were from South Africa or Eastern Europe, and were neither trained dancers nor especially beautiful. They were pure titillation: if an Indian woman performed in public as they did, she would certainly risk being called a prostitute. I wondered, as Anita and I watched the Kings XI girls warming up with their pompoms, whether the cheerleaders realised this. In the stark Himalayan light, before a semi-inebriated Punjabi crowd, they looked vulnerable and pathetic.

Punjab batted first, bringing Gilchrist and Paul Valthaty to the crease. Valthaty was the revelation of this IPL season. A 27-year-old journeyman from Mumbai, he had not yet played a single first-class game. He had previously drifted around the IPL, with a highest score of six. Kings XI was his third IPL team. But Gilchrist, his captain, had seen something in Valthaty, given him a chance to open the innings, and he had seized it. He had scored an explosive 120 against Chennai early on in the tournament, and was now vying with Tendulkar to be its top run-scorer. Largely due to his performances, Kings XI had an outside chance of making the semi-finals. But on this green-tinged pitch, the Delhi seamers were proving to be a handful.

Even Irfan was – he was bowling fast and bending the ball through the air like his old self. He looked a bowler transformed. Gilchrist played and missed at a couple of deliveries, then carted the last ball of Irfan's opening over for four. 'Grandiose!' flashed up on the scoreboard, as the cheerleaders hopped up to dance.

Gilchrist was soon out, caught at mid-on off Morkel. Yet the flurry of wickets that the Delhi bowlers deserved didn't come. Valthaty and the Australian Shaun Marsh clung on, rather flukily. Then they began flaying the Daredevils' second-string bowlers all around the small ground.

They put on a hundred and, though Delhi came back at the end, with Irfan getting three well-deserved wickets, Punjab's final score of 170 looked good on this pitch. The Daredevils had only twice chased so many runs all season, their star batsman Sehwag was out injured, and the swinging ball would be even harder to follow under floodlights. The light was now rapidly fading, casting the distant Himalayas in a pink glow.

The Daredevils started well, putting on fifty for the first wicket. But after losing both openers and with nothing left to play for in the tournament, they fell apart. After 15 overs, they had collapsed to 97 for six. As each wicket fell, the crowd boiled over, the cheerleaders pranced about and Preity Zinta, the Kings XI's film-star owner, swirled a red-and-silver Punjab flag for the cameras. Amrit, sitting slightly apart from us, was hunched forwards, holding his head in his hands.

After the game, I went to the Kings XI dressing-room to find Zinta. A native of Himachal Pradesh, she was in the process of telling Gilchrist what sightseeing he must do in Dharamshala. 'There are lots of natural temples, stones, caves, literally thousands of years old,' she was saying, fixing her doe-eyes on the Australian cricketer. 'But not idols,' she said, looking suddenly severe. 'Because I never worship idols, OK?' Gilchrist nodded, wearing a neutral expression.

Zinta was easily the IPL's biggest Bollywood draw after Shahrukh Khan, with whom she shared more than IPL ownership. The daughter of an army officer, she was another self-made star. She also had a head for business, which she had briefly studied at Harvard.

Zinta said she would be happy to chat, so we sat down together on boundary-side seats. I asked her why she had got into cricket.

'I was at a stage of my career where I was, you know, the number-one star in India and I was, you know, a little bored,' she said, flicking a wisp of black hair from her eyes. 'I'd lost my passion for movies so I decided to concentrate on cricket. I put my passion, my energy into it.' She shot me a confiding glance and leant forward. 'You know, I think I concentrated on cricket too much.'

'And what have you brought to your team?'

'Bums on seats. People come to the stadium to see me, even when we're losing. And of course I'm completely with the team. I'm the glue that binds them together,' she said, pursing her lips very prettily. 'When I'm with them, I fly economy. I'd never flown economy before.'

I agreed that must help a lot. 'And did you always like cricket?' I asked.

Zinta nodded, widening her light brown eyes. 'People asked me that a lot when I got into this. They said "what do you know about cricket?" And I said, I don't know much, you know, just fours and sixes. But that's Twenty20, isn't it? It's all fours and sixes. The normal Indian woman doesn't know who Irfan Pathan is. And I didn't know who Irfan Pathan was. Well, OK, maybe I did because after all he's exceptionally cute ...'

'Why else do you think the IPL's been such a hit?'

'It's because Indians are so proud of it, because it's our tournament and all the foreign stars are coming here to play ... I guess somewhere in our psychology we know that we were colonised and that we're a Third-World country, so it's a great thing to see these things changing in cricket.

'And, of course, it has to be T20. Five days of cricket? Forget it. Not in this fast-paced world. With full respect to Test cricket, we just don't have time for it.'

CHAPTER NINE

Twenty20 Vision

On a cloudy morning in west London in July 2011, India and England met to play the 100th Test match of their complicated rivalry. It was a great occasion, a full house at Lord's, brimming with conviviality. In the space-ship press box, as replicated in Rajkot, former Indian and English greats swapped war stories. Out on the pitch, Sharad Pawar and the top brass of the BCCI paraded on the lush green turf of cricket's home.

How different this was from the scene of India's first Test match – also at Lord's – in 1932. Then, the Indians came as colonial servants to learn cricket from their masters. They had no prospect of actually winning the game. Now, the Indian board was cricket's paymaster and India the world's top-ranked Test side and World Cup champions. In Sachin Tendulkar and Rahul Dravid, they had two all-time great batsmen. Tendulkar was a century away from his 100th international century, an unprecedented feat. Most Indians assumed he would get it, if not today, at some point during the ensuing four-match series. They also expected that India would win.

But as so often in Indian cricket, the mismatch between a nation's expectations and reality was jarring. The 1932 Indians surpassed the, admittedly very low, predictions for them. The exalted 2011 lot were blown away. England declared their first innings on 474 for eight, a score that included a magnificent double-century from Kevin Pietersen – which was doubly felicitous for him, considering he was about to negotiate terms with the Delhi Daredevils. They went on to win by 196 runs.

England won the next three Tests by even bigger margins: by 319 runs at Trent Bridge; an innings and 242 runs at Edgbaston; and an innings and eight runs at the Oval. This was a proper thrashing. The margins of India's defeats were even bigger than that of their inaugural defeat in 1932. Apart from Dravid, no Indian batsman scored a century in the series.

Later that year the Indians went to Australia, where they suffered another 4-0 pasting, again by huge margins. This constituted their worst run of away defeats since the 1960s. Even by Indian standards of inconsistency, it was a dramatic slide.

The euphoria that had followed the 2011 World Cup victory was now a faint memory. It was suddenly apparent that, despite the country's vast cricket-mad population, India had not one dependable fast bowler. They had no indisputably world-class spinner. They had one of the weakest batting line-ups in Test cricket. After the Australia debacle, Dravid and V.V.S. Laxman – players with 53 Test centuries between them – both retired. That left India with one batsman ranked in the world's top 20, Tendulkar. And he was 18th in the world, almost 40 years old, and rapidly fading.

In November 2012 England toured India, and caused a further upset. They were by no means a great team. They had been well beaten by South Africa earlier in the year, leading to the retirement of their captain Andrew Strauss. Many of the players had also fallen out with their best batsmen, Kevin Pietersen, a brittle, brilliant recruit from South Africa, who had never been loved by his team-mates or the English public. The argument was partly caused by Pietersen's unhappiness at being barred by England from playing a full IPL season, for which he could have earned around $2 million. But the divisions in the team were put aside as England gave the Indians another hiding.

They won the four-Test series 2-1, to record their first series victory in India since 1985. India's millionaire cricketers came off worst in every aspect of the game. Their spin-bowlers, Pragyan Ojha and Ravichandran Ashwin, were out-bowled by Graeme Swann and Monty Panesar, who took 40 wickets between them. The English batsmen were in commanding form – Alastair Cook, England's new captain, scored three centuries and averaged over 80. His opposite number, Mahendra Singh Dhoni, struggled to score a pair of fifties and had an otherwise wretched series.

His captaincy was criticised, his team looked demoralised, uninterested even. Sometimes so did Dhoni. Tendulkar fared worse. He scored a solitary fifty and came 16th in the series averages. By the end of it, even some Indian commentators were suggesting he should retire. On 23 December 2012, the little master announced his retirement from one-day cricket, a format in which he had scored a staggering 49 centuries for India.

At a time of great despondency in Indian cricket, there was just one fresh hope. This was a 25-year-old with a calm head and classical technique – Cheteshwar Pujara. After an 18-month absence from the India side – chiefly owing to an injury picked up in the IPL – Chintu was picked to replace Dravid in a short home series against New Zealand, sandwiched between the disastrous tours of England and Australia. In the first Test, in Hyderabad, he hit 159. It was a wonderful innings, calm, rhythmic and occasionally ruthless. I watched it, with growing delight as he neared his century, from the misty English countryside. Too bad the stadium in Hyderabad was barely a quarter full.

On 99, Chintu flicked the ball off his pads to fine leg and ran through for a single. Joy flooded his long, almost equine, features. As he raised his bat, he glanced at the sky and his lips moved in prayer. He was giving thanks, I supposed, for the dead mother who had predicted this success, or to his father Arvind, watching at home in Rajkot.

He still refused to go to the stadium to watch his son. Arvind said he would only be a bother to him; he had also been in poor health. Even when India began their next home series, against England, in the nearby city of Ahmedabad, he therefore declined to attend. In the first innings, Chintu scored 206 not out, and he scored 41 not out in the second, setting India up for a crushing victory. In the second Test of the series, in Mumbai, Chintu scored 135 in the first innings. Indian cricket had a new star, even if India were woeful.

What had gone so wrong? By the end of 2012, India had slid to fifth in the Test rankings – below their calamitous rivals, Pakistan – and third in the one-day rankings. An easy 4-0 Test victory against Australia, when they returned to India in early 2013 with a bafflingly reduced team, then papered over these failings. But this was still a desperately poor return on India's cricketing advantages. Astonishingly, India were not obviously better at cricket than when Tendulkar began his long career, despite the vast wealth that had flowed into Indian cricket in the intervening decades. India's captain, the small-town hero Dhoni, was reckoned to earn over $25 million a year, more than Usain Bolt or Wayne Rooney. Yet he was ranked merely the world's 40th best batsman in Tests, 30th in T20 and, to his credit, sixth in one-day internationals. Nowhere had the commercialisation of sport caused a greater imbalance between achievement and financial reward than in Indian cricket.

The same might be said of the BCCI, whose rulers should – but of course did not – take some responsibility for India's poor performances. It was not hard to see how they might address the issue. They could build thousands of pitches in India's teeming slums and villages. They could dispatch hundreds of cricket coaches to them, and distribute millions of willow bats and leather balls. They could bolster India's existing club and district tournaments, most of which struggle in penury, and launch new ones. The BCCI could easily afford these measures, and the results would be dramatic. India's unique and multitudinous passion for cricket, thus harnessed, would unleash a torrent of sporting talent unprecedented in the history of any game.

But it will not happen, because the good of Indian cricket is not the chief priority of the politicians who run the BCCI. They are mainly concerned to perpetuate their power. That is why they devote so much time to fighting their nasty civil wars and building Ozymandian stadiums where there are no cricket pitches for poor boys to play on. Yet it is these men that will increasingly decide cricket's future, in India and elsewhere. Not since the heyday of the MCC, when patrician figures such as Lord Harris presided over cricket in England and everywhere, has a single country exerted such influence over the game as India does today.

That comparison is interesting. Lord Harris was a haughty British aristocrat. He had, in the cold light of the 21st century, some repugnant views on Indians (as well as a genuine love for India). He also gave himself too much credit, as one historian has shown, for Indian cricket's early growth. Yet Lord Harris had a real regard and care for cricket. That was why, as MCC president, he supported India's bid for Test status. It is also why he helped arrange reciprocal tours between the two countries. He had no selfish reason to do so.

The BCCI, by contrast, accepts no responsibility for cricket's global health. Nor even for how it fares in its own neighbourhood. Consider, thus, the case of Bangladesh. In 2000 the BCCI successfully campaigned for it to be awarded Test-class status, thereby assuring itself of another captive vote at the ICC. Yet India's eastern neighbour looked unready for that promotion, and so it has turned out to be. By late 2012 Bangladesh had played 75 Tests, of which it had lost 65 and won three. And India, which bears prime responsibility for this fiasco, has done less than any other Test country to remedy it. It is the only front-rank cricket country never to have invited the hapless Bangladeshis on a Test-match tour.

As so often with Indian cricket, it is easy to see in the BCCI's behaviour a wider significance. India's recent economic growth has transformed its place in the world, giving it an important voice in international negotiations on climate change, trade, energy, security and much else. It has also sent far-flung governments scrambling to understand India's desires and the nature of Indian diplomacy and power. That is as it should be. Yet if they know cricket, the global arena most affected by India's new influence, they will be dismayed.

'Are we going to be like America? Will we think we're the biggest and so you're all going to do what we say? I fear we are,' the commentator Harsha Bhogle once told me. He spoke of cricket, but he might equally have been talking of climate change or trade. India is in so many ways an inspiring example to the world: with its liberal traditions, democracy and the ingenuity of its fiercely competitive people. But it can also be, as the world is starting to find, an awkward partner: self-absorbed, often corrupt and overly anxious to be no one's fool. India is becoming powerful; it will be a long time before it forgets how it felt to be weak.

The IPL is perhaps the chief illustration of the Indian board's disregard for cricket's future good. It is a splendid cricket romp, hugely popular and great fun for players and spectators. But its effect on international cricket has been destructive. When the West Indies arrived in England to play a three-Test series in May 2012, four of their best players were playing in the IPL. You could hardly blame them. Chris Gayle, a Jamaican hitter and one of T20's biggest stars, had been promised at least a million dollars by the Royal Challengers Bangalore for six weeks' work. That was several times more than the cash-strapped West Indies board could afford to pay him for a year of international cricket.

Such clashes could be avoided. If India would only request a six-week pause, or 'window', in the international cricket schedule for the duration of the IPL, other countries would be quick to agree to it. For sure, this would be unfair on the new copycat T20 contests in Australia, Bangladesh and elsewhere, for which there could be no such dispensation. But it would be a pragmatic recognition of India's power in cricket, which might well help shore up the international game. Yet the Indian board, at the time of writing, will not countenance this request. Suspicious and controlling, its bosses apparently fear such a window might make the IPL somehow accountable to other boards. As for cricket in the West Indies, it can go hang. 'It's a free world,' shrugged N. Srinivasan, the latest BCCI president, when asked what could be done about the splintering West Indies team. 'People and players make their choices and we can't compel a person.' Srinivasan is, of course, not wholly impartial in the matter. His family cement company owns the Chennai Super Kings. And perhaps that was a worry to him – because in 2012 the IPL hit serious trouble.

Its fifth rendition, won by the Kolkata Knight Riders, was the most entertaining yet. Roughly a third of the games were decided in the last over. The tournament also saw bigger and more enthusiastic crowds, not least in Delhi, where the expensively improved Daredevils almost made it to the final. Television viewership was steady.

But shortly after the tournament ended, it became clear that most of the team-owners were in serious financial difficulty. The ill-advised Kochi franchise had not even made it this far: it was dissolved by the board in September 2011 after its investors failed to pay their bills. Of the nine surviving teams, seven were owned wholly or partly by listed companies, all of which were massively indebted and seeing their stock prices plunge. Together they were estimated to have lost $25 billion in value since April 2008, when the IPL began. Suddenly, some of the exuberant investments that India Inc. had been making in the good times seemed less go-getting than foolhardy.

The King of Good Times, fittingly, was one of the main casualties. By mid-2012 Vijay Mallya was almost bust. His airline was saddled with $1.7 billion in debts. One of the main arms of his booze business, United Spirits, owed another $1.6 billion. Now at the mercy of the banks, Mallya cut his collar-length hair and swapped his silk tracksuits for sober business suits. He sought to tone down his reputation for excess. But the pressure on his company was becoming intolerable. After the wife of one Kingfisher manager hanged herself and left a suicide note complaining that her husband had not been paid for seven months, there were calls in parliament for Mallya to be arrested. In November 2012 he sold most of United Spirits to the British-based company Diageo, and thereby lost control of one of his main sources of wealth.

Deccan Chronicle Ltd, owner of the Deccan Chargers, was also struggling. It owed over half a billion dollars to 28 different banks, two of which were reported to have been assured of future revenues earned by the IPL team as collateral. This irked the cricket board, which considered it highly irregular. After the usual court battle, it dissolved the Chargers in September 2012.

The Sahara Group, owner of the Pune Warriors, had even bigger debts. It stood accused of misselling bonds to some 23 million small investors; in August 2012 the Supreme Court ordered it to repay at least $3 billion to them. Sahara – which also operated an airline, film production business and, in partnership with Mallya, the Sahara Force India Formula One team – was one of India's most unusual companies. Grown from nothing by Subrata Roy, the son of a poor mill-worker, it had powerful political connections and a rather eccentric corporate culture. Sahara's 700,000 employees hail each other by placing their right arm across their chest and saying 'Sahara pranam!' ('Greetings, Sahara!') The company now looked to be fighting for its survival.

Other IPL franchises had lesser troubles. The Rajasthan, Punjab and Delhi teams were all rumoured to be wholly or partly for sale. The IPL, it appeared, was in meltdown. Yet, in the midst of this tumult, the BCCI coolly resold the rights to the Hyderabad franchise to a Chennai-based television company, Sun TV, for $79.5 million. Worked out over five years, that was double what Deccan Chronicle had paid in 2008. Soon after, Pepsi bought the IPL's title sponsorship rights for over $70 million – twice what their previous owner, DLF, had paid. There will be more upheavals in the IPL. But the tournament, it seems, is not going away.

This would mean more bad news for international cricket, especially the Test match, cricket's greatest format. So long as the IPL continues, its investors are likely to demand, *sotto voce*, an expansion of the tournament. The current eight-week duration of the IPL is too short for most of the franchises to make a profit, even with the share of television and other revenues they get from the BCCI. Building a team brand, to attract lucrative sponsorship deals, is hard enough in a country with little tradition of club sport. It probably cannot be done satisfactorily in so short a season. To save costs, most IPL franchises are in fact hardly trying. For nine months of the year, they operate from tiny offices with skeleton staffs. But as their handouts from the BCCI are gradually reduced, this will have to change. To make money, the franchises will have to become serious, year-round businesses.

That would logically require either a longer IPL season or a second annual tournament. Either would create an even worse clash between club and country, which the moneybags IPL would probably win. Yet it is hard to imagine that the Indian board would not, in the end, facilitate such an expansion of the tournament. Indians want more tamasha. And if the board will not provide it, perhaps others will. The IPL franchise owners might even consider going it alone: they are already claiming a bigger role in running the tournament. Rather than risk that happening, the Indian board would probably bend to their demands, to the great detriment of international cricket.

For cricket tragics, it is a depressing outlook. India, a country that has so enriched cricket, is now the gravest threat to its most precious traditions. But then again, look closer at what cricket means to Indians, and it is hard to remain altogether disapproving. Cricket is, for millions of poor and recently poor Indians, a remarkable consolation, a rare moment of escape and excitement, sometimes a dream of advancement and leisure. It always has been, for 150 years now. And they, too, deserve the cricket they most want.

Asghar Husain sat at his aged mother's feet, looking up at a large flat-screen television still half-wrapped in shop plastic. It was showing the pre-match scenes at Eden Gardens, ablaze with light and colour. Mumbai Indians were about to play Kolkata Knight Riders in one of the last games of the third IPL season. Victory for the Knight Riders would put them through to the tournament's final qualifying round as one of the top two sides. Victory for Mumbai could put them through too.

Asghar nodded approvingly. 'Big game,' he said. Yet he was unhappy with his new television set. It was the third he had bought for his small flat on Ninety Foot Road, a busy thoroughfare on the edge of Dharavi slum in Mumbai, but he still wanted something better. 'Twenty-eight inches only,' he said, fiddling with the remote control. 'Now we're planning to go for 40 inches.'

Asghar was a small man, aged 30, wearing black jeans with a lot of zips and a white linen shirt piped with gold embroidery. He considered himself a Mumbai Indians diehard. 'First because of cricket, which is my passion. I watch all games whenever I have time,' he said. 'Also because it is Twenty20 – new generation cricket.'

T20 was the only kind of cricket for Asghar, a first-generation fan. He was uninterested in Test matches. He also found the 50-over game dull by comparison, though he liked it when India won. But there was another reason why Asghar, a son of poor north Indian migrants, liked the Mumbai Indians: 'Mumbai is my city.'

As he fiddled with the remote, Asghar's other arm was draped lightly across the knees of his septuagenarian mother, Khairunnisa. She was a tiny figure in an embroidered salwar kameez, perched like a small white bird on her chair. She did not understand English, so listened to us in uncomprehending silence.

Khairunnisa hailed from a village on the Ganges, close to Allahabad. She and Asghar's father, Husain, had migrated to Mumbai sometime in the 1970s. She didn't know exactly what year, any more than she knew her age. Khairunnisa was illiterate, as Husain had been, and she found ages and dates hard to get straight. The couple had landed up in Dharavi along with thousands of other poor migrants from all across India, driven by ambition, hunger and the innumerable other small tragedies that afflict the poor.

Husain found work in the slum's shack factories, block-printing patterns on to silk saris. The couple and their ten children – Asghar was the second youngest – lived in a tiny two-room hut. Yet a decade after coming to the city, Husain made a brilliant investment. He borrowed 7,000 rupees and sent his eldest son to Dubai to work as a silk embroiderer. 'That was the turning-point for our family,' Asghar said. His father died a month later. But Asghar's migrant brother worked hard and did well, and almost every dirham he earned he sent back to the slum.

Supported by his brother, Asghar graduated from Mumbai University with a degree in electrical engineering, and got a job in the oil industry. He had since worked on oil rigs all over the world, on contracts worth half a million rupees a month. He also owned five mobile phone shops

in and around Dharavi, each with an Arabic name. Al-something, this
is my trademark,' Asghar said proudly. 'Like Al-Barakat, which is
prosperity, or Al-Kair, which is goodness.'

Asghar was now richer, better educated and more independent than
anyone in his family could have imagined possible. A year earlier, he
had bought this flat and left the family slum-hut, taking his mother and
new bride with him. He was now awaiting delivery of a 4x4 Skoda, a
power car in India. 'Big family, so we need a big car,' he said, grinning.

The door was flung open and Asghar's young wife and one of his
sisters stepped inside, wearing billowing black burkhas over their faces
and bodies. As they entered, they were chattering gaily; seeing me, their
heads dropped and they swished silently through to the kitchen.

'Money is one thing,' Asghar said. 'But we have continued our
culture, just like before. Respect for our elders, respect for our parents,
respect for our elder brothers, just like in the village. This is our culture.
We are the same.'

At Eden Gardens the Knight Riders' innings was reaching a dramatic
conclusion. Jacques Kallis, the great South African, heaved consecutive
sixes off the New Zealander James Franklin. Kolkata were on 149 for
four with three more overs to bat. The stadium was alive with a churning
crowd and the Knight Riders cheerleaders jumping up and down like
anything. As the cameras closed in, they pumped their hips and busts,
brandishing their pompoms.

'How do you like that?' I asked.

'They're nice,' Asghar said, smirking, as his mother maintained her
inscrutable silence.

I had first visited Dharavi four years before, for a week-long stay. I
had wanted to understand how the slum ticked. In particular, I wanted
to know how so many poor people could live so crowded together,
apparently harmoniously. Dharavi has had bursts of Hindu–Muslim
rioting, including a bad one in 1992 in the wake of the destruction of
the Babri mosque. But there had been no repeat of this and everyday
crime in the slum was rare.

I stayed as the guest of two slum-dwellers, Raju Korde and Shashikant
Kwale, whom I had met more or less by chance. Raju was a portly
Maharashtrian, taciturn and watchful. He had a small printing business

and a couple of slum shops. 'I am a communist and an entrepreneur. There is no contradiction,' he used to say, a bit defensively. He lived with his wife, two children and widowed mother in a three-room slum house, where I stayed. Shashikant, known as Shashi, was also Maharashtrian and one of Raju's sidekicks in the local communist party. He was a tall, slightly stooped Dalit and, when I first met him, on hard times.

He was unemployed, single and badly shaken by a motorbike accident. He lived with his drunken parents in a tiny two-room hut, where I also spent a night. The rest of the time, I wandered the slum with Raju or Shashi as my guides, exploring its workhouses and mazy ghettoes, its Bengali, Dalit and Muslim quarters. I learned more about India in those days, about the dynamism and grit of its hardworking poor, than in weeks in my office in Delhi. In the shanties of Mumbai – a city where half the population lives in a slum – modern Indian society is being forged.

Whenever I was back in Mumbai, I tried to revisit Dharavi to catch up with Raju and Shashi and hear their news. In these boom times, it was almost always uplifting. A year after my first visit I returned to find Raju running a small cooperative bank. Shashi had opened a small recruitment agency from a cubbyhole office. A year after that, Raju had opened more shops and Shashi's business was growing. This is how economic growth looks among the weeds of a poor country: as a glorious burgeoning of opportunity.

Shortly before I was due to leave India, I returned to Dharavi one last time. I wanted to say goodbye to Raju, Shashi and the slum. I also wanted to fill a serious gap in my knowledge of it, by finding out what cricket there was in Dharavi.

As usual, I went first to Raju, who was now operating from a room in a half-finished office block on the edge of the slum. It was a big step up from the dingy communist party office, where I had first met him, with portraits of Marx, Lenin and Engels on the walls.

'Welcome to my law office,' Raju said, half-smiling, as I entered.

'But you're not a lawyer!'

'I am now. I'm a slum lawyer and also a slum developer,' he said, and paused to see my reaction. 'There is no conflict. I'm doing business like anyone else, only with honesty.'

For his first redevelopment project, Raju said he had raised $100,000 and he expected to make a big profit.

Shashi soon turned up, wearing beige shorts and a matching T-shirt printed with the legend 'Golden Age Flying 2'. His news was also cheering. Shashi's employment agency now specialised in providing hospital orderlies and had over 400 on its books.

I was very pleased for him. Good-humoured and sometimes alarmingly candid, Shashi was one of the nicest people I knew in India. He could also be very funny. He was prone to sudden bursts of enthusiasm, gushingly expressed in Hindi with just enough English words thrown in for him to swear he was speaking English.

'*Aray*, I have more ...' he continued.

Shashi had got married, though he had always said that this would be impossible. He had been unable to say why, but he had hinted at some humiliating damage resulting from his motorbike accident. Yet a few months before, a young midwife had walked into Shashi's office and, though she was north Indian and of high Hindu caste, he had married her two days later.

'Love-marriage!' he said triumphantly.

'Everything is good,' said Raju. 'Everyone is moving up.'

I asked Raju if I could stay at his place. 'You are always welcome,' he said and informed me that it had undergone a significant improvement: it now had a toilet. I also told Raju I wanted a cricket tour of Dharavi, and he rolled his eyes and smiled. He was used to my requests: to see where the potters lived, to visit Dharavi's tanneries and recyclers, or a slum dance-bar. But I don't think he ever minded them. Raju, born and raised in Dharavi, was as fascinated by the slum as I was.

'Asghar will guide you,' he said, nodding at a young man sitting quietly in the corner.

We went first to the Dharavi-Sion Sports Club, a half-hour walk away, and one of only three spaces easily available to Dharavi's cricketers.

On a Sunday afternoon, ahead of the evening's IPL game at Eden Gardens, it was packed, with at least 20 games in progress. The cricketers were tailors, embroiderers and cobblers, slum-workers, all enjoying a precious day off.

Asghar led me to a muscular middle-aged man, wearing a tracksuit, who was keeping a magisterial eye on the play. This was Babaji Ghule, who was regarded as an authority on Dharavi cricket. A keen player himself, he organised an annual knockout tournament, contested by 16 slum sides. It comprised six-over games of tennis-ball cricket, played over two days in January or February.

The teams were mostly defined by the caste or religion of their members. Around half were Muslim, including Princes XI, a side that Asghar played for as an off-spinning all-rounder.

'So it's a communal cricket tournament?' I asked.

Asghar translated the question. '*Nahi, baas!*' Babaji replied. '*Hum sab ekhai!*' – 'We are all together!'

Babaji said he had started the tournament in response to the 1993 riots, to rebuild trust between Dharavi's bereaved and resentful communities. 'We do not see caste or religion in cricket,' Asghar said firmly.

Babaji was another first-generation cricket fan. His father, a poor migrant from a parched Maharashtrian village, had only known wrestling and kabbadi. 'But now I want my son to play real cricket, with a season ball, that is the next thing,' he said. But it was not easy. Babji reckoned it could easily cost 15,000 rupees a year, in cricket kit and subscriptions, to send his boy to a gymkhana. 'Pukka cricket is an expensive game for us.'

Soon the cricket ground was cleared for the afternoon's main event. This was a six-over contest between one of Dharavi's Muslim sides, Khwaja Geri Nawaz, named after a revered Sufi shrine, and a team from a neighbouring slum. The game was played with great intensity in front of a laughing, catcalling crowd, and the local side won easily. This was chiefly due to the brilliance of their fastest bowler, a short and skinny slum-dweller, who bowled almost unplayable tennis-ball yorkers.

I went up to congratulate him after the game. He was an illiterate silk embroiderer called Wahid Khan and, though very shy, he seemed thrilled to be praised. 'I love cricket too much,' he said, beaming.

Wahid had recently been offered a few hundred rupees a week by a local club to play for it on the maidans. Yet he was unsure whether he should do so. He said he was scared the hard leather ball might injure his hands, which he used to make tiny stitches on silk saris, for which he was paid 7,000 rupees a month. Most of that went to his elderly parents.

I asked Wahid if I could have a bat against him and he nodded happily. But, to the delight of the crowd, he was too good for me. I blamed my embarrassment on the light, which was fading rapidly now.

'Everyone is coming up,' echoed Asghar, as we left the ground to find his shiny new motorbike. 'But, you know, slowly.'

Halfway through the evening IPL game, it was shaping up for an exciting finish. Kolkata Knight Riders scored 175 for five in their 20 overs. It was a stiff target, but gettable for the Mumbai Indians' superb batsmen. Yet Asghar and I had had enough of the game. Instead, joined by Shashi, we left the flat on Ninety Foot Road and headed out into the slum. I wanted to see who was watching the cricket in Dharavi.

The slum's alleys, so narrow and overbuilt they were almost tunnels, flickered with fluorescent television light and resounded with television noise. Without a breath of breeze, it was very hot. Many of the slum-dwellers had therefore left open the doors of their windowless huts, in which most had a TV set switched on at high volume.

We moved carefully through the alleys, listening to the general television din. At every step, there were snatches of Bollywood songs and the melodramatic chords of a Hindi soap. But most of the sets blared out the equally portentous sound of Ravi Shastri, overlaid with bursts of dance music and a white noise of cheering. Perhaps one in three huts, I estimated, was watching the IPL.

A small multi-coloured Hindu temple, writhing with gods, signalled that we had entered a Tamil area. We stopped to talk with one of its dark-skinned inhabitants, Anthony Kamraj. He was lounging outside the single-room hut he shared with his new wife and his brother and sister-in-law, wearing nothing but a tartan sarong. Two sets of plastic rosaries hung around his neck. He was chewing paan and watching the game.

Anthony said he was a fan of the IPL though he much preferred to watch India play. 'That is not just for relaxing, it is something I feel in my heart,' he said. I asked him if he ever watched Test cricket and he smiled and shook his head. A small boy's shrill voice piped up from the dark of the alley. 'Boring!' it said in English. An explosion of noise signalled that a wicket had fallen. But at 123 for four, Mumbai Indians were cruising now.

We moved on, criss-crossing trickling drains, to arrive outside a tiny two-storey hut in a gloomy corner of the slum. This was where Asghar had lived until recently with Khairunnisa and his many siblings. Now it was occupied by two of his brothers, their wives and some children, about ten people in all.

Next door was a taller, three-storey shack, with a mess of ropes and ladders providing access to its upper levels. From the third storey came a flicker of TV light and the sounds of Ravi Shastri. So Asghar and I clambered up to look inside.

It was a rectangular room, about 15 feet by ten, weakly lit by a single bulb. The floor was filled by three wooden frames, around which a group of skinny boys were crouched, making desultory stitches in bright silk saris. They stared up at us blankly, surprised more than afraid, but too streetwise to show it.

There were 14 of them living here, they said. By day they worked on the frames, embroidering saris and shawls; during the night they slept under them. They were skinny and gaunt and the youngest looked no more than 12 or 14.

Watching television was their Sunday treat, the boys said. At other times their boss, a local Bihari businessman, forbade them to turn the TV on lest it distract them from their work. The boys earned 2,500 rupees a month, a bit more than $40, which they mostly sent home to their impoverished parents in Bihar, Uttar Pradesh and West Bengal. Hanging beneath the television, on a row of wooden pegs, were a few grimy-grey shirts. These were their possessions.

I asked how they had spent their day off and every one of them said he had been playing cricket. An effeminate-looking Bengali called Shahrukh said he been playing at the Dharavi Sports Club. He wore a smudge of pink lipstick, a silver hoop in his right ear and said he was a fast bowler.

Cricket was a new hobby for Shahrukh. No one had played the game in his village in West Bengal. I asked him what he liked about the game and, though still watchful, he replied with all his heart. 'I play cricket with my passion and my emotion. It is my chance to be famous,' he said.

I asked what his ambitions were, expecting him to say something about cricket, and he looked embarrassed. 'Any human can dream ...' he said, reluctantly, shooting a glance at his workmates. 'I know I am fated to be small and poor but I can always imagine earning a lot of money.'

I asked how much he had in mind. 'Maybe 6,000 rupees a month,' he said.

This, then, is also where Indian cricket resides, far from the elite, the corrupt politicians, tycoons and turkey-cocking film stars who have laid claim to it. Here, in the slums and villages, what was once an English game thrills and unites millions – including those, like Asghar, accelerating away from poverty, and many more, like Shahrukh, who have not yet made the break. Cricket is their relief, their excitement, the main ingredient of national culture that they have embraced. It belongs to them too.

With that Asghar and I thanked the boys and turned to clamber back out into the alleyways of Dharavi, into the television noise and light. And, as we went, I noticed that Shahrukh had written his name, 'SHAHRUKH' in curly-blue capital letters all over his jeans.

Acknowledgements

During four years living and working in India I travelled thousands of miles to dozens of Indian cities and interviewed many hundreds of people. Yet I resolved to write *The Great Tamasha* on my doorstep in Delhi, watching a group of children playing games of cricket.

It seemed appropriate: cricket is India's and my shared passion. It was also more than usually in the news at the time because of the IPL, which was launched shortly after our arrival in Delhi and caused a great political uproar not long before we were due to leave. No news item was consistently bigger in India during these boom years between 2007 and 2010, both for the light the tournament shone on India's growth and progress, as well as its cricketainment 'wow'. At a time of gathering global interest in India, foreign correspondents also found themselves writing about Preity Zinta's glamour quotient and DLF maximums – even those, such as my counterparts at the *New York Times*, unfamiliar with the language of runs and wickets. That *The Economist* was interested in Lalit Modi's billion-dollar baby was less surprising. Unknown to most of its readers, the British weekly is a deeply cricket-loving organ: in the heart of many *Economist* editors and writers cricket love burns.

Yet having initially resolved to write the story of the IPL, I soon discovered that this would not do. To write so narrow a book on Indian cricket, one which paid no homage to Bombay's maidans, or to the Indians who have played and spread the game over the decades, or which ignored the many coincidences between cricket and the great events of Indian politics would have been a travesty. As I hope to have shown, I know of no better way to make sense of India, in its vastness and complexity, than through its passion for cricket. And the more I discussed my research with friends and journalistic contacts in Delhi, the clearer this became.

Experts in diverse fields, of politics, business or social affairs, most nonetheless turned out to have strong (sometimes very strong) views on cricket, too. These sources and friends are too many to list here. But of the many brains I have picked for this book, on cricket and otherwise, I owe particular thanks to: Ajay Agnihotri, Imtiaz Ali, Manoj Badale, Abbas Ali Baig, Bishan Singh Bedi, Surjit Bhalla, Pramod Bhasin, Harsha Bhogle, Bharat Bhushan, Adam Gilchrist, Shekhar Gupta, Cyrus Guzder, Peter Griffiths, Dipankar Gupta, Arun Jaitley, Tony Jesudasan, Aamir Khan, Ashok Malik, Amrit Mathur, Pratap Bhanu Mehta, Himanshu Modi, Lalit Modi, Raju Narisetti, T.N. Ninan, the late Tiger Pataudi, Aditi Phadnis, Sachin Pilot, Chandra Bhan Prasad, Arvind Pujara, Sundar Raman, Mahesh Rangarajan, Sunali Rohra, Rajdeep Sardesai, Ronnie Screwvala, Ashutosh Sharma, Uday Shankar, Lokesh Sharma, Parul Sharma, Y.S. Shatrusalyasinhji, Suhel Seth, Rajeev Shukla, Digvijay Singh, Manjit Singh, Manvendra Singh, Badri Narayan Tiwari and Yogendra Yadav.

I am especially grateful to those who fed and housed me on my travels for this book including: Vivek Narain, Sonia Jehan and Raju Korde in Mumbai, Najam Sethi and Jugnu Mohsin in Lahore, Declan Walsh in Islamabad, Sarah Webster in Delhi, Anwar Ali in Shahabpur and Utpal Pathak in Patna. I am especially grateful to John Haywood who, without a second's hesitation, gave me a room in his house in Nizamuddin to work from, and to John Driver for the same kindness in Tilton-on-the-Hill.

I am deeply indebted to a group of experts on Indian cricket for all manner of generous help. Gulu Ezekiel, Gideon Haigh, Ramchandra Guha, Ashis Nandy and Vasant Raiji gave me their wonderful books as well as their thoughts. Sandeep Dwivedi and Sharda Ugra, two brilliant cricket journalists, were encouraging and wise counsellors and always ready to help with their contacts. Varun Sood provided superb logistical and intellectual support in Mumbai, especially navigating Bollywood and the television industry. Madhusudhan Rama, a brilliant cricket statistician, ran rigorous and imaginative checks on the caste, religious and regional profiles of Indian cricketers over the decades. He and his colleagues at Cricinfo, one of the great creations of the internet age, are a beacon of hope for serious cricket fans. L.V. Krishnan at TAM was kindness itself in providing me with data on Indian television audiences. I am also extremely grateful to Leo Mirani, for skilfully negotiating the *Times of India* archives in Mumbai on my behalf.

I am also especially thankful to those who kindly read and commented on the manuscript: Gideon, Sandeep, Sharda, Sambit Bal, M.J. Akbar, Debjeet Kundu, Stephen Brown, Mark Bearn and Barney Ronay. Their criticisms rid it of many errors and infelicities, for which I am deeply grateful. Natasha Fairweather, my paragon of an agent at A.P. Watt, was an unfailing and patient support. I am profoundly grateful to Charlotte Atyeo and Matthew Engel, my outstanding and understanding editors at Bloomsbury. And I am particularly thankful to Indrani Bhattacharya, who runs *The Economist's* Delhi office and is a dear and generous friend, meticulous researcher and valued advisor.

I must thank, too, my colleagues at *The Economist* in London, especially Simon Long. A superb Asia editor and generous predecessor in Delhi, he encouraged me to roam and think freely about the subcontinent, after his own example. I am also grateful to John Micklethwait for sending me to Delhi, which gave me the opportunity to write this book, and then for giving me two bouts of book-leave to finish it.

But my greatest thanks are inevitably to those closest to me, who have put up with my absences while working on the book and have in many ways compensated for them. I owe enormous thanks to my parents-in-law, Rupert and Mary-Blanche Ridge, and to my siblings, Katherine, Matthew and Mark. I owe a big apology to my children, Francis, Tommy and Gabriel, and look forward to spending more time playing cricket with them than writing about it. Above all I am grateful to Mian Ridge, my wife, for her glorious company in India and elsewhere, and for her encouragement and tolerance of me, most of the time. But this book is dedicated to my parents, Michael and Jean Astill, who have a head-start in that regard.

Bibliography

Most of this book was researched from living sources, in scores of interviews with the great and small personages of Indian cricket. But many published records were also essential. In researching the historical sections of this book, I consulted primary or near-contemporary records where possible. On the pre-1947 origins of Indian cricket, the early Parsi cricket chronicles and several colonial memoirs were invaluable sources. The archives of the *Times of India* in Mumbai were extremely useful. But I was also indebted to several more recent histories.

Ramachandra Guha's brilliant *A Corner of a Foreign Field: The Indian History of a British Sport* was a peerless guide to the 19th-century Parsi struggle for a playing space in Bombay, as it was for the biography of Palwankar Baloo. Simon Wilde's *Ranji: A Genius Rich and Strange* was a formative rendering of Ranjitsinhji. Boria Majumdar's *Twenty-Two Yards to Freedom* provides the best account of the role of cricket in liberalising India's airwaves. Richard Cashman's *Patrons, Players and the Crowd* was often inspirational on the social composition and economy of Indian cricket's first independent decades. Mihir Bose's pioneering *A History of Indian Cricket* provided a wonderful introduction to the broad sweep of India's cricketing story.

For the later chapters on the IPL, especially the league's formation, I made great use of the archives of Cricinfo. They are likely to be the most reliable source for future aficionados.

Among all the books I consulted, the following were especially helpful:

A.G. Bagot, *Sport and Travel in India and Central America* (London: Macmillan and Co., 1897)

Derek Birley, *A Social History of English Cricket* (London: Aurum Press, 1999)

Rahul Bhattacharya, *Pundits from Pakistan: On Tour with India 2003–04* (Delhi: Picador, 2005)

Mihir Bose, *A History of Indian Cricket* (London: Andre Deutsch, 1990)

Mihir Bose, *A Maidan View: The Magic of Indian Cricket* (London: George Allen and Unwin, 1986)

Mihir Bose, *The Magic of Indian Cricket: Cricket and Society in India* (London: Routledge, Sport in the Global Society, 2006)

Mihir Bose, *Bollywood: A History* (Stroud: Tempus Publishing Ltd, 2006)

Geo W. Briggs, *The Chamars* (Calcutta: Association Press, 1920)

Richard Cashman, *Patrons, Players and the Crowd: The Phenomenon of Indian Cricket* (New Delhi: Orient Longman, 1980)

E. L. Docker, *History of Indian Cricket* (Delhi: Macmillan, 1976)

Framjee Dosabhoy, *The Parsees: Their History, Manners, Customs and Religions* (1858) (Delhi: Asian Educational Services, India, 2003)

Tony Greig, *Test Match Cricket: A Personal View* (Hamlyn, 1977)

Ramchandra Guha, *A Corner of a Foreign Field: The Indian History of a British Sport* (London: Picador, 2001)

Ramchandra Guha (ed.), *The Picador Book of Cricket* (London: Picador, 2002)

Ramchandra Guha, *Spin and Other Turns* (London: Penguin, 1994)

Ramchandra Guha, *Wickets in the East* (Oxford: OUP, 1992)

Ramchandra Guha, *India after Gandhi: The History of the World's Largest Democracy* (London: Pan Macmillan, 2008)

Gideon Haigh, *Sphere of Influence: Writings on Cricket and its Discontents* (Melbourne: Melbourne University Publishing, 2010)

C.L.R. James, *Beyond a Boundary* (London: Hutchinson, 1963)

Prashant Kidambi, *The Making of an Indian Metropolis* (Farnham: Ashgate, 2007)

Pradeep Magazine, *Not Quite Cricket: The Explosive Story of How Bookmakers Influence the Game Today* (Delhi: Penguin India, 2000)

Boria Majumdar, *Lost Histories of Indian Cricket: Battles off the Pitch* (London: Routledge, 2005)

Boria Majumdar, *Twenty-Two Yards to Freedom: A Social History of Indian Cricket* (Delhi: Viking, Penguin, 2004)

Boria Majumdar, *Indian Cricket Through the Ages: A Reader* (Oxford: OUP, 2005)

Nalin Mehta, *Indian on Television: How Satellite News Channels Have Changed the Way We Think and Act* (Delhi: Harper Collins, 2008)

Sujit Mukherjee, *Playing for India* (Delhi: Orient Longman, 1988)

Sujit Mukherjee, *Autobiography of an Unknown Cricketer* (Delhi: Ravi Dayal Publisher, 1996)

Ashis Nandy, *The Tao of Cricket: On Games of Destiny and the Destiny of Games* (Oxford: OUP, 2007)

J.M. Framji Patel, *Stray Thoughts on Indian Cricket* (Bombay: The Times of India Press, 1905)

Manekji Kavasji Patel, *History of Parsee Cricket* (Bombay: J.N. Petit Parsi Orphanage Captain Printing Press, 1892)

M.E. Pavri, *Parsi Cricket* (Bombay: J.B. Marzban and Company, 1901)

James Pycroft, *The Cricket Field* (1851) (Milton Keynes: Lightning Source UK Ltd., 2012)

Vasant Raiji, *India's Hambledon Men* (Bombay: Tyeby Press, 1986)

Vasant Raiji, *C.K. Nayudu: the Shahenshah of Indian Cricket* (Mumbai: Marine Sports, 1989)

N.K.P. Salve, *The Story of the Reliance Cup* (Delhi: Vikas Publishing House, 1987)

Captain James Trevor, *The Lighter Side of Cricket* (London: Methuen and Co., 1901)

Stephen Wagg (ed.), *Cricket and National Identity in the Postcolonial Age: Following On* (London: Routledge, 2008)

Simon Wilde, *Ranji: A Genius Rich and Strange* (London: the Kingswood Press, 1990)

Simon Wilde, *Caught: The Full Story of Cricket's Match-fixing Scandal* (London: Aurum Press, 2001)

Index